D0546909

METALITERACY

ALA Neal-Schuman purchases fund advocacy, awareness, and accreditation programs for library professionals worldwide.

METALITERACY
*Reinventing Information Literacy
to Empower Learners*

THOMAS P. MACKEY
and
TRUDI E. JACOBSON

An imprint of the American Library Association

CHICAGO   2014

© 2014 by the American Library Association

Printed in the United States of America

18 17 16 15 14   5 4 3 2 1

Extensive effort has gone into ensuring the reliability of the information in this book; however, the publisher makes no warranty, express or implied, with respect to the material contained herein.

ISBN: 978-1-55570-989-1 (paper).

Library of Congress Cataloging-in-Publication Data
Mackey, Thomas P.
      Metaliteracy : reinventing information literacy to empower learners / Thomas P. Mackey and Trudi E. Jacobson.
      pages   cm
      Includes bibliographical references and index.
      ISBN 978-1-55570-989-1 (alk. paper)
      1. Information literacy. 2. Information literacy—Study and teaching. 3. Information literacy—Study and teaching—Case studies. 4. Metadata. 5. Web 2.0. 6. Semantic Web.
   I. Jacobson, Trudi. II. Title.
      ZA3075.M327 2014
      028.7—dc23   2013051233

Cover design Kimberly Thornton.

Text design in the Chaparral, Gotham, and Bell Gothic typefaces.

♾ This paper meets the requirements of ANSI/NISO Z39.48-1992 (Permanence of Paper).

LIB
028.7
MAC
2014

This book is dedicated to all of our students who teach us, and to family, friends, and colleagues who expressed such great interest in this project as it moved forward.

—Tom Mackey and Trudi Jacobson

And to John, who spurs me forward.

—Trudi

Contents

Acknowledgments

WE ACKNOWLEDGE THE CONTRIBUTION OF COLLEAGUES AND friends as work on this book unfolded. The Metaliteracy Learning Collaborative was instrumental in moving theory to practice and talking us into using our own model in developing a SUNY-wide partnership to apply metaliteracy in several grant-related projects. This group includes Project Manager Emer O'Keeffe and Co-Principal Investigators Michele Forte, Jenna Hecker, Mark McBride, Michael Daly, and honorary member Kathleen Stone. Emer, Michele, and Kathleen played key roles in working with us on expanding and enriching the metaliteracy learning objectives to the format they take today. We appreciate the initial support we received for the book proposal from Charles Harmon. As always, we acknowledge the astute editing of Amy L. Knauer and thank Rachel Chance, acquisitions editor at ALA for taking us into the home stretch. Thanks as well to Angela Gwizdala, Don Chatham, Dan Freeman, and the entire team at ALA. We also acknowledge Sheila A. Webber for writing such a wonderful foreword.

We thank Deborah Lines Andersen for providing preliminary feedback on our research survey, which certainly improved the final instrument. Thanks as well to Gregory Bobish for writing a key section in Chapter 6 that effectively demonstrates metaliteracy in practice. We thank Roger Lipera, who developed our snazzy metaliteracy logo and the circular representations of both the metaliteracy model and the metaliterate learner. Additionally, Mary Casserly was very supportive of this project and offered helpful advice about the research analysis that informed Chapter 5. As we finished the book, we developed Metaliteracy MOOC and appreciate the inspiration for doing so from Betty Hurley-Dasgupta and Carol Yeager. We also thank our MOOC cohorts Jenna Hecker, Tor Loney, and Nicola Marae Allain, as well as all of our MOOC Talk presenters and participants. Thanks to James R. Kellerhouse for providing excellent feedback and for offering great suggestions about the book's title.

Tom and Trudi

Foreword

THESE ARE EXCITING TIMES FOR INFORMATION LITERACY. World headlines are captured by news stories about accessing, misusing, and authenticating information. In November 2013 the United Nations Educational, Scientific and Cultural Organization (UNESCO) (2013) voted in favour of a resolution on media and information literacy. For the first time there is an international policy document in which information literacy is explicitly the main focus. UNESCO member countries are encouraged to endorse this resolution at a national level: citizens can point to the resolution and demand of their governments "What are *you* doing about information literacy?" Indeed, as the authors of this book note in chapter 4, "the continued progression and transformation of information literacy is an international concern." The time when information literacy could be seen as a quaint preoccupation of librarians is past.

Intellectual engagement with the concept of information literacy has also blossomed. Different schools of thought about information literacy are emerging: the sign of a vigorous, healthy subject field. There is a greater body of research literature and a growing number of completed doctoral studies. All over the world people are exploring what information literacy means, in their country and culture, in the 21st century. The book you have before you provides a rich contribution to this intellectual debate.

As well as unfolding the thinking behind the metaliteracy model of information literacy, the authors provide a useful review of trends and theories that have contributed to the development of their model. It is also valuable to have examples of, and reflections on, practice.

The authors identify that they wish their model to be one which "allows lifelong learners to create meaning through an interactive and participatory social network" (chapter 1). In chapter 2, they note how, while social media could, in theory, empower everyone to create and interact, in fact the majority of people do not unlock social media's full potential. They give detailed examples in the final two chapters of how incorporating a metaliteracy approach into teaching practice can help with this process.

I have put collaboration and reflection at the heart of my teaching and assessment of information literacy ever since Bill Johnston and I developed a credit-bearing information literacy course for business school students in the late 1990s (Webber & Johnston, 2000, p. 388). The central role of metacognition and collaboration in the metaliteracy model is important. As the authors say, it "allows us to move beyond rudimentary skills development and prepares students to dig deeper and assess their own learning" (chapter 1). Nowadays, in our fast-moving and competitive world, it is a disservice to learners to deny them the opportunity to reflect explicitly on their information literacy and learning. All citizens deserve teaching that empowers them to self-develop and adapt to change in technology, culture, and society.

Librarians and faculty also need to be lifelong learners. The authors note that development opportunities abound via social media and through channels such as the MOOC which the authors have facilitated. However, books such as this one still have an important place in our learning experience.

Sheila A. Webber
Director of the Centre for
Information Literacy Research
Information School, Sheffield University

REFERENCES

United Nations Educational, Scientific and Cultural Organization. (2013). *Draft resolution: International Federation of Library Associations and Institutions (IFLA) Media and Information Literacy Recommendations.* http://unesdoc.unesco.org/images/0022/002242/224273e.pdf

Webber, Sheila, & Johnston, Bill. (2000). Conceptions of information literacy: New perspectives and implications. *Journal of Information Science, 26*(6), 381–397.

Preface

THE IDEA FOR THIS BOOK EMERGED FROM AN ARTICLE WE PUB-
lished in *College & Research Libraries* (*C&RL*) in January 2011 titled
"Reframing Information Literacy as a Metaliteracy." A year earlier, we presented on metaliteracy at the Information Literacy Research Seminar as
part of the Seventh International Conference on Conceptions of Library and
Information Science (CoLIS) at University College London. Energized by the
discussion at the conference, we developed the first outline for this book in
between sessions. During the research seminar at CoLIS we talked with Sheila
Webber and other participants about the metaliteracy framework. The article
itself was first made available by *C&RL* as a preprint online and then as an
essay within the openly available journal. The posting of the preprint made us
aware of the interest in metaliteracy through blogs, tweets, and social bookmarking, illustrating how information moves circuitously through a decentered social network. The issue of *C&RL* that included the final version of the
essay was the first published in a freely available open format. This change by
such a high-profile academic journal to an open publishing model suited the
themes of the article very well and allowed it to circulate even further.

In the fall of 2011 we presented on metaliteracy in a massive open online course (MOOC) that was hosted by State University of New York (SUNY) Empire State College on creativity and multicultural communication. This was the first ever MOOC offered in the SUNY system and was developed by Betty Hurley-Dasgupta and Carol Yeager. Our contribution to the MOOC allowed us to be a part of an innovative new online format that combined open education with a range of emerging technologies, such as video conferencing, blogging, Twitter, and Facebook. The MOOC reached an international audience that included over 500 participants (Yaeger, Hurley-Dasgupta, & Bliss, 2013). We also continued working on our courses, in person and online, thinking about how the metaliteracy framework informs practice.

We had several reasons for exploring a new way of thinking about information literacy and, in fact, redefining it to empower learners. In our own teaching, in the classroom and online, and through several edited book projects about faculty-librarian collaboration, we were keenly aware of the connections between information literacy and emerging technologies. The evolution of Web 2.0 and the revolution of social media and social networking required a fundamental shift in how to think about information literacy in the 21st century. Our own research and writing about information literacy has been informed by changes in technology and the relationships among the librarians, students, and faculty in social media. In addition, emerging literacies such as transliteracy, mobile literacy, and digital media literacy influenced our thinking that what we really needed, instead of yet another literacy type, was an overarching and unifying framework—a metaliteracy—for identifying a comprehensive model. Our first article on this topic and several presentations and conversations with peers and readers of the first essay inspired us to take this idea further with a full treatment in this manuscript.

Since we started writing this book, there have been several important developments, expanding the model and collaborating with others to extend its visibility and reach. A website, Metaliteracy.org, was created to serve as a central information point. It includes a blog with posts about metaliteracy-related issues, an explanation of what metaliteracy is, an expanded set of learning objectives, and examples of how metaliteracy is being used in practice. True to the collaborative nature of metaliteracy, we encourage others to post examples, suggestions, and comments. We have adapted the learning objectives based on helpful feedback we have received from several people.

We also secured an Innovative Instruction Technology Grant from SUNY for 2012–2013 (www.suny.edu/provost/iitg2012recipients.cfm). The project was initially named Developing a SUNY-wide Transliteracy Learning Collaborative to Promote Information and Technology Collaboration, but shortly into our work, we realized that metaliteracy was the more appropriate model for the work of the learning collaborative. The co-principal investigators for the grant included faculty members, librarians, and technology experts.

Depending on the particular project, we were also able to call on an instructional design expert and a number of additional faculty members. The learning objectives found on Metaliteracy.org originated from the group's work. So too did a metaliteracy badging system and a SUNY intercampus conference in the Conversations in the Disciplines program, Developing Metaliterate Learners: Transforming Literacy Across Disciplines.

In fall 2013 we offered Metaliteracy MOOC (http://metaliteracy.cdlproj ects.com), working with the same format originally designed by Betty Hurley-Dasgupta and Carol Yeager. Metaliteracy MOOC explored many of the key themes in this book and brought together colleagues from the Metaliteracy Learning Collaborative and scholars from around the world. Through this format, we united learners from the University at Albany and Empire State College, and the experience was entirely open to global participants interested in the metaliteracy model.

BOOK ORGANIZATION

This book is organized into seven interrelated chapters, providing a theoretical exploration of metaliteracy while grounding it in practice The first part of the book delves into the theory of metaliteracy and the context in which it was developed. In the first chapter, we introduce metaliteracy through an examination of how the term has been used in other contexts. We also explore the prefix *meta* in relation to our use of the term and conduct a literature review that looks at metacognition, multiple intelligence theory, multiliteracies, multiple literacies, transliteracy, convergence, and multimodal literacy. We frame this discussion through a postmodern perspective and also describe the impact of Web 2.0 and how metaliteracy expands upon our traditional understanding of information literacy. The second chapter examines issues related to how the expansive, decentered social media environment challenges our established assumptions about information literacy. Chapter 3 examines the role of metaliteracy and information literacy in the context of the burgeoning number of literacies focused on technologies (mobile literacy, for example) and formats (such as visual literacy). Each of these literacies has essential elements that would presume associated learning objectives. Chapter 3 therefore concludes with a set of objectives within four primary metaliteracy learning goals. The fundamental changes in the information environment identified in the first three chapters are examined in the context of global information literacies in the fourth chapter, providing an international perspective supporting a metaliteracy framework.

In the second part of the book, we shift from theory to practice. Chapter 5 provides an analysis of findings from an international survey of instructional librarians who incorporate emerging technology in their teaching. This chapter continues the global perspective established in Chapter 4 while grounding our metaliteracy structure in a quantitative and qualitative analysis of information literacy practices. The sixth chapter presents the first of two case studies, demonstrating that metaliteracy is more than a theoretical construct and has practical implications for today's information literacy instruction. This first case study examines the introduction of Web 2.0 tools in an information literacy course taught by a faculty librarian at a large research university and the development of a second course in order to focus in greater depth on the changing information environment. We close the book in Chapter 7 with a second case study that examines the use of social media tools in a course about digital storytelling to advance critical thinking and lifelong learning for online learners. This chapter illustrates the importance of metaliteracy approaches in an online course that does not necessarily require information literacy instruction but benefits from the integration of this comprehensive model.

ADVANCING METALITERACY THROUGH PRACTICE

In a social media age, the idea of developing discrete skills must be replaced by the formation of a comprehensive knowledge set, informed by multiple information sources through individual and collaborative practice. The 20th century saw the fixity of print and tangible documents in small and large collections evolve into online resources, open and online journals, and electronic books. These changes continue in the 21st century, but we have entered a new era defined by radical redefinitions of peer review, access, portability, sharing, and co-creation of new media documents. Today's libraries continue to play a central role in information literacy endeavors, reflecting the changes we have seen in emerging technology, and they are doing so through blended, online, mobile, and virtual modes, providing interactive access to digital materials and archives, electronic journals, e-books, and information commons. Librarians have embraced these technologies and interface with learners through blogs, microblogs, personal learning environments (PLEs), virtual spaces, and expansive social networks.

Without a common understanding about information literacy in these contexts, however, or how it relates to associated literacy formats, we end up with a fragmentation of discrete skills and disconnection among multiple literacies. Very often the development of a new technology sparks interest in learning related skills within educational and real-world contexts, but what are the overarching principles or characteristics to guide educators and learners? How does information literacy fit into this complex and fragmented conception of learning in open and social media spaces? What role does technology play in our understanding of literacy?

This book provides a theoretical and practical exploration of ideas, reinventing information literacy to empower learners. The theory is important
to understanding the argument, but it is grounded in practice through useful examples that can be applied in multiple settings. Faculty, librarians, and
instructional designers are already using emerging technologies and integrating social media into courses and programs. Our primary purpose with
this book is to provide a *meta* perspective for this work and a way to think
about information literacy today and in the future, building connections
among related literacy types that support learner success. This metaliteracy
model provides a way to frame information literacy efforts at your institution, offering a context for collaboration and the meaningful use of open and
social resources to advance critical thinking, metacognitive learning, and
empowerment.

REFERENCE

Yaeger, Carol, Hurley-Dasgupta, Betty, & Bliss, Catherine A. (2013). cMOOCs and
global learning: An authentic alternative. *Journal of Asynchronous Learning
Networks,* 17(2), 133–147. http://sloanconsortium.org/jaln/v17n2/cmoocs
-and-global-learning-authentic-alternative

1
Developing a Metaliteracy Framework to Promote Metacognitive Learning

IN THIS BOOK WE PRESENT A COMPREHENSIVE FRAMEWORK for information literacy that unifies related literacies to advance critical thinking and metacognitive learning. Metaliteracy builds on decades of information literacy theory and practice while recognizing the knowledge required for an expansive and interactive information environment. Today's lifelong learners communicate, create, and share information using a range of emerging technologies such as social networks, blogs, microblogs, wikis, mobile devices and apps, virtual worlds, online communities, cloud computing, and massive open online courses (MOOCs). Metaliteracy expands the scope of traditional information skills (determine, access, locate, understand, produce, and use information) to include the collaborative production and sharing of information in participatory digital environments (collaborate, participate, produce, and share). This approach requires an ongoing adaptation to emerging technologies and an understanding of the critical thinking and reflection required to engage in these spaces as producers, collaborators, and distributors. Metaliteracy is not about introducing yet another literacy format, but rather reinventing an existing one—information literacy—the critical foundation literacy that informs many others while being flexible and adaptive enough to evolve and change over time.

This first chapter examines the metaliteracy framework and how we arrived at this expanded conception of information literacy. In the first section of this chapter, "Metaliteracy," we provide an overview of the term and describe how it has been used in other settings. In the second section, "The *Meta* in Metaliteracy," we provide a background on the prefix *meta* as it relates to this redefinition of information literacy. Then, in "Metacognition," we outline a few key concepts related to this expansive and complex area of study and connect the term to our metaliteracy model, especially in relation to what it means to be a thoughtful metaliterate learner. The next section, "Toward a Metaliteracy Framework," identifies significant trends in information literacy and multiple approaches to literacy. Each section of this first chapter leads to a discussion of "The Metaliteracy Model" that provides a visual representation of the overall concept and integrated elements.

METALITERACY

The use of the term *metaliteracy* suggests a way of thinking about one's own literacy. To be metaliterate requires individuals to understand their existing literacy strengths and areas for improvement and make decisions about their learning. The ability to critically self-assess different competencies and to recognize one's need for integrated literacies in today's information environment is a metaliteracy. This metacognitive approach challenges a reliance on skills-based information literacy instruction and shifts the focus to knowledge acquisition in collaboration with others. The metaliterate individual has the capability to adapt to changing technologies and learning environments, while combining and understanding relationships among related literacies. This requires a high level of critical thinking and analysis about how we develop our self-conception of information literacy as metacognitive learners in open and social media environments.

The term *metaliteracy* has been applied previously in several different contexts and academic disciplines related to the study of literacy. According to Ingraham, Levy, and colleagues (2007), "when the focus is on interaction with information irrespective of medium, information literacy itself may be seen as a meta-literacy that in the net-worked environment embraces a range of other literacies" (p. 162). Although not fully developed as a comprehensive redefinition of information literacy, this assertion recognizes the all-encompassing potential of information literacy in relation to other literacies. Spitzer, Eisenberg, and Lowe (1998) argue that "visual literacy, media literacy, computer literacy, and network literacy" (pp. 23–26) are "implicit in information literacy" (p. 13). The authors define a clear link among related literacies and acknowledge technology-mediated influences on information literacy. According to the *Encyclopedia of Library and Information Science* (Kent, Lancour, & Nasri, 2000), "the metaliteracy revolution" is part of a larger communications revolution that includes transformations in language, literacy, and telepresence" (p. 135). While this previous definition predates the rapid growth of social media, the impact of computer-mediated communications and hypertext informs an understanding of metaliteracy based on significant changes in communications "in all possible forms—symbolic, oral, and telepresence" (p. 138). This recognition of multiple modes of communication through digital technologies is central to our definition as well, but with an added emphasis on social media.

In another example of metaliteracy terminology, Heather Lotherington (2004) argues that educators must consider the role of computer games on cognition and "how these sophisticated digital metaliteracies are increasingly required of contemporary communication" (p. 318). She also links metaliteracy to multiliteracies: "How children enact digital literacies and how they interweave modern and postmodern literacies requires a sophisticated organizing and orienting knowledge: a metaliteracy to access multiliteracies" (p. 312). Lotherington defines digital metaliteracies as "ways of entering the chaos of postmodern texts; ways of navigating digitized knowledge programmed into varying platforms" (p. 315). As we will see in this first chapter, Lotherington's rationale for metaliteracy, and its relationship to multiliteracies, is similar to the argument we present because it is inspired by radical changes in digital technologies and communications. Our conception of metaliteracy, however, pushes the boundaries further by promoting a comprehensive reinvention of information literacy for revolutionary social media environments.

Jen Webb and Tony Schirato (2003) examine Pierre Bourdieu's (Bourdieu, 1992; Bourdieu & Wacquant, 1992) conception of reflexivity as a form of metaliteracy. Webb and Schirato (2003) argue "reflexivity is best understood as a collective, rather than an individual process, and it is largely specific to those fields that have institutionalized, through the mechanisms of training and dialogue, a disposition for subjects to turn those mechanisms 'against themselves'" (p. 551). Bourdieu (2000) originally stated, "By turning instruments of knowledge that they produce against themselves, and especially against the social universes in which they produce them," individuals are prepared to escape "economic and social determinisms" (p. 121). According to this definition, reflexivity is a form of critical inquiry within a discipline that continuously reflects back on itself. Bourdieu (2000) provides a theoretical perspective that extends beyond the individual to a larger discipline. At the same time, Webb and Schirato (2003) assert that this reflexive approach to a field of study has implications for individuals as well because they are a part of the larger collective and contribute to the conversation within a community (p. 551).

Bourdieu's work is relevant to metaliteracy because he asserts a critical social theory that challenges individual bias to consider the disciplinary and social contexts for intellectual thought and knowledge (Bourdieu & Wacquant, 1992, pp. 39–40). In the book *An Invitation to Reflexive Sociology* by Pierre Bourdieu and Loic J. D. Wacquant (1992), reflexivity "is cursorily defined as the inclusion of a theory of intellectual practice as an integral component and necessary condition of a critical theory of society" (p. 36). Based on this explanation, "its primary target is not the individual analyst but the *social and intellectual unconscious* embedded in analytic tools and operations" (p. 36). This approach emphasizes the social context of knowledge production. To further underscore this point, reflexivity is seen as "a collective enterprise rather than the burden of the lone academic" (p. 36). Ultimately, "reflexivity aims at increasing the scope and solidity of social scientific knowledge" (pp. 36–37). Although Bourdieu and Wacquant (1992) do not explicitly refer to metaliteracy in this particular work, the intellectual process they describe in the social sciences is a critical theory that emphasizes the importance of collective knowledge. This is a valuable perspective as today's social media environments are similarly focused on how we create and share knowledge within a common network. The individual is a key part of this process, but the social context helps shape the experience. Social media environments are socially constructed spaces that rely on the contributions of individuals to create meaning. Metaliteracy expands the scope of how to use these spaces as individuals and requires a critical perspective that reflects on the networked environment itself and how knowledge is produced and shared.

In *Understanding Bourdieu*, Webb, Schirato, and Danaher (2002) argue, "If literacy involves the capacity to read the situation and game from a particular perspective, metaliteracy involves the capacity to move strategically into different positions in one's reading of the situation and the game" (p. 143). This definition suggests a high level of critical awareness that requires an understanding of the diverse perspectives of others within a larger social environment (p. 143). The authors provide the example of a group of students working on a multimedia project. They describe a team of students with varying skill levels, such as the students who have the capacity for multimedia production techniques and those students who may not be as well versed in digital imaging but have an understanding of marketing (p. 143). According to the authors, "In each case, the students have *literacies*: but they will only develop *metaliteracy* to the extent that they are able to understand each other's areas of knowledge and respond to the different perspectives other people may bring to multimedia" (p. 143). In this example, metaliteracy emphasizes the social setting for multimedia production and not just the individual skills required to produce a technology project.

In a social media environment, the larger social context extends beyond the classroom to include a network of users and participants. The development of a social media project, and not just multimedia, requires another layer of understanding about communication and interaction across a vast network. Social media requires virtual collaboration that could take place from any location, at any time, and connects users with a wide range of skills and knowledge.

The concept of metaliteracy has also been explored in relation to how children read picture books (Arizpe & Styles, 2003) and as an expansion of critical information literacy in electronic environments (Kerka, 2000). In addition, metaliteracy has been described as a set of strategies for indigenous populations to counter traditional narratives and assumptions to participate in academic discourse (Gilmore & Smith, 2005). The term *metaliteracy* is found throughout the literature in varying contexts, although not as a fully developed expansion of how information literacy is envisioned.

The purpose of this book is to build on our previous work in this area to develop metaliteracy as a reinvention of information literacy. We see this approach as a comprehensive framework for open, online, mobile, and social media environments. In our preceding article on this topic, "Reframing Information Literacy as a Metaliteracy," we argue:

> Metaliteracy promotes critical thinking and collaboration in a digital age, providing a comprehensive framework to effectively participate in social media and online communities. It is a unified construct that supports the acquisition, production, and sharing of knowledge in collaborative on-line communities. Metaliteracy challenges traditional skills-based approaches to information literacy by recognizing related literacy types and incorporating emerging technologies. Standard definitions of information literacy are insufficient for the revolutionary social technologies currently prevalent online. (Mackey and Jacobson, 2011, pp. 62–63)

The primary goal of this reframing is to repurpose information literacy for the 21st century by identifying associations to relevant literacy types, such as visual literacy, digital literacy, mobile literacy, and media literacy. Our reason for using the term *metaliteracy* as part of this redefinition is to build on earlier information literacy research and practice while reconfiguring the term to reflect the dramatic changes in today's social media environment. We also see this as a way to transcend any particular literacy and instead to focus on the overall knowledge required to critically engage in today's networked settings. While many theories have emerged focusing on multiple literacies, and multiple intelligences, metaliteracy provides a core concept for revising information literacy to meet the pedagogical challenges of the social media age. Our goal is to recast information literacy to make it relevant in networked learning environments and to provide examples in later chapters, through case studies, for how this can be done.

THE *META* IN METALITERACY

As part of this dynamic model, metaliteracy identifies inherent connections to related literacy types. The term *meta* traces back to the Greek origins of the prefix that has multiple meanings. According to *A Dictionary of Ecology*, the term is defined in this way: "The Greek *meta*, meaning 'with' or 'after', used as a prefix implying change and meaning 'behind', 'after', or 'beyond'" (Allaby, 2011). For instance, the word *metamorphosis* from Greek mythology describes significant change or transformation and is applied in multiple disciplinary contexts in the arts and sciences (Mazzolini, 2003). The *Oxford English Dictionary (OED)* emphasizes similar meanings by defining the term as "denoting change, transformation, permutation, or substitution." In addition, the *OED* states that the term *meta* is "prefixed to the name of a subject or discipline to denote another which deals with ulterior issues in the same field, or which raises questions about the nature of the original discipline and its methods, procedures, and assumptions." This definition allows us to envision metaliteracy as a way to raise critical concerns about literacy and information literacy in a social media age. Metaliteracy is a form of critical inquiry that provides a way to question our basic assumptions about information literacy and how we have been teaching it. While literacy is focused on reading and writing, and information literacy has strongly emphasized search and retrieval, metaliteracy is about what happens beyond these abilities to promote the collaborative production and sharing of information. Metaliteracy also includes a metacognitive component and openness to format and mode that is less pronounced in information literacy.

The prefix *meta* has also been used to explain key components of our complex Internet environment. For instance, a *Dictionary of the Internet* defines the term as "a prefix placed before a word in order to describe properties about the original word. For example a metafile is a file which contains data about files, metadata is data about data" (Ince, 2009). Similarly, the *OED* recognizes *meta* as a prefix "to technical terms to denote software, data, etc., which operate at a higher level of abstraction." Our use of the word *metaliteracy* in this book describes a unifying construct that combines literacies while acknowledging fundamental changes in the information environment. Metaliteracy moves beyond traditional definitions of information literacy as an ordering of discrete skills to create a comprehensive framework that supports collaborative knowledge acquisition, which is ideal for learning in participatory social media settings.

The prefix *meta* also reflects a postmodern reinvention of information literacy. According to Roberts (2000), "At the most basic level, the word 'postmodern' suggests a period that comes after the modern" (p. 112). Postmodernism is a theoretical construct that emerged in the late 20th century and has been applied in the arts, literature, cultural studies, architecture, and philosophy to describe a break from the modern era. While modernism emphasized the notion of the artist or writer working in isolation on individual and ambitious expressions or narratives, postmodernism describes a shift to a multiplicity of ideas and styles that challenges linear narratives and historical assumptions. This is a useful perspective as we consider the nonlinear nature of information in today's networked environments and the role of metaliteracy as a way to challenge some of our assumptions about information literacy as only skills based.

As Jean-François Lyotard (1984) asserts in *The Postmodern Condition: A Report on Knowledge*, "A work can become modern only if it is first postmodern. Postmodernism thus understood is not modernism at its end but in the nascent state, and this state is constant" (p. 79). Lyotard's definition of postmodernism describes an end to a movement or period of time but also acknowledges the beginning of a new era. We have seen a similar shift in how we understand information, from discrete elements in print and paperbound journals that were previously accessed and retrieved through single or binary pathways to the creation and publishing of various forms of digital information in dispersed social environments. Lyotard argues that "knowledge is altered as societies enter what is known as the postindustrial age and cultures enter what is known as the postmodern age" (p. 3). We have seen the realization of this new era, defined by rapid technological change in computing, the Internet, the World Wide Web, and social media. As Lyotard states:

> As for the second function, it is common knowledge that the miniaturization and commercialization of machines is already changing the way in which learning is acquired, classified, made available, and exploited. It is reasonable to suppose that the proliferation of information-processing machines is having, and will continue to have, as much of an effect on the circulation of learning as did advancements in human circulation (transportation systems) and later, in the circulation of sounds and visual images (the media). (p. 4)

The "miniaturization and commercialization of machines" is most evident in our various mobile devices for communicating, creating, and sharing information. For instance, the cell phone has morphed into a multipurpose smart device with a variety of applications, from gaming to texting to digital imaging, for both individual and collaborative use. In addition, our familiarity with the "information superhighway" in the 1990s identifies a similar parallel between the expanse of transportation systems and the rapid emergence of digital information in various forms through the Internet and web (Andrews, 1993). This terminology is now outdated because the information superhighway has given way to a collaborative social network. Information in this decentered environment is fragmented and transient, requiring new approaches to literacy education. Technology itself is an ever changing and unpredictable part of this dynamic. As such, we must consider how emerging trends like social media influence our literacy archetypes and, for the purpose of this book, a metaliteracy model.

While modernism was primarily about the author and artist working on individual expressions, postmodernism defines a multiplicity of ideas and practices in decentered nonlinear environments. This postmodern vision has been demonstrated most recently in a hypertext web environment that offers the user numerous pathways and links in a collaborative network. The purpose of a metaliteracy is to identify relationships among literacies in a networked reality. Although we describe our metaliteracy model as an overarching framework, this is not intended to be a hierarchical theory but rather a comprehensive one that allows lifelong learners to create meaning through an interactive and participatory social network.

Lyotard (1984) critiques the "grand narratives" of the modern age and defines postmodernism as "incredulity toward metanarratives" (p. xxiv). He argues, "This incredulity is undoubtedly a product of progress in the sciences: but that progress in turn presupposes it" (p. xxiv). This is a theoretical challenge to many modern assumptions about technological progress and determinism that offers a new way to think about the development of knowledge in society. Our use of the prefix *meta* in metaliteracy is not intended to invoke yet another meta- or grand narrative but rather to acknowledge the fragmented and decentered nature of information in the postmodern age. Metaliteracy is a critical perspective that raises questions about our pedagogical assumptions and the linear ways we have been teaching information literacy. This approach combines disparate parts in a comprehensive and evolving structure but does so without creating yet another linear narrative about absolute knowledge or praxis. We expect the components of metaliteracy to change over time, as technologies and the needs of our learners vary, but we need a way to bridge cognate literacies and to incorporate the social dimension of today's expansive learning network.

METACOGNITION

Metaliteracy is a conceptual model to unify cognate literacies and to expand the traditional definition of information literacy. This new approach places a stronger emphasis on social technology and emphasizes knowledge acquisition instead of just skills development. In our original article on this topic we examined metaliteracy from a primarily library and information science (LIS) viewpoint. In this first chapter, we expand our initial argument beyond the field to include a metacognitive perspective with a particular focus on the groundbreaking work of John H. Flavell.

According to Thomas O. Nelson (1992), "*Metacognition* is defined as cognition about one's own cognition" (p. 1). The use of the prefix *meta* suggests a high level understanding of one's own knowledge and cognitive abilities. Nelson (1992) argues, "Metacognition is also closely related to the topic of *consciousness*, which has always been a central topic in philosophy, especially the philosophy of mind" (p. ix). Today's interest in metacognition extends beyond the fields of philosophy and psychology to influence much broader disciplinary and interdisciplinary perspectives. In her book *Metacognition in Learning and Instruction: Theory, Research and Practice*, Hope J. Hartman (2002) argues that metacognition "is generally defined as cognition about cognition or thinking about one's own thinking, including both the processes and the products" (p. xi). Hartman refers to Flavell's research and identifies the impact of metacognition on "acquisition, comprehension, retention and application of what is learned, in addition to affecting learning efficiency, critical thinking, and problem solving" (p. xi). Information literacy instructors are similarly interested in how learners acquire, comprehend, retain, and apply what is learned about the information environment in an effective and efficient manner. In addition, both critical thinking and problem solving are essential learning outcomes of information literacy education. A metacognitive approach to information literacy builds on these elements and challenges us to prepare our students to think about their own learning. This is particularly relevant to how students self-assess their participation in highly social information environments. It also requires us to develop collaborative and interdisciplinary strategies for metacognitive learning opportunities that build on basic skills instruction. Further, this approach demands an effective assessment plan that incorporates metacognitive approaches in our learning design.

Metacognition has also been examined in literacy education, particularly related to reading and writing. Griffith and Ruan (2005) suggest that an emphasis on metacognition prepares independent and successful learners. They argue that "learners with high levels of metacognitive abilities are able to monitor and regulate their learning processes to accomplish the learning goals they set" (p. 16). This supports a process beyond skills development that prepares individuals to take control of their learning by gaining a deeper understanding of what is needed to set and achieve goals. This is the kind of empowerment we strive for in information literacy education, although the traditional emphasis on teaching discrete skills and the time constraints of one-shot library sessions (or other skills-based instructional modes) do not make this method possible. A metacognitive approach to information literacy prepares learners to gain new insights about their own learning and shifts the focus from skills development to knowledge acquisition through deep reflection on the learning process itself.

In his landmark essay "Metacognition and Cognitive Monitoring: A New Area of Cognitive–Developmental Inquiry," Flavell (1979) defines metacognition as "knowledge and cognition about cognitive phenomena" (p. 906). Flavell expands the description of cognition by adding a meta layer to the conceptualization of how we think and learn. Central to his theory is the idea that "cognitive monitoring" takes place in a wide range of activities, including "memory, comprehension, and other cognitive enterprises" (p. 906). As a part of this approach, Flavell identifies four interrelated dimensions of metacognition, including "(a) metacognitive knowledge, (b) metacognitive experiences, (c) goals (or tasks), and (d) actions (or strategies)" (p. 906). He defines "metacognitive knowledge" as "stored world knowledge that has to do with people as cognitive creatures and with their diverse cognitive tasks, goals, actions, and experiences" (p. 906). At its most basic level, this refers to knowledge gained and how individuals understand or perceive what they know. In addition, Flavell defines "metacognitive experiences" as "any conscious cognitive or affective experiences that accompany and pertain to any intellectual enterprise" (p. 906). This is generally understood as the process of thinking about one's knowledge and consciously making decisions or taking actions to enact or pursue further knowledge. As part of this interconnected framework, he argues, "Goals (or tasks) refer to the objectives of a cognitive enterprise. Actions (or strategies) refer to the cognitions or other behaviors employed to achieve them" (pp. 906–907). For the purposes of this chapter, we will focus specifically on metacognitive knowledge and metacognitive experience with the understanding that goals and strategies are related to this construct and necessarily emerge from our instructional practices.

Flavell (1979) offers several examples that could be easily applied in a range of settings today, although his work does not specifically address digital technologies or information literacies in relation to thinking and learning. The scenarios he describes are universal and transcend any particular learning environment. As an example of "metacognitive knowledge," Flavell describes "a child's acquired belief that unlike many of her friends, she is better at arithmetic than at spelling" (p. 906). In our own experience teaching information literacy, we relate this example to our observations as well.

For instance, we have observed students with similar self-assessments of their information competencies. Some learners believe they are stronger in searching the Internet than conducting research through library databases, and other learners believe they are better with technology than writing or research. In addition, what many of us see quite often are students who think they are very good web searchers, when actually they are not. We also know that, while technology is ever-present in our culture, some students struggle with technology competencies and may assess their own technology skills as low compared to other learners. Many students are excellent consumers of the latest technology products and may feel confident in the uses of these devices, but they may not necessarily be sophisticated users or evaluate the technology critically. We also know through experience that some learners may think they have a good understanding of intellectual property issues but then make the mistake of plagiarizing materials or incorrectly citing resources. Some learners may not be aware of ways to protect their privacy in social media environments because of assumptions they make about privacy online or lack of knowledge in this area. These discrepancies between perceived skills and actual abilities support an increased emphasis on the development of metacognitive knowledge about information literacy competencies, or what we define as metaliteracy. Learners are continually immersed in beliefs about their own capabilities and knowledge, although this may not be made explicit or foregrounded in our teaching and learning practices.

In terms of "metacognitive experience," Flavell (1979) provides the example of "the sudden feeling that you do not understand something another person just said" (p. 906). Learners may not explicitly state this feeling but continually analyze and process an assessment of their own learning. Unless students ask questions to clarify, we may not be aware that this is what they are experiencing. Flavell also illustrates his approach to metacognitive experience with a scenario in which "you may feel that you are liable to fail in some upcoming enterprise, or that you did very well indeed in some previous one" (p. 908). These examples point to our analysis and understanding of a particular cognitive situation. If we feel that we may fail at an upcoming test or assignment, we may reuse and refine a strategy or goal in response to this belief. At the same time, if we believe that we did well in a previous exercise, perhaps we will have the confidence to develop the same strategy for success.

This process of thinking about our own cognition can be similarly applied to information literacy instruction. Our learners are constantly engaged in the same reflective situations. In a search assignment, for instance, learners make decisions based on previous experience with search engines and their feelings or beliefs about their search knowledge. The decisions they make in a new search may be informed by the success or failure of previous experiences. But what if students perceive a successful search strategy that only skims the surface without digging deeper into the range of sophisticated approaches available to them via new technologies? In this example, we want to teach students more than how to search; we want them to gain high-level critical thinking abilities to better understand their own search processes and what they learned from that experience. We want them to adapt to changes in technologies as well as changes in their own cognitive development. An ongoing reflective practice that prepares students to be critical readers of the technology and their own thinking about technology may allow them to continuously improve their own processes. This requires a metacognitive perspective that informs how we teach information literacy and how students learn these concepts, and not just the skills for conducting an effective search.

Overall, both aspects of metacognition, metacognitive knowledge and experience, identify individuals' awareness of and beliefs related to intellectual abilities. Flavell (1979) argues:

> Investigators have recently concluded that metacognition plays an important role in oral communication of information, oral persuasion, oral comprehension, reading comprehension, writing, language acquisition, attention, memory, problem solving, social cognition, and various types of self-control and self-instruction; there are also clear indications that ideas about metacognition are beginning to make contact with similar ideas in the areas of social learning theory, cognitive behavior modification, personality development, and education. (p. 906)

This suggests an expansive role for metacognition related to how we communicate information, contribute to oral and written discourse, collaborate with one another, understand concepts, and solve problems. It also describes an interdisciplinary set of concerns for thinking about cognition. Flavell concludes that this focus on metacognition is important because it influences learning theory and pedagogy in practice. He asserts, "the ideas currently brewing in this area could someday be parlayed into a method of teaching children (and adults) to make wise and thoughtful life decisions as well as to comprehend and learn better in formal educational settings" (p. 910). This is a critical point because the author argues that metacognitive abilities can be developed through teaching strategies and that metacognition has an impact on lifelong learning. The emphasis on knowledge and experience also suggests a role for formal and informal learning in this process. Formal learning takes place in higher education settings while informal learning is a part of life experience and open learning opportunities.

The terms *metacognitive knowledge* and *metacognitive experience* provide us with a useful context for how we think about and enact the *meta* prefix in metaliteracy while raising important questions about how we apply metaliteracy in practice. For example, if we look at information literacy from a *metacognitive knowledge* perspective, would we be more effective in teaching information literacy if we emphasized self-assessments and encouraged students to think about their own information competencies? This suggests an expanded role for journaling, blogging, tweeting, and even compiling the standard annotated bibliography because these activities provide a context for students to focus on their knowledge about information literacy, or met-aliteracy. In addition, if we consider *metacognitive experience* in relation to information literacy instruction, would learners gain deeper insights about their own literacies if we asked them to foreground their experiences with the research process through an exchange with peers? This method provides a rationale for collaboration in the classroom and online so that students share their experiences and learn from one another, expanding their metaliteracy in dialogue with others. It also supports the integration of information literacy with experiential learning, service learning, open learning, and prior learning based on the assessment of life experience. In these situations, learners gain insights about their own knowledge through real-world practice and critical engagement with communities.

As we have seen, Flavell's (1979) definition of *metacognition* describes a high-level critical thinking process related to the ways individuals understand their own cognitive abilities. Flavell's work does not explicitly refer to the impact of digital technologies on learning, or the role of information literacy in an information age, and his work was too early to address the influence of social media. If we apply metacognition to information literacy, however, we see that metaliteracy is similarly focused on critical awareness of one's own knowledge. As a metacognitive concept, metaliteracy expands traditional defi-nitions of information literacy to explicitly emphasize the impact of critical thinking about one's own thinking and learning. Metaliteracy prepares our learners to critically engage in social media, but we need to prepare them to self-assess their capabilities in these settings. Through metaliteracy, learners become aware of what is needed to strategize and set goals in collaboration with others in networked information environments. Metaliterate individu-als recognize the intersections among literacy formats through self-reflection, and they connect literacy needs to specific technologies and abilities.

A metacognitive approach to information literacy allows us to move beyond rudimentary skills development and prepares students to dig deeper and assess their own learning. Rather than simply learning a skill and how to apply it, learners build on basic skills with deep thinking related to the activity and process, allowing for adaptability to new settings and situations. Metaliterate students will be prepared to fill the gaps in learning and develop strategies for understanding more than what we, as teachers, present or dis-cuss. Through this process, the learner is also a teacher and each individual is a collaborative partner in the learning experience. If learners gain new insights about their knowledge in these areas, they will be better prepared to criti-cally evaluate information and technology systems common today and in the future. To become metaliterate, then, is about more than integrating literacies and adapting to new technologies; it also supports a profound and analytical understanding of one's own literacy. Metaliteracy is more than descriptive; it identifies how learners critically evaluate and understand their knowledge as individuals and participants in social learning environments.

Information literacy is the ideal starting point for developing a metaliteracy because it has evolved over time with a primary emphasis on critical thinking and lifelong learning. In addition, one of the foundation elements of information literacy, to "determine the extent of information needed" (ACRL, 2000, p. 2), suggests a higher order ability to know when and where to start in the research process. This is usually one of the first parts of the standard definition, along with the ability to access, evaluate, incorporate, use, and understand information. Gaining the ability to know when and where to begin a research process, however, requires learners not only to scan the information environment for choices, but also to critically self-assess one's own ability to do so. This is a capability that develops over time and is not always part of a sequence or starting point. The ability to make such a determination about an information need requires one to step back, think about what one knows, and apply a new strategy to each information situation. As we will see in later chapters, this ability to "determine" is unique to information literacy, especially when compared to other literacy types. This further supports information literacy as a metaliteracy in a social media age because it connects to other literacy formats while providing an overarching framework for multiple literacies. Metaliteracy builds on the standard characteristics of information literacy by adding the competencies to produce, collaborate, participate, and share in social media environments. It provides us with a model to think about what our learners may need to develop as self-aware individuals with the ability to adapt to ongoing changes in information and technology.

TOWARD A METALITERACY FRAMEWORK

As we have seen, metaliteracy is a reinvention of information literacy for a postmodern social media age. It prepares our learners to engage in the information environment as active, self-reflective, and critical contributors to these collaborative spaces. The timing is right to reconfigure information literacy, and several developments in the field have already challenged our assumptions about traditional definitions of the term. The postmodern era has influenced the many dimensions of learning, with theories about multiple literacies, multiple intelligences, and metacognition. While our approach to metaliteracy expands the standard definitions of information literacy and our model has some connection to previous theories related to the integration of related literacy types, we are also asserting a new idea. That is, metaliteracy provides an overarching model for connecting related literacies with an emphasis on emerging technologies. We argue that, based on a metacognitive perspective, learners develop skills and acquire knowledge through self-reflective awareness and understanding of their own literacies. This is accomplished when students apply a range of literacies in an associative way in collaborative learning environments. By applying a metacognitive approach to information literacy we open a multitude of possible learning strategies. Rather than simply teaching students how to gain skills, we prepare them to build on their skills and to think about their learning in novel ways. As active producers and publishers of original digital information, learners continuously reflect on their thinking and adapt to changing technologies. In this book we build on our initial call for reframing information literacy to a reinvention of information literacy through an increased emphasis on metacognition.

Multiple Intelligences

The complexity of individual experience and the need for an expanded understanding of interrelated competencies is exemplified in the work of Howard Gardner (1993) and his theory of "multiple intelligences" (pp. 8–9). Gardner has had a profound impact on the dialogue in many disciplines related to human intelligence and in helping us appreciate the importance of diverse learning styles. This is an essential perspective for developing a metaliteracy that acknowledges multiple information competencies and links related literacy types. In his book *Frames of Mind*, Gardner (1993) argues that "there is persuasive evidence for the existence of several relatively autonomous human intellectual competences" (p. 8). Gardner identifies various and interconnected ways of knowing as "multiple intelligences," and he asserts that "these are relatively independent of one another, and that they can be fashioned and combined in a multiplicity of adaptive ways by individuals and cultures" (pp. 8–9). Gardner's research offers an expanded and multipart understanding of human intelligence that challenges previously one-dimensional perspectives.

In *Multiple Intelligences: New Horizons*, Gardner (2006) recognizes the seven original intelligences that defined his multiple intelligence (MI) theory, including musical, bodily-kinesthetic, logical-mathematical, linguistic, spatial, interpersonal, and intrapersonal (pp. 8–18). At the core of Gardner's framework is that "intelligences always work in concert, and any sophisticated adult role will involve a melding of several of them" (p. 8). Gardner's MI theory distinguishes multiple ways of knowing, acknowledging that all individuals have different strengths and combine intelligences in diverse ways. In a post-modern age, single methods for understanding intellectual capabilities have been replaced by the multiplicity of Gardner's MI theory. This approach also recognizes a more complex self, based on the capability for various ways of knowing within a social context.

Multiliteracies

As with MI theory, we have seen similar changes to literacy that shifted from single to multiple perspectives. In 1996 the New London Group published the first paper on "multiliteracies" based on conversations that took place among this group in 1994 (p. 62). According to this team of ten researchers, the term *multiliteracies* recognizes two key aspects of literacy pedagogy based on social, cultural, and technological changes. First, this group argued for changes to literacy pedagogy based on the multiplicity of linguistic and textual forms in a global environment. Second, the multiliteracies methodology was influenced by the emergence of the Internet, multimedia, virtual communities, and desktop publishing. According to the authors, the first part of a multiliteracies pedagogy "relates to the increasing multiplicity and integration of significant modes of meaning-making, where the textual is also related to the visual, the audio, the spatial, the behavioral, and so on" (p. 64). The multiliteracies approach to literacy education acknowledges the multimodal communications and virtual environment evident at the time with television, advertising, and an emerging Internet. The second part of the term *multiliteracies* also provides "a way to focus on the realities of increasing local diversity and global connectedness" (p. 64). The multiliteracies movement places an emphasis on the importance of social settings in the development of literacy education based on real-world and virtual communities within international contexts.

According to the New London Group (1994), "When learners juxtapose different languages, discourses, styles, and approaches, they gain substantively in meta-cognitive and meta-linguistic abilities and in their ability to reflect critically on complex systems and their interactions" (p. 69). This rationale for exploring the interconnections of multiple literacies suggests a higher level of cognitive and linguistic capabilities and critical thinking than does focusing on a single approach. It also impacts learning design because, according to the authors, "metalanguages" are used in this context to "describe and explain patterns of meaning" and include several key elements of design: "Linguistic Design, Visual Design, Audio Design, Gestural Design, Spatial Design, and Multimodal Design" (p. 78). The different forms of design reflect the dynamics of multimedia environments and real-world social contexts. Design and meaning are interrelated in this framework and design itself is central because it asserts an active role for both teacher and learner (similar to envisioning learners as producers rather than just consumers). It also reveals multiple layers of complexity within an active learning and critical thinking framework.

The multiliteracies methodology and MI theory are similar because of the emphasis on the multiplicity of literacies and intelligences in a postmodern world of technology-mediated environments. Both theories also focus on high-level or metacognitive capabilities through the intersection of multimodal methods for learning.

As we will see, there is some similarity between multiliteracies and our metaliteracy model as well, but as a reinvention of information literacy, metaliteracy is focused much more directly on the foundation elements of information literacy (determine, access, evaluate, understand, incorporate, and use) and the intersections with related information literacies (media literacy, digital literacy, visual literacy, etc.). Metaliteracy is also a response to the convergence of social media, social networking, and mobile, online, and open learning. Gardner's MI theory and the multiliteracies approach of the New London Group do not fully address the social dimension of learning technologies. Today's virtual environment is very different from even a few years ago and it continues to evolve, requiring a pedagogical response from information literacy educators that challenges and expands existing frameworks.

Multimodal Literacy

The prevalence of emerging technologies in an ever-changing information environment influenced the development of multimodal literacy. According to Sean Cordes (2009), "Although reading and writing are still the foundation of knowledge, literacy in this age means more than the ability to read and write; it requires a complex set of skills including: access, analysis, synthesis, evaluation, and use of information in a variety of modes" (p. 1). As with metaliteracy and other expanded literacy frameworks in a social media age, multimodal literacy recognizes the need for a confluence of integrated abilities. It also situates the library as an essential part of this dynamic, as a space for documents in various forms and as a means for literacy instruction. This approach requires librarians to be familiar with multiple dimensions of information and technology to expand instructional practices. Cordes defines multimodal literacy as "the synthesis of multiple modes of communication" and as "a union of literacies in multiple modes" (p. 3). Within this framework, "communication can result in a transformation of the singular modes into a form that often contains new or multiple meanings" (p. 3). As such, communication moves across various media formats and informs how the messages are conveyed and understood.

Multimodal literacy builds on previous approaches to multiliteracies by integrating information literacy, visual literacy, multicultural literacy, and media literacy as a core group of literacies in a comprehensive multimodal framework (Cordes, 2009, pp. 2–3). It also recognizes the individual and collaborative abilities required to communicate and create in an increasingly complex information environment. Multimodal literacy is similar to MI theory and multiliteracies because it expands the scope of individual intelligences and skills to include several different characteristics and perspectives. It is also similar to metaliteracy because it combines multiple literacy types such as media and visual literacy. At the same time, however, multimodal literacy considers information literacy as just one of the combined literacies within a group, while our metaliteracy model identifies information literacy as the core literacy in an expanded and comprehensive structure for related literacy types.

Transliteracy

Transliteracy emerged outside the field of library and information science, but it has been embraced as a transformative theory within the field. It has also been discussed in relation to metaliteracy, although we see it as distinct from our model. According to Sue Thomas and colleagues (2007), *transliteracy* is defined as "the ability to read, write and interact across a range of platforms, tools and media from signing and orality through handwriting, print, TV, radio and film, to digital social networks." The use of the prefix *trans* in this context suggests the ability "to go across and beyond literacy to transliteracy" (Thomas et al., 2007).

Rather than focus on the integration of separate literacies, transliteracy provides a way to conceptualize and practice active engagement with different media formats through reading, writing, and interactivity. This approach reflects the multimodal and multimedia dynamics of our interconnected Web 2.0 environments while acknowledging that transliteracy is informed by and central to these revolutionary changes. The prefix *trans* in this context suggests movement, transformation, transferability, and adaptability across multiple media settings, from print to hypertext and multimedia. According to Tom Ipri (2010), "Despite the fact that transliteracy originated outside the library realm, librarians should follow the development of this concept because so much of transliteracy overlaps concerns much at the heart of librarianship" (p. 567). In many ways this has happened with the emergence of transliteracy conferences, blogs, and writings about transliteracy in relation to libraries and information literacy instruction.

This framework has captured the imagination of librarians because it overtly addresses the influence of emerging technologies on literacy rather than viewing technology as a secondary consideration. Librarians know that social media continues to have significant impact on our students and that we need a pedagogical response to this networked participatory environment. As Ipri notes, transliteracy "analyzes the relationship between people and technology, most specifically social networking, but is fluid enough to not be tied to any particular technology" (p. 532). This point suggests learner adaptability to new technologies that continuously transform at a rapid rate. As such, transliteracy provides a unified approach to literacy, rather than developing a new discrete literacy every time a new technology emerges.

At the same time, transliteracy does not address information literacy directly, although the theory certainly relates to how we understand information in relation to technological developments. By contrast, metaliteracy places information literacy at the center of 21st-century competencies as part of an expanded, overarching, and integrated framework. Metaliteracy builds on the information literacy foundation and recasts it for social media environments while challenging us to prepare students as active and self-aware producers of information. This framework connects to related literacy types to find commonality among multiple literacies in relation to the information literacy core principles. It is important to note that whether we are looking at a multi-, trans-, or metaliteracy, the postmodern era of multimedia and networked learning has demanded a pedagogical shift from a linear perspective to a multidimensional one that is based on multiplicity and associative ways of viewing one's world and perhaps oneself.

Michelle Kathleen Dunaway (2011) refers to both transliteracy and metaliteracy in her argument that the learning theory connectivism supports the goals of information literacy in today's networked learning environment (p. 676). Dunaway examines transliteracy and metaliteracy as emerging literacy frameworks that demonstrate evidence for a connectivist approach to information literacy. Connectivism is a learning theory developed by George Siemens (2004), who argues:

> The starting point of connectivism is the individual. Personal knowledge is comprised of a network, which feeds into organizations and institutions, which in turn feed back into the network, and then continue to provide learning to individual. This cycle of knowledge development (personal to network to organization) allows learners to remain current in their field through the connections they have formed.

This networked approach to learning situates the individual within an interactive social environment that is informed by the interrelated connections of participants. Knowledge is gained through personal and organizational connections within this expansive and evolving space. According to Siemens, connectivism has implications for our understanding of management and leadership, the media, news and information, personal knowledge, organizational knowledge, and how we design learning spaces.

Dunaway (2011) applies this theory specifically to information literacy instruction, with a particular emphasis on transliteracy and metaliteracy as new literacy concepts influenced by social media and emerging technologies.

SIMMS LIBRARY ALBUQUERQUE ACADEMY

According to Dunaway, transliteracy and metaliteracy "are central to the principles of the theory of connectivism, which postulates that communities, connections, information networks, and information technologies are central to the learning process" (p. 680). By exploring transliteracy and metaliteracy in relation to connectivism, Dunaway reinforces the need for collaborative learning that promotes the integration of related literacies in a comprehensive framework. This requires us to redesign our technology infrastructure to support networked learning and to rethink our instructional practices to include engagement with dynamic resources and online communities.

Dunaway also identifies a limit in the existing Association of College and Research Libraries (ACRL) *Information Literacy Competency Standards for Higher Education* (2000) by arguing that "the idea of learning networks, the central element of the theory of connectivism and arguably an important concept in emerging models of information literacy, is not clearly articulated in the ACRL standards, indicators, and outcomes" (p. 682). As with our metaliteracy model, Dunaway argues that the revolutionary changes in today's social learning environment require a new look at existing assumptions about information literacy education. As Dunaway points out, there are connections between transliteracy, metaliteracy, and connectivism. Although she argues that connectivism is more of a learning theory than either transliteracy or metaliteracy, all three approaches support fundamental changes in the learning environment and a necessary rethinking of how we learn through collaborative networks.

Metacompetency and Convergence

Prior to our use of the term *metaliteracy*, the idea of developing information literacy as a metacompetency was introduced by Annemaree Lloyd (2003), who argues: "As a meta-competency, information literacy enables the effective adaptation of existing information competencies, and the acquisition of new skills related to specific contexts such as the workplace" (p. 90). Lloyd explores this idea specific to workplace settings that require individuals to solve problems and make decisions as part of daily practice (p. 90). Within these particular information environments, the information literate individual builds on a foundation of skills while continuously adapting to change, acquiring new abilities, and applying one's knowledge. In 2007 Joan K. Lippincott identified a divide between information and technology literacy, arguing for "a convergence of literacies" in a unified framework that prepares students to actively produce information (p. 16). According to Lippincott, "It is time to frame the discussion of literacies in the context of academic work products rather than in the context of organizational structures (e.g., library, computing, English department, media department)" (p. 17). Lippincott argues that we need to bring together information and technology literacies to support learners as active content creators while challenging higher education organizational structures that prevent convergence.

The impact of participatory Web 2.0 environments on our conception of information literacy has informed new frameworks for information literacy instruction. For instance, Sharon Markless (2009) proposes an approach to the design of digital learning environments that would "support student choice in learning rather than information literacy teaching" (p. 34). This shift from a linear instructional mode to a decentered learning style focuses on the choices made by the student and reflects the nonlinear format of online spaces. According to Markless, "The impact of context on learning should lead students to make different choices about which strategies to employ in which order and which skills to draw on depending upon the nature of their current task and the wider social context in which they are operating" (p. 34). She outlines a "non-sequential" model for "information and critical literacies" based on "connecting with information," "interacting with information," and "making use of information" (pp. 35–36). The model she describes is effective in reminding us that learners do not necessarily engage with information in sequential order and that our instructional practices and online spaces should reflect learner choice. The nonlinear and asynchronous nature of online learning is ideal for this approach.

Greg Bobish applies constructivist principles in a unifying essay that examines the integration of social media in information literacy instruction. Bobish (2011) argues that five Web 2.0 tools relate directly to the ACRL (2000) *Information Literacy Competency Standards for Higher Education* and provides specific assignment examples for each standard. This mapping of tools to outcomes provides a practical and detailed argument for combining social media resources with information literacy instruction. According to Bobish (2011):

> By designing instruction in which students actually use current tools to create information as an author does, as well as more skillfully consuming information in all formats, we enable students to understand both the process of evaluating and using these tools and the visceral differences between posting and discussing something publicly as opposed to handing it in to one person (the instructor). (p. 63)

Bobish challenges instructors to know the tools our students are already familiar with but to do so in ways that improve information literacy skills. This approach exemplifies the "convergence of literacies" that Lippincott (2007) called for because Web 2.0 tools are integral to the learning outcomes within a constructivist framework that supports collaboration and participation. He also suggests that the consumer-producer binary is not a mutually exclusive one because we need both effective consumers of information and creative and well-informed producers. Overall, Bobish (2011) provides a constructivist methodology for effectively engaging learners with the technologies that reflect their real-world experience. He aligns specific Web 2.0 tools with the established ACRL Information Literacy Competency Standards. By doing so he supports a learner-centered approach to teaching information literacy that moves beyond the critical consumption of information to an expanded role in creating information with technology. This is a useful starting point for connecting the active production of information with an existing framework, but it will need to expand and change as the standards are revised and then continue to evolve over time.

■ ■ ■

Through this review of the literature we see that learning and literacy take multiple forms, are socially constructed, and are continuously mediated by new forms of technology. Developments in social media, social networking, and Web 2.0 have transformed the information landscape, requiring us to rethink our traditional assumptions about information, information literacy, and our instructional practices.

THE METALITERACY MODEL

The visual model for metaliteracy (figure 1.1) illustrates an integrated approach to information literacy. All of the core elements of the ACRL (2000) standard information literacy definition (determine, access, evaluate, understand, incorporate, and use) are components of this model. We, however, expand these characteristics to include four essential elements for today's social media environment: collaborate, participate, produce, and share. As discussed in this book, social media and social networking require additional competencies to address the interactive and participatory nature of such online and mobile resources as Facebook, Twitter, LinkedIn, Pinterest, YouTube, and many other evolving technologies. In today's social networking environment, learners engage with information as producers, collaborators, and distributors of original digital content in various forms. Our information literacy instructional practices must move beyond a search-and-retrieval mode to acknowledge the interactive social resources for creating original materials such as shared texts and hypertexts, tags, bookmarks, digital images and audio, multimedia, and virtual worlds. The standard definition of *information literacy* is not sufficient for these revolutionary changes and must be expanded to include these elements in collaborative, networked learning spaces.

Previous visual representations of information literacy have illustrated connections to related literacies and specific technologies, including the social

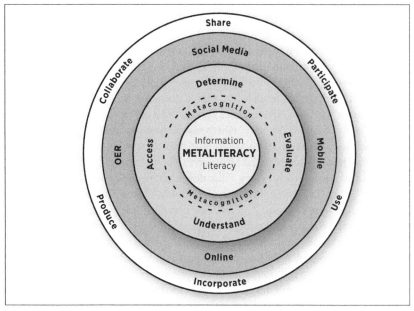

FIGURE 1.1
Metaliteracy Model

resources available with Web 2.0. Before we look at our metaliteracy model, we will review two other visual illustrations that emphasize learners as producers of information. For instance, in his discussion of information literacy practices in Germany, Thomas Hapke (2008) identifies the influence of collaborative social technologies on users as active and collaborative producers of information. He argues that "in the world of social software the 'users' or now better 'co-producers' take part in building up the content of the information systems like weblogs, wikis, etc." (p. 174). He points out that in this social environment users learn from other users and not just from the information system. Hapke visualizes the impact of these technologies on information literacy through a conceptualization of "Information Literacy 2.0" (p. 176). At the center of Hapke's holistic model is "Information Literacy 2.0" surrounded by four dimensions that include "Key competencies," "Web 2.0," "Learning," and "Learning about information" (p. 176). Each of these components includes specific examples, such as "weblog, wikis, and podcasts" in the Web 2.0 section and "story-telling and E-Portfolios" in the Learning section (p. 176). This is a useful framework because it acknowledges the impact of Web 2.0 on information literacy and it emphasizes specific social media resources and approaches to learning in these environments through storytelling and e-portfolios. This visual model also expands the standard competencies to include an emphasis on the social dimension of learning as well as the "competence of reflection" and the "competence of action," both key elements of a metacognitive approach.

In another integrated visual model, Mackey and Ho (2005) present a "convergent model for information literacy" that combines both research literacy and web literacy (p. 541). Similar to Hapke's holistic approach, Mackey and Ho present "a dynamic model that places students in active roles as author and producer" (p. 548). The authors conducted a research study that included a factor analysis of survey data, which was facilitated in an upper-level information literacy course that required students to develop original web pages. This research study identified a strong correlation between information literacy and information technology skills development and concluded that information literacy "is significantly associated with" three dimensions, including "web development knowledge," "web environment knowledge," and "research skills" (p. 553). This model combined specific research literacy skills, such as searching databases and writing and revising research essays, with web literacy skills in coding HTML and XML documents. Although this model was prior to Web 2.0 and did not provide a universal framework that could be easily applied in a range of educational settings (because of the strong focus on web design), this example demonstrates a convergence of information literacy and information technology proficiencies with a particular emphasis on the student as author in participatory web environments.

The metaliteracy model we present in this book reimagines information literacy through interrelated concentric circles (see figure 1.1). At the center of our circular model is the metaliteracy core, representing a revision of the original information literacy construct. The inner circle is surrounded by "metacognition" as a permeable layer that represents this key concept in relation to information literacy. The dashed circular line that surrounds metacognition illustrates the influence of this reflective approach throughout the other dimensions.

The metaliteracy model presents a circular visual representation of a collaborative approach to information literacy. Moving outward from the metaliteracy core, the next domain or sphere includes the ability to determine, access, evaluate, and understand information, all essential aspects of the original ACRL (2000) standard definition. As we discuss in chapter 3, these core elements are still relevant for social media and social networking and inform related literacy types such as visual literacy, digital literacy, and media literacy.

The next sphere includes specific reference to several significant trends in open and online learning, including social media, Open Educational Resources (OERs), mobile technologies, and online communities. All of these evolving technologies and social environments mediate how we determine a specific need for information as well as how we access, evaluate, and understand information. These are no longer individualized activities only, and a reinvention of information literacy must account for the influence of collaborative online communities. Social media includes any online or mobile resources that link users through interactive and participatory media; OERs are freely available educational resources for sharing and reuse; mobile technologies include smartphones, digital tablets, and mobile media players; and online communities include formal and informal spaces for groups to interact virtually about a range of topics, issues, or concerns. Over time, this mediation sphere will include other emerging technologies and trends that influence the related competencies in this evolving framework.

The outer sphere of this model includes the ability to incorporate and use information but also expands the domain to include the ability to produce and share information, and to collaborate and participate in social media settings. While incorporating and using information requires production, collaboration, and the sharing of digital resources, we need a more direct assertion of these concepts than currently available in the standard definition. As the interrelated and fluid domains of this metaliteracy model illustrate, the ability to collaborate and participate in socially constructed and networked spaces are key competencies as well. Through collaborative practice, learners determine, access, evaluate, and understand information as individuals and in partnership with others. Social environments expand how these central elements are understood and realized, shifting the emphasis from the individual to a community of users in a range of open, online, and mobile spaces.

This reinvention of information literacy places all of the essential characteristics in a nonlinear, circular, and transparent framework. This integrated design recognizes that users approach information from multiple perspectives and may start and end an information process (search, retrieval, creation, and distribution of information) from any point and not necessarily in sequential order. The original definitions of information literacy often suggested a particular sequence of skills development, but in a nonlinear and asynchronous online learning environment users apply these characteristics as needed and do not always follow the same pathway (even if instructed to do so). It is important for us to recognize that gaining information literacy knowledge is individualized and does not follow the same direction for all participants. While there is a scaffolding of skills in this process, learners are unique, bringing with them varying levels of prior knowledge and gaining new skills in an individualized manner. The circular nature of the visual metaliteracy model (see figure 1.1) offers flexibility and illustrates an open framework that could be approached from any point. The scaffolding that takes place in this context is decentered, building on the experiences and strengths of the individual while increasing skills and knowledge through active engagement with information in collaborative online and mobile settings.

The following two scenarios illustrate this model in practice. First, imagine a learner who approaches the metaliteracy model from the outer sphere as a producer and distributor of digital content in an informal setting that is outside the walls of the academy. In this example, the learner takes a picture or records a video of a public art display with a smartphone or portable tablet. This individual then uploads the digital image or movie instantly to a social media site or course wiki. After posting the digital materials online, the learner may gain new insights about the art object from comments made by a community of users. The act of sharing also informs others, sparking curiosity about the image, location, background, and perhaps a variety of community experiences or memories related to the object. In this scenario, learning about this public art object takes place on the spot and at the very moment of taking the picture, while opening a dialogue with others that may lead to new information and perspectives at different times.

Second, consider another scenario in which a learner starts from another point of access through a library website to locate a journal article for a research paper on public art. The learner may compare this document with freely available OERs on the same topic and then discuss it with a user community online. An expert on the topic may have informed the search process or provided background information through a blog or micro blog posting. This student will gain insights from many sources and will need to evaluate all of the materials as a critical reader of both traditional and online resources in several formats. This work may lead to the production of an individual or collaborative paper, project, or presentation in text, audio, video, or a combination of media elements, which will then be shared via a social learning environment, virtual world, blog, or wiki.

In both scenarios, the learners may have included a pre- and post-research process. For instance, the student who took the picture of the public art display may have conducted an informal Google search or a more refined search of resources via the local or college library website or app. This activity may have informed where and when to take the picture or video and essential background information about the artist and location. In the second scenario, the student who started with the formal search may have conducted a less formal pre-research process through the synthesis of tweets, dialogue in online communities, or the exploration of freely available OERs. The research topic itself may have been inspired by random access to the public art object in a community or online. Further, both learners may have included a post-research process with journaling of the experiences to self-assess how the information was accessed, evaluated, and created, or through tweets or blog postings that commented on different aspects of the inquiry. The learners are also making decisions on the fly and building their own knowledge as they go. This requires them to think about their own knowledge and to make decisions about what they need to know in order to take the next step. This process would allow for deeper insights about one's own metaliteracy, providing opportunities for reflection to build on existing knowledge. The possible scenarios for applying information literacy in social media settings are endless, requiring a comprehensive understanding of this construct for today's information environment.

While the information competencies may vary in both scenarios, depending on the prior knowledge of the learner and the information task at hand, the combination of several elements within the metaliteracy model supports multiple pathways to learning. Metaliteracy provides a solid foundation to effectively collaborate and participate in a variety of open and social media spaces as active and critical thinkers.

This integrated visual model (figure 1.1) supports our definition of *metaliteracy* for a social media age as a new way to think about information literacy as a dynamic and collaborative approach to knowledge. This model combines multiple competencies and is informed by links to related literacy types in a collaborative network for learning. The idea of *meta*literacy shifts the focus from the discrete skills of any particular literacy type and avoids the ongoing drift to embrace the latest literacy. Metaliteracy is a larger framework for literacy itself that adapts to changes in technology and unites associated literacies. In this context, information literacy is the unifying structure for all related literacy types. The basic principles that traditionally defined information literacy (define, access, evaluate, understand, incorporate, and use) provide a relevant foundation for integrated literacies, but these terms must be reimagined in a networked, participatory, virtual, and open social media environment. In addition, information literacy must be reinvented for the social media age to reflect the ongoing changes in this environment (collaborate, participate, produce, and share). The term *meta* is used as a prefix to suggest a fundamental change in how we conceptualize information literacy and to describe the comprehensive nature of this construct. As such, metaliteracy is literacy about literacy. As we argued in our original essay, "Reframing Information Literacy as a Metaliteracy," "Many of the information literacy characteristics are central to multiple literacy perspectives, defining a literacy framework about literacy. Metaliteracy provides an integrated and all-inclusive core for engaging with individuals and ideas in digital information environments" (Mackey & Jacobson, 2011, p. 70). This approach presents a way to continually examine and revise our approaches to information literacy through reflection and reinvention. Rather than simply respond to the latest technology with a new literacy type, we need to identify connections to related literacies within an expanded framework. This comprehensive model shifts the emphasis from discrete skills development to an inclusive, collaborative, and self-reflective approach to knowledge.

CONCLUSION

As this first chapter demonstrates, views on literacy and learning continue to evolve and include a multiplicity of formats and approaches. As a starting point for this book, we outlined relevant developments in postmodernism, metacognition, multiple intelligences, multiliteracies, transliteracy, connectivism, metacompetency, convergence, and multimodal literacy. This review of the literature reinforces a need for expanding information literacy with a particular emphasis on the collaborative production and sharing of information in many forms. Rather than discard or replace the work that has already been done in the area of information literacy, we argue for a new concept that builds on this critical foundation and reinvents information literacy as a metaliteracy.

The metaliteracy model (figure 1.1) is a flexible and transparent visual representation of a wide-ranging and expanded information literacy framework. We added to the standard information literacy competencies the creation, sharing, and distribution of original digital content through a participatory social media network. This framework also includes a metacognitive component that supports the deep understanding and potential spur to growth of one's own information literacies. This approach challenges us to teach students to self-assess and reflect on their own learning. A metaliteracy framework informed by metacognition supports a self-reflexive process that includes such activities as journaling, peer interaction, collaborative problem solving, and the use of social media tools for the original development of ideas and to continuously reflect on one's education. These interactive competencies reinforce the collaborative nature of emerging technologies and recognize that individuals are complex beings with multiple ways of learning and knowing. Our learners are both individual and collaborative, developing strong connections to portable gadgets and devices while building formal and informal relationships among other participants in a range of open and online communities.

This expansion of the information literacy competencies is only the first part of this process. In the next chapter we examine many of the key trends in open learning and social media that have inspired our metaliteracy model. We also explore how our understanding of information itself has changed in these networked spaces. This reinvention of information literacy as a metaliteracy will allow us to rethink our instructional practices and prepare our students for critical engagement with socially and technologically mediated information environments. Metaliteracy empowers learners to be active and collaborative participants while encouraging metacognitive reflection.

REFERENCES

Allaby, Michael. (2011). Meta-. In *A dictionary of ecology* (4th ed.). Oxford Reference Online. Oxford University Press. www.oxfordreference.com/views/ENTRY .html?subview=Main&entry=t14.e3479

Andrews, Edmund L. (1993, September 15). Business technology; policy blueprint ready for data superhighway. *The New York Times*. www.nytimes.com

Arizpe, Evelyn, & Styles, Morag. (2003). Picturebooks and metaliteracy: Children talking about how they read pictures. In Evelyn Arizpe & Morag Styles (Eds.), *Children reading pictures: Interpreting visual texts* (pp. 190–201). London, England: RoutledgeFalmer.

Association of College and Research Libraries. (2000). *Information literacy competency standards for higher education*. American Library Association. www.ala.org/ala/mgrps/divs/acrl/standards/standards.pdf

Bobish, Greg. (2011). Participation and pedagogy: Connecting the social web to ACRL learning outcomes. *The Journal of Academic Librarianship, 37*(1), 54–63.

Boonstra, Claire. (2009, December 1). Layar 3.0 launched: 5 cases to show the power of the platform [Blog post]. http://layar.com/blog/2009/12/01/layar-30-launched-5-cases-to-show-the-power-of-the-platform

Bourdieu, Pierre. (1992). *The logic of practice* (Richard Nice, Trans.). Stanford University Press.

Bourdieu, Pierre. (2000). *Pascalian meditations* (Richard Nice, Trans.). Stanford University Press.

Bourdieu, Pierre, & Wacquant, Loic J. D. (1992). *An invitation to reflexive sociology*. The University of Chicago Press.

Cordes, Sean. (2009, August). *Broad horizons: The role of multimodal literacy in 21st century library instruction*. World Library and Information Congress: 75th IFLA General Conference and Council, Milan, Italy. www.ifla.org/annual-conference/ifla75/index.htm

Dunaway, Michelle Kathleen. (2011). Connectivism: Learning theory and pedagogical practice for networked information landscapes. *Reference Services Review, 39*(4), 675–685.

Flavell, J. H. (1979). Metacognition and cognitive monitoring: A new area of cognitive–developmental inquiry. *American Psychologist, 34*(10), 906–911.

Gardner, H. (1993). *Frames of mind: The theory of multiple intelligences* (10th-anniversary ed.). New York, NY: Basic Books.

Gardner, H. (2006). *Multiple intelligences: New horizons*. New York, NY: Basic Books.

Gilmore, Perry, & Smith, David M. (2005). Seizing academic power: Indigenous subaltern voices, metaliteracy, and counternarratives in higher education. In *Language, literacy, and power in schooling* (pp. 67–88). Mahwah, NJ: Lawrence Erlbaum.

Griffith, Priscilla L., & Ruan, Jiening. (2005). What is metacognition and what should be its role? In Susan E. Israel, Cathy Collins Block, Kathryn L. Bauserman, and Kathryn Kinnucan-Welsch (Eds.), *Metacognition in literacy learning: Theory, assessment, instruction, and professional development* (pp. 3–18). Mahwah, NJ: Lawrence Erlbaum.

Hapke, Thomas. (2008). Information literacy activities in Germany between the Bologna Process and the web 2.0. In Carla Basili (Ed.), *Information literacy at the crossroad of education and information policies in Europe* (pp. 165–183). Rome: Consiglio Nazionale delle Ricerche.

Hartman, Hope J. (Ed.). (2002). *Metacognition in learning and instruction: theory, research and practice*. Boston, MA: Kluwer Academic Publishers.

Ince, Darrel. (2009). Meta. In *A dictionary of the Internet*. Oxford Reference Online. Oxford University Press. www.oxfordreference.com/views/ENTRY .html?subview=Main&entry=t12.e209

Ingraham, Bruce, Levy, Phil, McKenna, Colleen, & Roberts, George. (2007). Academic literacy in the 21st century. In Gráinne Conole & Martin Oliver (Eds.). *Contemporary Perspectives in E-learning Research: Themes, methods and impact on practice* (pp. 160–173). London, England: Routledge.

Ipri, Tom. (2010, November). Introducing transliteracy: What does it mean to academic libraries? *College & Research Libraries News, 71*(10), 532–567. http:// crln.acrl.org/content/71/10/532.full.pdf+html

Kent, Allen, Lancour, Harold, & Nasri, William Z. (2000). *Encyclopedia of library and information science* (Vol. 67).

Kerka, Sandra. (2000). Extending information literacy in electronic environments. *New Directions for Adult and Continuing Education*, (88), 27–38.

Libraries and Transliteracy (n.d.). What is transliteracy? [Blog post]. http:// librariesandtransliteracy.wordpress.com/what-is-transliteracy

Lippincott, Joan K. (2007, November/December). Student content creators: Convergence of literacies. *Educause Review, 42*(6), 16–17. www.educause. edu/EDUCAUSE+Review/EDUCAUSEReviewMagazineVolume42/ StudentContentCreatorsConverge/162072

Lloyd, Annemaree. (2003, June). Information literacy: The meta-competency of the knowledge economy? An exploratory paper. *Journal of Librarianship and Information Science, 35*, 87–92.

Lotherington, Heather. (2004). Emergent metaliteracies: What the Xbox has to offer the EQAO. *Linguistics and Education, 14*, 305–319.

Lyotard, J. (1984). *The postmodern condition: A report on knowledge* (G. Bennington & B. Massumi, Trans.). Minneapolis, MN: University of Minnesota Press.

Mackey, Thomas P., & Jinwon, Ho (2005). Implementing a convergent model for information literacy: combining research and web literacy. *Journal of Information Science, 31*(6), 541–555.

Mackey, Thomas P., & Jacobson, Trudi E. (2011). Reframing information literacy as a metaliteracy. *College & Research Libraries, 72*(1), 62–78.

Markless, Sharon. (2009). A new conception of information literacy for the digital learning evironment in higher education. *Nordic Journal of Information Literacy in Higher Education, 1*(1), 25–40.

Mazzolini, Renato G. (2003). Metamorphosis. In J. L. Heilbron (Ed.), *The Oxford companion to the history of modern science.* Oxford Reference Online. Oxford University Press. www.oxfordreference.com/views/ENTRY. html?subview=Main&entry=t124.e0463

Meta. (2011). In *Oxford English dictionary (OED) online.* Oxford University Press. www.oed.com/viewdictionaryentry/Entry/117150

Middle States Commission on Higher Education. (2006). *Characteristics of excellence in higher education: Eligibility requirements and standards for accreditation* (12th ed.). www.msche.org/publications/CHX06060320124919.pdf

Nelson, Thomas O. (1992). *Metacognition: Core readings.* Boston, MA: Allyn and Bacon.

Roberts, A. (2000). *Fredric Jameson.* Florence, KY: Routledge.

Siemens, George. (2004). Connectivism: A learning theory for the digital age. *elearnspace: everything elearning.* www.elearnspace.org/Articles/connectivism .htm

Spitzer, Kathleen L., Eisenberg, Michael B., & Lowe, Carrie A. (1998). *Information literacy: Essential skills for the information age.* Information Resources Publications, Syracuse University. www.eric.ed.gov/ERICWebPortal/ detail?accno=ED427780

Thomas, Sue, Joseph, Chris, Laccetti, Jess, Mason, Bruce, Mills, Simon, Perril, Simon, & Pullinger, Kate. (2007, December 3). Transliteracy: Crossing divides. *First Monday, 12*(12). www.uic.edu/htbin/cgiwrap/bin/ojs/index.php/fm/article/ view/2060/1908

Transliteracy Research Group. (2010). Transliteracy Blog. Retrieved December 3, 2011. http://nlabnetworks.typepad.com/transliteracy

Webb, Jen, & Schirato, Tony. (2003). Bourdieu's concept of reflexivity as metaliteracy. *Cultural Studies, 17*(3/4), 539.

Webb, Jen, Schirato, Tony, & Danaher, Geoff. (2002). *Understanding Bourdieu.* London, England: Sage.

2
Metaliteracy in the Open Age of Social Media

N OW THAT WE HAVE ESTABLISHED A THEORETICAL FRAME-
work for metaliteracy as a metacognitive approach to information literacy, this chapter will examine the rapid expanse of social technologies
that influence open and collaborative approaches to learning. Today's social
media environment is a participatory network for consuming, producing,
and sharing information. The use of Facebook, for instance, has significantly
altered the types of digital content that are reused and shared online among
a network of friends and acquaintances. We have seen the democratization
of media through self-publishing in many forms including the distribution
of original ideas in individual and collaborative blogs. Twitter has created a
tweeting and re-tweeting culture of original and reusable content based on
140-character blurbs of information. The creators and distributors of these
materials do so on the fly through portable devices that allow for instantaneous mobile communications. The process of highlighting and sharing articles and online readings of interest has become an open practice with social
bookmarking sites including Delicious, StumbleUpon, and Reddit. A new form
of visual networking through Pinterest provides a space for collecting digital

artifacts with virtual pin boards. Tagging content in all forms including both visual and textual information allows participants to connect ideas thematically and to optimize search engine results based on key concepts. In addition, the massive open online course (MOOC) has revolutionized open and online learning on a monumental scale and has challenged educators to think in new ways about the creation and delivery of teaching and learning.

These profound changes in media formats and conceptions of higher education have had a significant impact on our understanding of information itself as something collaboratively produced and distributed. Our schools and libraries have been challenged by these radical developments. This has required faculty to think carefully about how and when learning takes place and through which modality. At the same time, librarians have tried to respond to this revolution when time for both preparation and instruction in social media and open learning environments are so limited and the one-shot library session is still the norm at many institutions.

The information age, which initially inspired the information literacy movement, has transformed into a post-information age of decentered content producers in an expansive global network. This cultural shift has resulted in the open age of social media, exemplified through countless social technologies and defined by democratic participation in transparent systems. While these changes seem ideal, tensions play out between open and closed systems, freely available and commercial endeavors, as well as old and new conceptions of information literacy. Metaliteracy provides a frame for rethinking our teaching and learning practices in these networked environments while encouraging innovation and change in traditional library instruction. It also challenges us to think beyond the library as the sole provider for information literacy instruction and instead to envision metaliteracy as embedded throughout the curriculum and supported by the entire institution.

We start this chapter with "Trends in Social Media" to describe the expansive use of social networking sites such as Facebook and Pinterest. We also review self-publishing trends in blogs and microblogs, and the emergence of global mobility through the use of portable networked devices around the world. This section illustrates why we need a flexible, open, and collaborative metaliteracy model to reflect these socially constructed virtual spaces. Then, in the next part of this chapter, "From Information Age to Post-Information Age," we take a close look at the transformation of the information age to a post-information age. This section provides a theoretical exploration of information as it has morphed from linear entities within hierarchical systems to non-linear fragments collectively produced and shared through connected networks. We follow this section with "The Open Age of Social Media" to describe participatory design and open learning in today's social media environment. This includes a discussion of metadata initiatives and the Semantic

Web for developing connected, open, and interoperable spaces for knowledge production and sharing.

TRENDS IN SOCIAL MEDIA

Several indicators suggest considerable changes in the way we communicate with one another and manage information through social media. According to Roger E. Bohn and James E. Short in a 2009 report on information consumption, *How Much Information?*, "a full third of words and more than half of bytes are now received interactively" (p. 7), pointing to a major shift in how we use information, from passive consumption to interactive engagement. In addition, this report noted the influence of social media and argued that "Web use was changing due to the rapid uptake of social networks such as Facebook and MySpace" (p. 20). As the consumption and production of information continued to increase over time, the site MySpace was eventually replaced by Facebook as the dominant social network of choice. We have seen a diversification of social media resources and a tension between freely available tools and proprietary interests.

Social media connects us with one another in a global network using a range of resources and devices. These spaces integrate multimedia and promote the sharing of information that is visual, textual, and auditory. Social media is both synchronous and asynchronous allowing real-time discussions with chat and video conferencing while providing delayed communications through discussion boards, gaming, and e-mail. For instance, Facebook features multiple modes of communication and promotes virtual interaction with status updates, chat, games, e-mail, photo sharing, and tagging. We have also seen the emergence of Pinterest, a rapidly expanding resource to collect and share visual artifacts online and through mobile technologies.

Social and Visual Networking

As trends in social media continued to advance quickly, Facebook reached a significant milestone in October 2012 with one billion users internationally (Smith, Segall, & Cowley, 2012). The Nielsen ratings service acknowledged Facebook's rise as the primary social networking medium in the United States and globally: "Among the most visited websites around the world, Facebook had roughly 152 million unique U.S. visitors in March 2012—or, more than two out of three Americans who were active online visited Facebook" (Nielsen Wire, 2012b). Based on Nielsen's analysis, Facebook is the top social networking site in 11 out of the 12 countries examined, including Brazil, Italy,

Spain, and France. At the same time, we have seen a diversification of social media choices and the adoption of social networks beyond Facebook. Nielsen reports: "While Facebook is the top social network globally, many netizens visit multiple social media sites; in Japan blog sites are more popular in the social media category (Facebook is ranked 5th), and in Brazil sites like Tumblr and Google+ are growing quickly as well" (NielsenWire, 2012b). This expanding set of options and the mixed response to the initial public offering of Facebook in 2012 may indicate the emergence of an international social network that is open to variation and nonproprietary solutions and less focused on one dominant provider (Morgenson, 2012). The open learning movement, for instance, extends beyond commercial interests and instead promotes interoperable systems, shared resources, and collaborative practices that advance universal participation and learning.

A research study published by the Pew Internet and American Life Project, titled "Why Most Facebook Users Get More Than They Give," sheds some light on the expanded use of Facebook and how users interact in this environment. The authors note, "Half the adults and three-quarters of the teenagers in America use social networking sites and Facebook by far is the most popular of these sites" (Hampton et al., 2012). This indicates widespread use of Facebook as the primary social networking site among adults and teenagers in the United States. The same report identifies "power users" who are much more active in this environment than the typical user (Hampton et al., 2012). While the number of Facebook participants continues to increase, the type of use varies considerably and a core group of "power users" drives much of the interaction: "When we explored the density of people's friendship networks, we found that people's friends lists are only modestly interconnected" (Hampton et al., 2012). This study challenges one of the basic assumptions about how people are linked via social networking. That is, while the Facebook community continues to increase in size, the extent to which users are actually associated and active in this space is not the same among all participants. The authors argue:

> These power users, who, depending on the type of content, account for 20% to 30% of Facebook users in our sample, "like" other users' content, tag friends in pictures, and send messages at a much higher rate than the typical Facebook user. Power users tend to specialize. Some 43% of those in our sample were power users in at least one Facebook activity: sending friend requests, pressing the like button, sending private messages, or tagging friends in photos. Only 5% of Facebook users were power users on all of these activities, 9% on three, and 11% on two. It is this intensive set of users on each activity that explains why, when we look at the average amount of content sent and received in a month,

> it appears that Facebook user[s tend] to receive more than they give (Hampton et al., 2012).

This is probably not a surprise to most Facebook users, but the way individuals interact within this space and apply different features varies within a network of friends. Less than half of the respondents in this report are especially energetic in using key interactive features, such as tagging, liking, and private messaging. A much smaller proportion of users apply all of the features available through this interface. This one study suggests a divide among participants in engagement and perhaps a hierarchical relationship among those who produce and share information and those who receive it. Overall, this report suggests a need for continued research into the nature of online relationships and what it means to be "friends" within these social spaces. In the Facebook era, the definition of friendship has changed considerably from the traditional connotation of a close personal relationship to work colleagues, acquaintances, family members, and casual links within a worldwide network.

Presently, with one billion users globally, Facebook is clearly the primary social networking site of choice (Smith, Segall, and Cowley, 2012). At the same time, according to the "Social Media Update 2013" by the Pew Internet and American Life Project, "Facebook is the dominant social networking platform in the number of users, but a striking number of users are now diversifying onto other platforms" (Duggan and Smith, 2013, p. 1). As the field of options continues to expand, other social media formats are emerging with distinctive features that appeal to users interested in producing, organizing, and sharing information. For instance, Pinterest is a virtual pin board site that is a popular social space for sharing visual information within a social network. According to Nielsen: "Like Tumblr, Pinterest is a visually-oriented social media site that is also growing rapidly, with over 10 million unique U.S. visitors in December 2011, almost double their audience from October" (NielsenWire, 2012a). The popularity of Pinterest demonstrates the evolving social trends in collecting and sharing visual information via the web and mobile devices. Pinterest users collect and arrange visual information based on their own creations or via digital images and virtual artifacts they discover and share online. The Pinterest site offers many examples of virtual pin boards, including recipes, fashion, patterns, furniture, accessories, flowers, wedding plans, and design ideas.

Pinterest and other social media resources are easily integrated with Facebook, so while there is a variation of social media choices, many lead back to Facebook as users share their discoveries with Facebook friends and often invite them to participate in new environments. Facebook is proprietary and connects users to commercial resources for advertising, travel, gaming, news, and photo sharing. These partnerships allow Facebook to link more users than it could in isolation and expands its influence beyond one site to countless web and mobile resources. As other social networks gain in popularity, Facebook is strategically placed at the center of these commercial interests as the primary interface to link and share. As a profit-making site, Facebook is also highly competitive and makes design decisions based on innovative trends in social media. For instance, Hayley Tsukayama (2012) reports that "Pinterest's simple pinboard design has resonated with social media users since the site took off earlier this year. But it's faced competition from bigger social networks, such as Facebook, which have adapted that simple, grid-like layout into their own products to let users display things or products that they like." Tsukayama (2012) describes the way design decisions are made in a highly competitive environment that seeks new consumers. Pinterest integrates well with the Facebook interface but also introduces novel ways to display information that Facebook and other sites then replicate in their own design.

Blogs and Microblogs

The blog is a popular format for self-publishing user-generated content in a range of media formats. According to Technorati (2011), "Nearly 90% of bloggers are using some form of multimedia on their blogs, the most popular form being photos. Half of all bloggers surveyed use video on their blog, while another 10% use audio." Technorati also notes that more than half of bloggers are sharing repurposed multimedia information rather than original materials: "Among respondents who create assets, 48% of the multimedia they post is their own creation. This is down significantly from 67% in 2010." This decrease in the posting of original material may be due to the increased video resources available online through YouTube, and/or the continued acceptance of digital materials with Creative Commons licensing. This statistic demonstrates the importance of both producing and sharing information online, as social media promotes both functions through a variety of interactive resources. Technorati reports that "Wordpress is the most popular blog hosting service among all respondents, used by 51%. Blogger and Blogspot hosting services are also popular (21% and 14%)." These freely available sites make it easy for users to develop blog content, without having to code web pages. The standard blog includes interactive functionality with comments from users, RSS feeds, archive, and the integration of Facebook and Twitter updates.

The re-tweeting of information through Twitter further emphasizes the nature of sharing ideas in social media settings. Re-tweeting allows users to highlight and share the tweets of those followed by individuals in Twitter. In addition, users are informed when their tweets are shared, adding a status dimension to the original message. This works like a virtual citation because a re-tweet means that the original message was important enough to share with an individual's followers, similar to the way citations mark the importance of a scholarly work. In many ways we have become a re-tweeting culture that participates in an asynchronous conversation based on 140-character fragments of information. The sharing of ideas is continuous and circuitous within this global network. Although the use of Twitter is not as extensive as Facebook, the acceptance of this microblogging site has increased, especially as it has shifted to mobile devices. According to Aaron Smith (2011), in a research study titled *Twitter Update 2011* conducted for the Pew Internet and American Life Project, "As of May 2011, 13% of online adults use the status update service Twitter," which was an increase from the 8 percent of users reported in 2010. Smith also reports that half of those surveyed indicated that they used a mobile device to access Twitter, illustrating the changes we have observed in how people access and use the Internet based on mobility rather than standard computers. Further, Twitter feeds have been incorporated into blogs and websites and linked to other social media resources such as Facebook, providing additional venues for sharing this microblogging tool.

Global Mobility

In an article published by *Wired Magazine*, Chris Anderson and Michael Wolff (2010) proclaim, "The Web Is Dead: Long Live the Internet." The authors argue that we have shifted from a reliance on web navigation for searching information to the use of mobile apps with specific functions for performing tasks. They predict that within five years "the number of users accessing the Net from mobile devices will surpass the number who access it from PCs," which is a profound change in how we communicate, as well as access, create, and share information. Since 2010, for instance, mobility has had a significant impact on how we navigate the Internet, communicate with other users via social media, interact through text messaging and e-mail, and play games. It has spawned an apps culture that continues to grow exponentially with a host of portable resources related to news and entertainment, weather information, music downloading, mapping, e-books, and search. Mobility has also expanded our portable productivity functions for writing, presentations, spreadsheets, and calendar functions as well as for interactive consumer resources related to banking, retail, and travel. Further, mobility has been incorporated into learning management systems such as Moodle and Blackboard and the adoption rates for mobile devices continue to advance in the United States and internationally.

The Pew Internet and American Life Project published a report that examines the smartphone adoption rates in the United States. Aaron Smith (2012) argues, "Nearly half (46%) of American adults are smartphone owners as of

February 2012, an increase of 11 percentage points over the 35% of Americans who owned a smartphone last May." Smith (2012) reports that the increases have taken place across multiple demographics, allowing for a fairly broad adoption rate that has leveled the playing field through many different populations. Some groups, however, such as seniors and individuals who do not possess high school diplomas, have increased smartphone usage at only modest rates (Smith, 2012). This suggests that while strides continue to be made in bridging the digital divide through mobility, we still have some work to do in providing equal access to everyone through this innovative technology.

In a special edition of *Open Learning: The Journal of Open and Distance Learning*, guest editor Agnes Kukulska-Hulme (2010) discusses mobility as an international movement for transforming learning. She introduces several examples of mobile learning from around the world and argues that portable devices provide access to previously underrepresented groups. In her editorial that presents this collection of essays, the author emphasizes equal access to mobile learning as a central concern internationally:

> Learning is open to all when it is inclusive, and mobile technologies are a powerful means of opening up learning to all those who might otherwise remain at the margins of education. Mobile learning can reach those who have missed out on the opportunity to learn, and those who have been disappointed in their previous experiences of learning which did not seem to be compatible with their personality or which did not fit in with other priorities or busy schedules. (Kukulska-Hulme, 2010, p. 184)

Mobile devices offer great potential for closing the digital divide through a usable, accessible, and relatively inexpensive means for creating and communicating information. As Kukulska-Hulme suggests, mobile technologies such as netbooks, portable media players, and smartphones are being incorporated into learning practices in locations around the world. The author argues, "Many mobile phones now perform all the functions of a computer, whilst other lightweight devices such as personal media players, notebooks, slates and tablets make learning truly personal and portable" (Kukulska-Hulme, 2010, p. 184). Global mobility extends the classroom to sites beyond the traditional classroom settings by connecting a network of learners at a distance, and transforming any location in the real world to a learning space by engaging students where they are. This approach reinforces mobile learning as a social activity that is shared among multiple points of portable access.

Global statistics provide further evidence that the use of these portable devices is rapidly expanding around the world. In some countries mobility exceeds the use of fixed computers to access the Internet. According to the International Telecommunication Union (2012), we have nearly six billion cell phone users globally and "with 5.9 billion mobile-cellular subscriptions, global penetration reaches 87%, and 79% in the developing world." In some countries mobile broadband has provided access to the Internet in a way that would not have been possible otherwise. For instance, "in Africa mobile-broadband penetration has reached 4% compared with less than 1% for fixed-broadband penetration" (International Telecommunication Union, 2012). In some parts of the world it has been beneficial to bypass fixed computing as a mode of access to the Internet in favor of mobile devices. This trend offers much potential for the future since mobile devices are less expensive than other computing solutions, but we need to design for mobility in order to take full advantage of this technological revolution. When doing so, we create learning environments and activities that promote interactivity and collaboration among mobile participants. This will bridge the digital divide and inform the design of user interfaces that make it easy to create and distribute all forms of content from any location in the world. Designing for mobility provides opportunities for thinking about the learning experience and interface itself, and how our communications are mediated by mobile technologies. As part of this process, metaliteracy encourages self-reflection and metacognition through journaling, posting, tagging, tweeting, and re-tweeting information with an emphasis on critical thinking and the analysis of shared content.

UNESCO (2012b) promotes global mobility as a resource for lifelong learning through a series of working papers, online resources, and the establishment of "Mobile Learning Week." According to Mark West (2012), "there are a staggering 5.9 billion mobile phone subscriptions on a planet with 7 billion people" (p. 6). This expansive reach offers considerable potential to increase portable and interactive approaches to learning internationally. West also argues that "over 70% of mobile subscriptions worldwide come from the developing world, and thanks to rapidly declining prices, powerful mobile handsets previously available only to wealthy individuals are increasingly within reach of the poor" (p. 6). Mobility has started to close some aspects of the digital divide in different parts of the world by providing access to reasonably priced technology devices in places where other computing options have been cost prohibitive. According to West, "Access to robust mobile networks is nearly universal: 90% of the world's population and an impressive 80% of the population living in rural areas are blanketed by a mobile network" (p. 6). This level of global access to portable learning resources resolves some of the traditional access barriers based on financial constraints, location, and technology format. But according to West, we still need to address some of the perception problems with mobile learning and what he sees as "a stigma that can and should be overcome" (p. 7). For instance, he states that mobile devices "are commonly viewed as isolating, distracting and even dangerous to young people, providing access to inappropriate content and enabling destructive behaviours such as cyber-bullying" (p. 7). These concerns definitely need to be addressed as part of the mobility revolution and will require users to gain a critical-thinking perspective about this technology. At the same time, however, the benefits gained from improved access to information through global mobility cannot be underestimated. In order to take full advantage of mobile resources, we need a pedagogical and policy strategy that supports open access and an emphasis on expanded and integrated literacies. Metaliteracy provides a way to address these concerns through its comprehensive framework that encourages the effective use of emerging technologies. It challenges users to embrace new tools while asking critical questions about the design and application of these resources.

The 2012 Horizon Report asserts that mobility is changing how we use and share information. According to Johnson, Adams, and Cummins (2012), mobile apps and tablets are the top two "technologies to watch" within the first 12-month period of the report's publication. The authors of this report recognize that today's learners have access to a variety of mobile devices (from phones to tablets) and "expect to be able to work, learn, and study whenever and wherever they want to" (p. 4). The development of mobile apps is a rapidly increasing industry that includes both commercial and educational resources. The popularity of tablet computing has led to a collaborative user experience for sharing information in remote settings that expand beyond the traditional classroom. According to the 2012 Horizon Report:

> Because tablets are able to tap into all the advantages that mobile apps bring to smaller devices, but in a larger format, higher education institutions are seeing them not just as an affordable solution for one-to-one learning, but also as a feature-rich tool for field and lab work, often times replacing far more expensive and cumbersome devices and equipment. (Johnson, Adams, & Cummins, 2012, p. 7)

Tablet computing makes possible a tactile dimension to learning based on touch-screen functionality. The portability of these devices allows learning to take place in any location, outside the traditional classroom. This promotes interactivity in face-to-face learning environments and provides a bridge to online learning, for creating and distributing information collaboratively. Portable tablets enhance both individual and team based learning, supporting face-to-face, blended, and online instruction.

The 2013 version of The Horizon Report emphasized both MOOCs and tablet computing as the top two "technologies to watch" (Johnson, et. al., 2013, p. 4). According to the report, "Tablets have proven to be a solid fit with today's always-connected university students, and the recent expansion of the tablet market is presenting them with a wide array of affordable options" (Johnson, et. al., 2013, p. 4). While the increasing use of tablet computing is transforming the traditional campus environment, by providing university students with continuous access to educational resources, this trend also expands the scope of when and where learning takes place worldwide. Tablets extend the classroom to anywhere the learner happens to be, while also opening educational opportunities to anyone in the world with a mobile device. The synergy between tablet computing and OERs offers great potential for expanding learning and literacy across the globe by providing portable access to information within an interactive network.

■ ■ ■

Based on this review of trends in social media, metaliteracy has a role to play in how learners interact in social and visual networking environments such as Facebook and Pinterest. Metaliteracy challenges learners to analyze and use social spaces such as blogs and microblogs for self-publishing and sharing reusable content. These interactions often take place through a mobile network that is international in scope. Since metaliteracy considers the relationship between technology and learning, a meta perspective recognizes emergent trends such as global mobility and prepares reflective creators and distributors of information in these settings. Metaliterate individuals adapt to changing technologies and think about their own learning in these spaces. This metacognitive emphasis prepares students to ask questions about how systems function and how to be active contributors as the social environments evolve. Metaliteracy is a framework for thinking about ways to democratize an online environment that may not be as egalitarian as many assume. For instance, Facebook and other online communities include participants who are more active than others. In these networked spaces, a metaliterate individual would ask critical questions to be aware of this dynamic and consider ways to effectively engage in this group setting.

Metaliteracy fosters active engagement online and provides learners with a means to develop the specific competencies to produce, arrange, and communicate visual information in socially networked environments. It inspires the critical consumption of information that is created and shared by others. For instance, Pinterest requires a critical thinking perspective related to the quality and purpose of digital objects within a particular pin board collection and how these materials are organized and distributed. A metaliterate individual would gain insights about how to develop criteria for a collection of visual and virtual objects in this space. A meta perspective would challenge participants to improve the quality of images found and shared, leading to a coherent organization of materials in this environment.

Overall, metaliteracy prepares learners to navigate social spaces as individuals while learning about community building and how to interact in meaningful ways. This approach moves beyond skills development only to maximize the creative and democratic potential of social and visual network-ing sites for the dynamic production of new knowledge. In addition, consistent with the foundation elements of information literacy, metaliteracy includes an emphasis on ways to define the relevance and credibility of information in social media settings. For instance, how do we advance the critical evaluation of information created by multiple participants? What are the specific compe-tencies for the assessment of information when everyone is a contributor in a decentered network? How do we effectively differentiate between personal and professional perspectives online while validating formal and informal approaches to learning? All of these questions require an expanded concep-tion of information literacy as a metaliteracy to build on the information lit-eracy foundation and to develop linkages with related literacy types.

We will continue to see changes in how people use emerging social tech-nologies, and refinements in design are inevitable, especially as the modes change so quickly. But as recent trends in social media show, the move to networked spaces with collaborative potential continues to advance. We are also seeing a revolutionary emphasis on global mobility, requiring us to rede-sign information literacy to reflect the times and to meet the needs of socially engaged learners from around the world.

FROM INFORMATION AGE TO POST-INFORMATION AGE

The Information Age

The interconnected nature of today's networked environment has radically altered our conception of information. When we trace back to the origins of information literacy, we can see how it was a response to another revolutionary time of change. As a 20th century idea, information literacy emerged from an information age that was in transition from print to text. Information literacy defined the essential skills for all lifelong learners in an information society. The early framers of this movement understood the need for advancing infor-mation skills in higher education and as a practice of lifelong learning, while promoting the critical role of libraries in this process. Breivik and Gee (1989) argue that "the library plays a crucial role in an information society—connect-ing, integrating, and managing informational resources—and nowhere have computers been more empowering than in library operations and services" (pp. 3–4). The authors establish the connections among library, user, and com-puters in a rapidly developing information society. In this definition, however, the library is primarily place-based, not virtual, and the information itself is fixed in books and journals, not searchable and shared across an expansive social network.

The relationship between information and technology was encapsulated in the *ALA Final Report of the Presidential Committee on Information Literacy*: "Information is expanding at an unprecedented rate, and enormously rapid strides are being made in the technology for storing, organizing, and accessing the ever growing tidal wave of information" (ALA, 1989). At the time, information literacy efforts originated primarily from print-based environments, including pre-Web academic and public libraries that provided access to paperbound materials. But the continued influence of computers, and then the rapid growth of the Internet, increased the scope of the information society considerably. The link between information literacy and technology has always been evident, and libraries have consistently adapted to these changes, but there has also been a careful distinction between information competencies and the associated need for computer or technology skills. The ACRL (2000) *Information Literacy Competency Standards for Higher Education*, in particular, mapped out the higher level academic skills required for individuals to be informed citizens, effective researchers, and lifelong learners in the information age. Metaliteracy presents a way to advance information literacy by focusing directly on the relationships among cognate literacies and by clearly identifying the influence of emerging technologies on mobile, open, and networked learning.

Today's 21st century learners take the information age for granted and are immersed in a social media environment of instantaneous communication, transient documents, and collaborative discourse. The information society has transformed into an interactive social network of collaborative developers, authors, editors, and consumers. This is a fundamental change from one-way modalities such as print, television, film, radio, and advertising to the multiple pathways available online and through mobile devices, such as Facebook, Wordpress, YouTube, Pinterest, and Google, in an expansive social network.

Claude Shannon (1948) established the field of information theory with his analysis of communication systems based on his sender-receiver model (p. 2). He argued, "The fundamental problem of communication is that of reproducing at one point either exactly or approximately a message selected at another point" (p. 1). Shannon described communication as a sequential process with multiple parts and established the foundation elements of information theory including *source, transmitter, channel, receiver, and destination* (p. 2). The social media environment, however, is more than a one-way flow between sender and receiver and is better understood as a dynamic system with multiple streams in an interactive and fluid dialogue. The Shannon model is still relevant in defining the essential binary process that underlies all digital systems, especially since he also argued, "The system must be designed to operate for each possible selection, not just the one which will actually be chosen since this is unknown at the time of design" (p. 1). This perspective acknowledges the importance of designing for the variance of message type, and how our systems must be built to adapt to these changes over time. Shannon's model is still at play in our social media systems, but as a conceptual model for how we communicate, the sender-receiver approach does not fully represent today's distributed network. In social media, learners are both senders and receivers of information, as they produce and consume digital materials. They interact with systems and other participants in these environments when searching, accessing, creating, and sharing information, but they may not be as knowledgeable about how to engage in these activities in online spaces as they may think.

Our understanding of information in this complex environment has been radically altered by a revolution in authority, challenging the notion of expert, and replacing it with the new distributed authorities of networked participants. For instance, Wikipedia has changed the way we think about writing and peer review as previously emanating from scholarly experts and established institutions only to an open community of writers and editors. While many instructors discourage the use of Wikipedia as a reliable academic source of information, this is an evolving open resource that is user-driven with checks and balances among a peer community. Rather than discount this global knowledge resource, learners would gain insights about collaborative writing and peer review in this environment that would complement learning about traditional sources of information including standard encyclopedias and academic journals. Learners must be exposed to a full range of digital assets, including the emerging ones, to compare and contrast resource types and to understand the shifting landscape of choices. The use of technology as a consumer of information does not automatically lead to an understanding of authorship, authority, peer review, copyright, or intellectual property. Changes in technology require us to engage learners in the emerging environments, including Wikipedia, Facebook, Twitter, Pinterest, and Wordpress, as producers and distributors of information while also reflecting on the associated issues that are raised by these spaces. Barring the use of such resources prevents active engagement and metacognitive reflection. Metaliteracy foregrounds the rapid changes we have seen in emerging technologies and places individuals at the center of this activity. It also builds on the foundation elements of information literacy to understand copyright and intellectual property through the academic research process.

The Post-Information Age

The information society has been radically transformed by what Nicholas Negroponte (1995), in *Being Digital*, describes as a "post-information age" (p. 164). Negroponte argues that the post-information age was defined by personalization and a redefinition of place: "In the post-information age, we often have an audience the size of one. Everything is made to order, and information is extremely personalized" (p. 164). This user-centered revolution is evident in the lower-case "i" that we have seen in the iPhone, iPod, iTouch, iBook, iPad, and other personalized portable devices. The "i" nomenclature introduced by Apple reflects both a brand distinction and a personalized relationship with micro and nano devices. The mobile aspect of these devices has changed our relationship to place. Negroponte argues that the post-information age will defy geographic boundaries:

> In the same ways that hypertext removes the limitations of the printed page, the post-information age will remove the limitations of geography. Digital living will include less and less dependence on being in a specific place at a specific time and the transmission of place itself will start to be possible. (p. 16)

Nearly two decades after this prediction we have witnessed the emergence of a post-information age that offers a new relationship to place with immediate access to information and communication through portable devices and a popularized understanding of cartography via geographic positioning systems (GPSs). We are constantly on the go as transient digital citizens, and technology is used to get us there and to create and share information in multiple forms (text, image, video, voice, map) from any location along the way.

In today's social media environment, the personalization that Negroponte (1995) describes has been extended through collaboration in a networked community of users. We are more than digital beings; we are also mobile, networked, interactive, virtual, and multimodal selves. Today we are both individual and social through our selective engagement with mobile technologies and online communities. Digital documents have morphed into transient fragments of information, constantly undergoing independent publishing and community review through the exchange of tweets, text messages, comments, status updates, and other snippets of information. We identify and post our transient visits to real places based on the public sharing of GPS coordinates online. The idea of authoritative information in fixed formats such as books and journals, located in buildings and stacks, has been replaced by interactive user-generated information, written in, referenced to, and shared through a sprawling social network. This revolution in access to information requires a greater emphasis on critical thinking than previous information situations ever did. Researchers in this environment do more than locate, understand, and synthesize information. They constantly create and distribute it through numerous channels and media formats previously unimagined.

In her book *University of Google: Education in the (Post) Information Age*, Tara Brabazon (2007) examines the challenges of teaching and librarianship in a post-information age that has privileged Google as the dominant mode of search. She makes a clear distinction between technological and scholarly ways of organizing, evaluating, and understanding information by stating, "Google is not a library catalogue" and "The Internet is not a library" (p. 38). Brabazon's distinctions do not acknowledge the blurring of lines between actual and virtual spaces, or between professional and novice approaches to knowledge acquisition, because she identifies a clear difference between the library and online search. She argues, "The characteristic of a library—the organization of knowledge into preservable categories—has left few traces on the internet" (p. 38). She describes the complexity of this changing environment and the continued relevance of libraries and librarianship in education and scholarship in a Web 2.0 world. According to Brabazon:

> A catalogue of accessible holdings is not a collection of numbers but a sequence of ideas. This ordering is not an archaic relic of the analogue age, but holds a social function: to allow users to search and assess information and build larger relationships to broader subjects, theories and ideas. While the web may appear to remove the physicality of information, we are yet to make this leap conceptually. The digital library is determined as much by research training, database instruction, computer support and document delivery as the availability of search engines. (pp. 38–39)

While the library has expanded to digital environments, the "social function" Brabazon describes is not unique to social media or social networks but is critical to the research process itself (p. 39). By engaging students in a process of discovery, they move beyond their own perspectives to engage and interact with the ideas of others. We know, for instance, that requiring students to develop a reference page is more than a process of citing their sources and documenting where they have been. Compiling a list of references, and knowing how to read the specific citations documented by others, also provides the opportunity to continuously share new pathways to knowledge. It opens to a world of scholarship. This is a core principle of all research activity, to engage with, interact, and reveal discoveries, while making a unique contribution to the scholarly conversation.

At the same time, however, we should not minimize the influence of an online social network in this process because it offers the opportunity to extend individual and collaborative research to audiences beyond a particular assignment or course. Considering these dramatic changes, the days of sending students to the basement stacks are over. Today information is everywhere and in continually shifting forms. We need to prepare learners for this new reality. In many ways social media is ideally suited for research if we recognize these collaborative spaces as a means for effectively creating and sharing knowledge in diverse modes, and not just for informal social interactions.

Brabazon (2007) supports a central role for information literacy in educating learners about these radical changes in modality. Her approach, however, is to provide the instructional and technological academic support for these virtual spaces that depend on more than freely available search engines. She states, "In a (post) information society, strategies are required for responding to multiple modes of communication" (p. 63). This approach suggests a strategic educational response to the technological changes and recognizes the need for a new pedagogical approach to these environments. She argues:

> Information literacy integrates documents, media, form, content, literacy and learning. The expertise of librarians and teachers must—overtly rather than implicitly—support new modes of reading, writing and communicating, integrating and connecting discovery, searches, navigation and the appropriateness of diverse resources. (p. 39)

Brabazon asserts a central role for information literacy as a way to make sense out of these changes and to explicitly educate learners about new forms of research and communication. As she suggests, the popularization of Google has overly simplified this process and has led to a superficial reading and understanding of information: "Books can be flicked through just as a hypertext link can be jumped, but web-based search engines encourage a smash and grab style of reading, rather than a smoother, more reflexive engagement" (p. 39). Brabazon is interested in foregrounding the differences in mode and providing students with the knowledge to differentiate among a vast array of sources in print and online. This suggests a metacognitive approach to understanding the information and mode of delivery, allowing for a deeper reading that "must be done slowly and returned to, drifting along with the sensuality of the words, so that reflexive meanings may emerge" (p. 39). This idea aligns well with the goals of metaliteracy to provide students with a high level of understanding that builds on skills and promotes collaboration to support knowledge acquisition and a self-reflexive thinking process.

Today's post-information environment has moved beyond search and retrieval to the making, mixing, and sharing of knowledge through multimodal and constantly shifting technologies. The idea of a "post-information" age suggests a postmodern definition that signals the end of information. The "post" prefix in this context, however, primarily describes an end to the concept of information as we knew it, as something simply accessed and retrieved in a one-way modality in print to networked ways of knowing through social media. Brabazon (2007) cautions that there is more at play than the transition from one technology format to another and that we also need to consider how we teach information literacy in these environments. By reinventing information literacy as a metaliteracy for the social media age, the integrated relationship to cognate literacies and evolving forms of social technologies will be even more obvious than the traditional print-based definitions of the same term suggests. It will promote a metacognitive reflexivity that prepares students to raise questions about their assumptions in these spaces and to continuously think about their own learning.

THE OPEN AGE OF SOCIAL MEDIA

Participation

In a time of post-information, the age of social media has emerged with the fragmentation of media sources, multiple modes of communication, and continuous social interaction. This new era has created numerous pathways for user participation that includes both open and commercial endeavors. In this collaborative information environment, users create meaning through active participation in online communities and through the creation and sharing of original and reusable content. Social media promotes community involvement on many levels, through social networking sites, blogs, microblogs, and so forth, and through the blurring of actual and virtual spaces evident in the flash mob phenomenon (Nicholson, 2009) and crowdsourcing (Howe, 2006). Flash mobs are public gatherings that are created when users connect via the convergence of social networking sites and mobile devices. Crowdsourcing is a form of virtual "outsourcing" that involves employing a community of users online to solve problems or contribute to projects or work tasks (Howe, 2006). As part of his original definition of Web 2.0 in 2005, Tim O'Reilly (2005) describes the process of "harnessing collective intelligence" as one of the primary differentiators between Web 1.0 and Web 2.0. He argues, "Network effects from user contributions are the key to market dominance in the Web 2.0 era." O'Reilly describes the way that Wikipedia creates "a profound change in the dynamics of content creation" through a community of writers and reviewers. He also mentions other trends that were emerging at the time, such as the digital imaging site Flickr, the open source movement, and the development of blogs as collaborative and dynamic examples of a new era based on the "architecture of participation." In this new socially connected world, peer communities flatten traditional hierarchies through active engagement online.

While O'Reilly's (2005) definition of Web 2.0 emphasizes a business model, Henry Jenkins (2010) has been careful to differentiate between commercial and pedagogical approaches to participation. In 1992, Henry Jenkins initially proposed the concept of "participatory culture" through his analysis of television fans. Jenkins describes "an alternative conception of fans as readers who appropriate popular texts and reread them in a fashion that serves different interests, as spectators who transform the experience of watching television into a rich and complex participatory culture" (p. 23). This argument challenges the traditional notion of television viewers as passive recipients of information to active participants who create meaning through their own involvement in the spectacle itself as part of dedicated fan groups. Jenkins (2006) expands this perspective to include digital media as part of a larger trajectory of participation from the printing press through ever-expanding media sources (p. 258). According to Jenkins, "convergence represents a paradigm shift—a move from medium specific content toward content that flows across multiple media channels, toward multiple ways of accessing media content, and toward ever more complex relations between top-down corporate media and bottom up participatory culture" (p. 243). Content produced for social media takes many forms and is created and shared across multiple platforms. For example, television content is easily accessible through the web and mobile devices and of course newspaper articles have moved beyond print to circulation via websites, Twitter feeds, and RSS. While the formats and modalities are more transparent than ever before, this permeability has also had a significant impact on authority, replacing our reliance on print journalism and television news with access to a multitude of resources available online and through mobile apps. The field of journalism itself has experienced radical changes in how news content is produced and delivered, as it struggles to find relevance in this new world.

As the work of O'Reilly and Jenkins demonstrates, this revolutionary shift to social media is dramatic and raises questions about our critical understanding of the authority, reliability, and accuracy of information. According to Jenkins (2006):

> The emergence of new media technologies supports a democratic urge to allow more people to create and circulate media. Sometimes the media are designed to respond to mass media content—positively or negatively—and sometimes grassroots creativity goes places no one in the media industry could have imagined. The challenge is to rethink our understanding of the First Amendment to recognize this expanded opportunity to participate. (p. 258)

For Jenkins the challenges posed by a revolution in authority present us with an opportunity to better understand democracy in these environments. He is interested in closing the "participation gap" created by such factors as the digital divide and educational barriers that prevent learners from fully engaging in these open participatory environments (Jenkins, 2006, pp. 258–259). According to Jenkins, literacy education can play a central role in closing the participation gap but must be focused on involving learners in active engagement with new media resources. Jenkins critiques traditional approaches to media literacy that discourages active engagement with these environments. For example, when "media are read primarily as threats rather than as resources," learners are prevented from active engagement with the very tools that would promote participation (p. 259). We see this play out, for instance, when Wikipedia and Facebook are prohibited by instructors as discredited resources rather than as new modes for constructing and sharing knowledge.

Metaliteracy is similarly focused on new media as a means to advance critical thinking and collaboration. Rather than discount the importance of emerging technologies and social media, metaliteracy integrates these resources into core information competencies. Participation is central to this approach because learners are encouraged to collaborate, create, and share information using new and expanding resources that will continue to evolve over time. Rather than discourage the use of Wikipedia, for instance, metaliteracy encourages learners to create their own encyclopedia entries collaboratively and to observe how a community of peers edit and transform these contributions over time. Rather than consider Facebook as a threat to the research process, metaliteracy encourages the development of Facebook communities to engage in online conversations, connect with peers, and share links to original and repurposed content. Metaliteracy promotes active involvement with open, online, and mobile resources to advance self-reflection and critical thinking.

Openness

Openness is another dimension of the social media age because it provides a conceptual framework for sharing diverse information types among a community of users and educators. Open education is not a new concept and predates social media, but it has been revitalized in new ways through innovative technologies such as the MOOC that has opened the online classroom to a global audience of thousands of participants. The emergence of open publishing formats has transformed book culture and replaced our reliance on the printed page with e-books and a variety of freely available digital resources. We have seen dramatic changes in how content is produced and distributed in open, online, and mobile environments and our traditional understanding of copyright and intellectual property has been altered. Openness also refers to open access to education and provides us with a way to open doors for everyone. The brick-and-mortar classroom and print-based libraries have given way to networked spaces for learning and a global movement in OERs.

International trends in open learning require us to change how we teach information literacy in participatory environments. Open education is as much a mode of learning as it is a teaching philosophy. Openness requires us to collaborate and to share the teaching and learning process. This includes open courses, assignments, teaching plans, syllabi, wikis, learning objects, online and mobile resources, and inter-institutional partnerships that promote openness. Among the many open learning innovations, for instance, MOOCs are expanding the audience for learning beyond a set course at one institution to an open online environment that includes learners from around the globe. George Siemens, Stephen Downes, and Dave Cormier collaborated to develop and facilitate successful MOOCs such as Personal Learning Environments Networks and Knowledge (PLENK) 2010 and Change MOOC (2011–2012). In fall 2011 Stanford University launched an open course on Artificial Intelligence that reached over 160,000 registrants in 190 countries worldwide (Lewin, 2012). The authors of this book presented on transliteracy and metaliteracy as part of the first MOOC at Empire State College, SUNY, developed by Betty Hurley-Dasgupta and Carol Yeager in fall 2011, on the overarching theme of Creativity and Multicultural Communication (www.cdlprojects.com/cmc11blog). In fall 2013, we developed a metaliteracy MOOC using the same connectivist platform as this first MOOC offered in the SUNY system (http://metaliteracy.cdlprojects.com).

In one of the first efforts to make course materials freely available online, Massachusetts Institute of Technology (MIT) announced the Open Course-Ware project in 2001 and a year later it had 50 open courses (http://ocw.mit.edu/about/our-history). Carnegie-Mellon's Open Learning Initiative emerged around the same time, with planning in 2001 and a funded proposal a year later (http://oli.cmu.edu/get-to-know-oli/learn-more-about-oli). In 2012, a decade after establishing open courseware in the United States, MIT and Harvard combined forces to create EdX to offer free and open distance education courses (https://www.edx.org/about). Coursera is another open course initiative that makes available open online courses from such institutions as Princeton, Stanford, University of California, Berkeley, University of Michigan-Ann Arbor, and the University of Pennsylvania (https://www.coursera.org/about). Internationally, the African Virtual University has been successful in opening course materials for such areas as biology, chemistry, and information communication technology (ICT) (www.avu.org). In addition, open communities have emerged for educators to share materials and practices related to open education, such as WikiEducator (http://wikieducator.org), OpenCourseWare Consortium (www.ocwconsortium.org), and the OER Commons (www.oercommons.org). Many of these initiatives raise questions about how to credential open learning resources, and the Open Educational Resources university (OERu) has taken on this issue directly as it works toward a model for credentialing inter-institutional OERs and develops courses within this context (http://wikieducator.org/OER_university/Home). These ongoing developments in open learning show how the creation and use of educational materials is transitioning in revolutionary ways from individual to shared experience.

OERs have emerged internationally as reusable instructional materials for informal and formal learning. The term was first adopted by UNESCO (2012a) in 2002 as a result of the Global Forum on Open Courseware and is defined as "teaching, learning or research materials that are in the public domain or released with an intellectual property license that allows for free use, adaptation, and distribution." OERs signal a profound change in how we understand teaching, learning, and research, from a closed process that generally takes place in a classroom or online course to an open experience that is a shared and fluid enterprise among instructors and learners. In 2012 OERs gained considerable momentum through the adoption of the Paris Declaration at the 2012 World Open Educational Resources (OER) Congress. The declaration makes several recommendations, including the first, to "Promote and use OER to widen access to education at all levels, both formal and nonformal, in a perspective of lifelong learning, thus contributing to social inclusion, gender equity and special needs education. Improve both cost-efficiency and quality of teaching and learning outcomes through greater use of OER" (UNESCO, 2012c, p. 1). OERs provide a non-proprietary means for sharing materials globally among a community of educators and learners. With UNESCO's support and leadership in this area, OERs are bridging the digital divide internationally by providing free access to educational materials.

Within these innovative open and online learning spaces, the one-shot library session is simply insufficient as a mode for teaching information literacy. In the new open paradigm the learner is an active agent in accessing OERs and in seeking learning opportunities. This is very different from envisioning the learner as a passive recipient of information through a single presentation format. As the open learning environment evolves, so must our approaches to information literacy. Considering the diverse range of materials now available to teachers and learners online and through mobile technologies, metaliteracy is especially imperative as a way to unite cognate literacies that prepare learners to raise critical questions about open resources and to adapt to ever-changing social technologies. It also has the potential to play a role in how we recognize open learning by providing a literacy framework for credentialing open resources. This could help shape the methods for translating open learning experiences to college credits and in defining learning objectives for open courses.

Metadata and the Semantic Web

Openness is evident in the creation and use of metadata in digital library environments and with meta tags in Hypertext Mark-Up Language (HTML).

Metadata has opened access to information and created a revolution in how information is created, searched, retrieved, and distributed. It is based on the basic premise that all information should be easily described and shared in open interoperable environments. Metadata such as meta tags demonstrate that there is more to data than just data and more to tags than just tags. According to the *Structural Metadata Dictionary for LC Digital Objects*, metadata is defined as:

> Information that refers to one or more other pieces of information that can exist as separate physical forms. In short, data about data. Any type of description can be considered metadata. Examples include library catalog information, encoded text file headers, and driver's license data. In the information technology world the term is often used to indicate data which refers to digital resources available across a network. (http://memory.loc.gov/ammem/techdocs/repository/gengloss.html)

Metadata provides multiple layers of information to organize digital resources and collections. It provides a logical and shared system to search and retrieve a multitude of digital documents in library collections. For instance, the Library of Congress has developed "Metadata for Digital Content (MDC)" for "Developing institution-wide policies and standards at the Library of Congress" (www.loc.gov/standards/mdc). According to the Library of Congress:

> Over the years the Library of Congress' digital projects have generated many digital objects and these objects have been given various levels and types of descriptive metadata. The Library has assembled several use cases that require a more coordinated and standardized approach to the creation and management of this descriptive metadata. (www.loc.gov/standards/mdc)

As part of this metadata initiative, the Library of Congress identifies several examples of specific use, including *Geographic navigation of Library of Congress digital content, Temporal navigation of Library of Congress digital content,* and *Exchange video and audio data with external services.* Metadata enriches the library experience through increased access to digital documents in multiple forms and expanded information about information. The metadata standards for doing so are collaboratively developed and openly available via the Library of Congress website, further opening the initiative to anyone interested in learning more about this specific process.

As a basic form of metadata, meta tags in HTML documents provide added layers of data about the document itself, including meta information that identifies the author, date of creation and last modified, institution affiliation, and keywords. Meta tags are placed in the Head of the HTML document, providing descriptive information about the document itself. In another example, the Resource Description Framework (RDF) "is a declarative language and provides a standard way for using XML to represent metadata in the form of statements about properties and relationships of items on the Web" (www .w3.org/Metadata/Activity.html). RDF was developed by the World Wide Web Consortium (W3C) and provides a framework to "associate metadata with a Web page, a graphic, an audio file, a movie clip, and so on" (www.w3.org/ Metadata/Activity.html). W3C offers several examples to apply RDF, including *Thesauri and library classification schemes, Web sitemaps, Description of the contents of Web pages,* and *Descriptions of device capabilities* such as mobile devices (www.w3.org/Metadata/Activity.html).

The Dublin Core Metadata Initiative (DCMI) applies the RDF model as a standard language and is described as "an open organization supporting innovation in metadata design and best practices across the metadata ecology" (http://dublincore.org). This project originated in the 1990s and today it "provides core metadata vocabularies in support of interoperable solutions for discovering and managing resources" (http://dublincore.org/about-us). The DCMI is an open initiative for developing metadata standards and documentation, building community around metadata issues, advancing education and training related to metadata, and building a global community to advance interoperability and access to information (http://dublincore.org/about-us).

As inventor of the web, Tim Berners-Lee established the World Wide Web Consortium (W3C) and Web Accessibility Initiative (WAI) to chart the future direction of the web and clearly articulate the importance of accessibility. He also articulated the goals for a Semantic Web and interoperable systems designed to create meaning across a vast network. The WAI promotes "strategies, guidelines, resources to make the Web accessible to people with disabilities" (www.w3.org/WAI). This expansive resource provides guidelines, standards, presentations, and tutorials to support universal web accessibility. It also addresses emergent technologies such as cell phones to include a discussion of "mobile accessibility" (www.w3.org/WAI/mobile/Overview.html). According to Berners-Lee, "The power of the Web is in its universality. Access by everyone regardless of disability is an essential aspect" (www.w3.org/stan dards/webdesign/accessibility). This is an open and inclusive vision for the web that removes technical barriers to provide universal access to all participants. The use of metadata is integral to making this vision a reality in daily practice. For instance, web content is accessible to all when we provide alternative text descriptions or "alt tags" for digital images. These tags allow screen readers to provide audio descriptions of visual content for individuals with visual impairments (www.w3.org/standards/webdesign/accessibility). The general principles of web accessibility are based on reasonable guidelines for providing equivalents for audio, video, textual, or multimedia content that cannot be accessed by individuals with disabilities. The extent to which these guidelines are actually applied is not yet universal, resulting in a web interface that is not fully accessible, although the means for doing so are clearly defined and based on good design practices.

The W3C advances the development of specific metadata standards "to use the Web to document the meaning of the metadata" and to do so in "a way that allows Web pages to be properly searched and processed in particular by computer" (www.w3.org/Metadata/Activity). This original goal for "meta-data activity" was established in 2000 but eventually evolved into a vision for a "semantic Web." Berners-Lee envisions the web as an open, navigable, and semantic interface, allowing everyone to access and create freely avail-able content. From the start, Berners-Lee understood the dual nature of the web as a network for both accessing and producing content. In his book *Weaving the Web: The Original Design and Ultimate Destiny of the World Wide Web*, Berners-Lee (2000) "imagined the information space as something to which everyone has immediate and intuitive access, and not just to browse, but to create" (p. 157). The second part of his vision considers the way computers interact in a *Semantic Web* in which "machines become capable of analyzing all the data on the Web—the content, links, and transactions between people and com-puters" (p. 157). Collaboration is central to this two-part vision. First, indi-viduals interact collaboratively to access and create information and, second, machines dialogue through agreed upon standards and protocols. Berners-Lee argues, "Once the two-part dream is reached, the Web will be a place where the whim of the human being and the reasoning of a machine coexist in an ideal, powerful mixture" (p. 158). Berners-Lee considers the web an ongoing work in progress and all of his efforts continue to advance an intuitive and interop-erable system that is open to all for accessing and producing information in partnership with others.

W3C plays a central role in the continued development of the Semantic Web. According to the W3C's *Semantic Web Activity Statement*:

> The goal of the Semantic Web initiative is as broad as that of the Web: to create a universal medium for the exchange of data. It is envisaged to smoothly interconnect personal information management, enterprise application integration, and the global sharing of commercial, scientific and cultural data. Facilities to put machine-understandable data on the Web are quickly becoming a high priority for many organizations, indi-viduals and communities. (www.w3.org/2001/sw/Activity)

The Semantic Web creates meaning through the description of informa-tion and connectivity in an interoperable system. Many of today's comput-ing resources, including mobile devices, are increasingly intuitive, providing open access to a wealth of information sources and creating connectivity with multiple users. At the same time, these user interfaces are highly proprietary in nature, creating some barriers to interoperability and adding a layer of commercial mediation to the online and mobile experience. This is evident in competing Internet providers, rival mobile carriers, as well as search engines and social networking sites that are driven by commercial advertising. Many of our innovative mobile products such as smartphones and tablets promote proprietary apps that are unique to a specific company. While the Semantic Web includes a focus on *commercial data*, the proprietary nature of the web presents some challenges to the idea of universal access and interoperability.

The age of social media advances a connected vision for all users but is constantly influenced by advertising and commercial interests. A form of semantic meaning is created through sharing of information at social networking sites, blogs, and microblogs, but most of these spaces contain commercial advertising or collect and share information about users. For instance, social bookmarking sites provide the chance to share information and bloggers identify ideas through tagging of information. In addition, Facebook users easily tag images, share links, and write status updates for an audience of personal and professional "friends" and acquaintances, but this space is mediated by confusing definitions of privacy, security, and competing commercial interests. The Semantic Web offers a vision for open access and networking, including the machine level, but much of what we have seen in social networking interconnectedness is based on competition among commercial enterprises and the analysis of user-behavior as a means to provide advertising space and links to ads. The commercial interests also drive much of the innovation, especially in the consumer marketplace, so we should not completely discount this influence either. But the distinction between a Semantic Web and proprietary interface further supports the need for a metaliteracy that prepares learners to distinguish between open and commercial interests. It also reinforces the need to develop non-proprietary OERs that are produced and shared among a community of educators for the benefit of lifelong learning internationally.

As information expanded from discrete documents in print and paper to digital formats created, stored, searched, and accessed across a vast network, metadata standards have created common agreements about how to make this information easily available. This formal approach has also given way to less formal agreements within a community of users that have created links and tags to personal and professional information. Metaliteracy is expansive in scope while building connections among related literacies and linking precise descriptions of information to create meaning. It encourages users to be aware of the multiple layers of information and to gain knowledge about metadata conventions to be effective consumers and developers of meta information.

Further, metaliteracy is literacy about literacy that recognizes both formal and informal learning. This approach provides us with an opportunity for big-picture thinking to examine how networked technologies impact knowledge creation and collaborative learning. It allows us to recognize the experiential nature of lifelong learning in creating meaning with emerging and open social technologies. Metaliteracy is a response to changes in the information environment and recognition that an expanded information literacy framework is relevant in an open social media age.

CONCLUSION

As we demonstrate in this chapter, trends in social media show that we are immersed in online and mobile information environments for interaction and participation. We have moved beyond the static web with individual pages that are connected by hyperlinks to a Semantic Web that is open, mobile, and social. The extent to which we are all truly connected varies considerably and requires further research, but we have definitely transitioned to socially constructed and portable environments that blend information and technology in new ways. We have also seen the emergence of proprietary interests that have significant impact on how we navigate these resources. Open initiatives that fulfill the vision for a Semantic Web provide a sharp contrast to social spaces and search engines that ultimately sell a product, but very often it may be difficult for our learners or for us to differentiate between the two. The immediacy and convenience of social and mobile environments often raise questions about the accuracy, reliability, and authority of information, as well as about how we search, retrieve, consume, produce, and share information in collaboration with others.

In the open age of social media, the traditional definitions of information literacy are inadequate for such revolutionary changes in information and technology. Many of the core characteristics, however, still have value, and as we will see in the next chapter, most of the terms share some of the same objectives as other literacies. Many differences exist among the new literacies as well. These contrasts in definition and description will allow us to introduce new ideas and elements to an integrated metaliteracy framework. Through an expansion of the original information literacy definition, and a mapping of key characteristics to related literacy types, we argue for a comprehensive metaliteracy that meets the needs of technology-mediated and socially immersed learners.

REFERENCES

American Library Association. (1989). *Presidential Committee on Information Literacy: Final report*. www.ala.org/ala/mgrps/divs/acrl/publications/whitepapers/ presidential.cfm

Anchin, Matt. (2012). *Data and design—Looking at data visualization*. NielsenWire. http://blog.nielsen.com/nielsenwire/media_entertainment/data-and-design -looking-at-data-visualization

Anderson, Chris, & Wolff, Michael. (2010). The web is dead. Long live the internet. *Wired* September 2010. www.wired.com/magazine/2010/08/ff _webrip/all/1

Association of College and Research Libraries. (2000). *Information literacy competency standards for higher education*. American Library Association. www.ala.org/ala/ mgrps/divs/acrl/standards/standards.pdf

Berners-Lee, Tim. (2000). *Weaving the web: The original design and ultimate destiny of the world wide web*. New York, NY: HarperCollins.

Bohn, Roger E., & Short, James E. (2009). *How much information? 2009 report on American consumers*. Global Information Industry Center, University of California, San Diego. http://hmi.ucsd.edu/pdf/HMI_2009_ConsumerReport _Dec9_2009.pdf

Brabazon, Tara. (2007). *University of Google: Education in the (post) information age*. Abingdon, Oxon, GBR: Ashgate Publishing Group.

Breivik, Patricia Senn, & Gee, E. Gordon. (1989). Taking a new look at libraries. In *Information literacy: Revolution in the library*. New York, NY: Macmillan, pp. 1–29.

Duggan, Maeve, & Aaron Smith. (2013). *Social Media Update 2013*. Pew Internet and American Life Project. www.pewinternet.org/~/media//Files/Reports/2013/ Social%20Networking%202013_PDF.pdf

Hampton, Keith, Goulet, Lauren Sessions, Marlow, Cameron, & Rainie, Lee. (2012). *Why most Facebook users get more than they give*. Pew Internet and American Life Project. http://pewinternet.org/Reports/2012/Facebook-users.aspx

Howe, Jeff. (2006, June). The rise of crowdsourcing. *Wired*. www.wired.com/wired/ archive/14.06/crowds.html

International Telecommunication Union. (2012). *The world in 2011: ICT facts and figures*. www.itu.int/ITU-D/ict/facts/2011/material/ICTFactsFigures2011.pdf

Jenkins, Henry. (1992). *Textual poachers: Television fans & participatory culture*. London, England: Routledge, Chapman, and Hall.

Jenkins, Henry. (2006). *Convergence culture: Where old and new media collide*. New York, NY: New York University Press.

Jenkins, Henry. (2010, May 24). Why participatory culture is not web 2.0: Some basic distinctions. *Confessions of an Aca-Fan: The Official Weblog of Henry Jenkins*. http://henryjenkins.org/2010/05/why_participatory_culture_is_n.html

Johnson, L., Adams, S., & Cummins, M. (2012). *NMC Horizon Report: 2012 Higher Education Edition*. Austin, TS: The New Media Consortium. www.nmc.org/ publications/horizon-report-2012-higher-ed-edition

Johnson, L., Adams Becker, S., Cummins, M., Estrada, V., Freeman, A., & Ludgate, H. (2013). *NMC Horizon Report: 2013 Higher Education Edition*. Austin, TX: The New Media Consortium. www.nmc.org/publications/2013-horizon-report-higher-ed

Kukulska-Hulme, Agnes. (2010). Mobile learning as a catalyst for change. *Open Learning: The Journal of Open and Distance Learning, 25*(3), 181–185. http://oro.open.ac.uk/23773/2/Open_Learning_editorial__Accepted_Manuscript_.pdf

Lewin, Tamar. (2012, March 4). Instruction for masses knock down campus walls. *The New York Times*. www.nytimes.com/2012/03/05/education/moocs-large-courses-open-to-all-topple-campus-walls.html

Mackey, Thomas P., & Jacobson, Trudi E. (2011). Transliteracy and metaliteracy: Emerging literacy frameworks for social media. In massive open online course *Creativity and Multicultural Communication*. Betty Hurley-Dasgupta and Carol Yeager (Course facilitators). www.cdlprojects.com/cmc11blog/contents/week-4-untitled

MIT OpenCourseWare, Massachusetts Institute of Technology. (n.d.). Our History. License: Creative Commons BY-NC-SA. http://ocw.mit.edu/about/our-history

Library of Congress (2011). Metadata for Digital Content (MDC): Developing institution-wide policies and standards at the Library of Congress [Web page]. www.loc.gov/standards/mdc

Literacy. (2012). In *Oxford English dictionary (OED) online*. Oxford University Press. www.oed.com/view/Entry/109054?p=emailAca24wNhiFpOw&d=109054

Metadata (1999). In *Structural metadata dictionary for LC digital objects*. National Digital Library Program: Digital Repository Development Project. http://memory.loc.gov/ammem/techdocs/repository/gengloss.html

Morgenson, Gretchen. (2012, May 19). Facebook gold rush: Fanfare vs. realities. *The New York Times*. www.nytimes.com/2012/05/20/business/in-facebook-stock-rush-fanfare-vs-realities.html?smid=pl-share

Negroponte, Nicholas. (1996). *Being digital*. New York, NY: Vintage Books.

The New Media Consortium. (2010). *The horizon report*. http://wp.nmc.org/horizon2010

Nicholson, Judith A. (2009). Flash! Mobs in the age of mobile connectivity. *The Fibreculture Journal*. http://six.fibreculturejournal.org/fcj-030-flash-mobs-in-the-age-of-mobile-connectivity

NielsenWire. (2012a). Buzz in the blogosphere: Millions more bloggers and blog readers. http://blog.nielsen.com/nielsenwire/online_mobile/buzz-in-the-blogosphere-millions-more-bloggers-and-blog-readers

NielsenWire. (2012b). Global and social: Facebook's rise around the world. http://blog.nielsen.com/nielsenwire/global/global-and-social-facebooks-rise-around-the-world

Open Learning Initiative, Carnegie Mellon University. (n.d.) Learn more about OLI. http://oli.cmu.edu/get-to-know-oli/learn-more-about-oli

O'Reilly, Tim (2005). What is web 2.0: Design patterns and business models for the next generation of software. http://oreilly.com/web2/archive/what-is-web-20.html

Shannon, C. E. (1948). A mathematical theory of communication. Reprinted with corrections from *The Bell System Technical Journal, 27*, 379–423, 623–656. http://cm.bell-labs.com/cm/ms/what/shannonday/paper.html

Smith, Aaron. (2011). Twitter update 2011. Pew Internet and American Life Project. www.pewinternet.org/Reports/2011/Twitter-Update-2011/Main-Report.aspx

Smith, Aaron. (2012). Nearly half of American adults are smartphone owners. Pew Internet and American Life Project. http://pewinternet.org/Reports/2012/Smartphone-Update-2012/Findings.aspx

Smith, Aaron, Segall, Laurie, & Cowley, Stacy. (2012). Facebook reaching one billion users. CNNMoney. http://money.cnn.com/2012/10/04/technology/facebook-billion-users/index.html

Technorati. (2011). State of the blogosphere 2011: Part 3. http://technorati.com/social-media/article/state-of-the-blogosphere-2011-part3

Tsukayama, Hayley. (2012, November 8). Pinterest to roll out "secret" boards. *The Washington Post.* Technology. www.washingtonpost.com/business/technology/pinterest-to-roll-out-secret-boards/2012/11/08/e51ba3f2-29b0-11e2-96b6-8e6a7524553f_story.html

United Nations Educational, Scientific and Cultural Organization (UNESCO). (2012a). Communication and information: Open educational resources. www.unesco.org/new/en/communication-and-information/access-to-knowledge/open-educational-resources

UNESCO. (2012b). ICT in education: UNESCO mobile learning week produces tangible results. www.unesco.org/new/en/unesco/themes/icts/single-view/news/unesco_mobile_learning_week_produces_tangible_results

UNESCO. (2012c). 2012 Paris OER Declaration. 2012 World Open Educational Resources (OER) Congress UNESCO, Paris, June 20–22. www.unesco.org/new/fileadmin/MULTIMEDIA/HQ/CI/CI/pdf/Events/Paris%20OER%20Declaration_01.pdf

West, Mark. (2012). Turning on mobile learning: Global themes. UNESCO. www.unesco.org/new/en/unesco/themes/icts/m4ed/mobile-learning-resources/unescomobilelearningseries

WordPress. (2012). How many people read blogs on WordPress.com? http://en.wordpress.com/stats

World Wide Web Consortium, Technology and Society Domain. (2002). Metadata Activity Statement. www.w3.org/Metadata/Activity

World Wide Web Consortium, Technology and Society Domain. (2013). Semantic Web Activity Statement. www.w3.org/2001/sw/Activity

World Wide Web Consortium, Web Accessibility Initiative. (2013). Mobile accessibility. www.w3.org/WAI/mobile/Overview.html

World Wide Web Consortium, Web Design and Applications. (2013). Accessibility. www.w3.org/standards/webdesign/accessibility

3

Developing the Metaliterate Learner by Integrating Competencies and Expanding Learning Objectives

L ITERACY HAS CHANGED OVER CENTURIES, FROM ORAL TRADI-
tions to pictographs, to diverse languages, print, and media. Specific literacy formats have emerged in response to spoken, visual, and textual information. Competencies vary depending on the disciplinary framework, mediating technology, and educational context. According to the *Oxford English Dictionary (OED)*, literacy is defined as "the quality, condition, or state of being literate; the ability to read and write." This explanation underscores the centrality of reading and writing to being literate in any environment. At the same time, literacy has a complex relationship to technology. The printing press revolution, for instance, led to mass-produced books and the emergence of book culture, library collections, and the acceleration of literacy around the world. Eventually, the surfacing of mass media and the information society inspired the development of information literacy as a pedagogical response to these changes. Several related literacies emerged as well including critical literacy, media literacy, visual literacy, and information fluency. The expansion of the Internet and web generated new approaches to digital literacy, cyberliteracy, and information communication and technology (ICT) literacy. Current

trends in social media that combine verbal, visual, textual, and aural information continue to inspire integrated approaches to literacy such as transliteracy, new media literacy, and metaliteracy. In addition, UNESCO's media and information literacy (MIL) places MIL at the center of several emerging literacies such as mobile literacy (Wilson et al., 2011, p. 19). As each new literacy type has advanced, particular technologies have been central to the development of the literacy that followed. Mobile literacy, for instance, focuses on the effective use of portable devices while media literacy emphasizes the competencies needed to critically evaluate and produce multimedia content. Topical issues have also informed approaches to literacy, advancing such terms as health literacy, financial literacy, and environmental literacy.

Considering all of these sweeping changes in technology and the emergence of so many different literacy formats, how does metaliteracy contribute to this conversation and how does it relate to existing literacies? Given the social evolution of the information environment as well as the cultural shifts from modern to postmodern, and information to post-information, how does any literacy format encompass such dramatic twists and turns? Our approach to metaliteracy challenges the notion that any one literacy type, independent of all others, is the only way to address such radical changes in dynamic information settings. As a part of this new framework, we are interested in identifying relationships among cognate literacies while foregrounding a reinvention of information literacy as primary. As we have introduced in this book, metaliteracy is a metacognitive approach to information literacy that expands the original term and recasts it as an overarching structure for related literacies.

As we will see in this chapter, the foundation elements associated with information literacy are shared by other literacies in a metaliteracy framework (see table 3.1). In the same way that reading and writing define literacy, the abilities to determine, access, locate, understand, produce, and use information are needed for understanding all information environments, including digital, mobile, and open spaces. At the same time, however, these basic competencies do not go far enough for today's social media environment and must be repurposed to include the creation and distribution of digital documents in collaborative networks. We need to break away from a skills-based approach to information literacy and move beyond the one-shot library sessions to integrate metaliteracy practices throughout the curriculum. We also need to move beyond traditional views of curriculum as fixed and proprietary to develop Open Educational Resources (OERs) that are freely available and accessible to learners around the world. Metaliteracy is a model that integrates related literacies because it recognizes and builds on common principles found in information literacy and other relevant literacies. This chapter will delve into these unified relationships further to support this broad conception of metaliteracy for the open age of social media.

TABLE 3.1

Metaliteracy and related literacies

Literacy		Characteristics									
Meta (IL)	Determine	Access	Evaluate	Understand	Use	Incorporate	Produce	Collaborate	Participate	Share
Media		Access	Evaluate	Analyze		Create			Participate	
Digital		Access	Evaluate	Understand	Use	Create	Publish		Participate	
Cyber		Access	Evaluate	Understand	Write	Critique	Design		Participate	
Visual	Determine	Find and access	Interpret, analyze, evaluate	Understand	Use	Create	Design	Participate		Share
Mobile		Access	Credibility detection	Understand	Spatial awareness	Create	Hyper-Connect	Collaborate		Share
Critical		More than access	Critically evaluate systems	Understand discipline	Use	Solve problems	Produce	Community		Share reading and interpretation
Health		Access to info, services, health care	Evaluate credibility and quality	Analyze risks and benefits	Locate health information	Interpret test results	Calculate dosages	Community partners		Shared responsibility between patient and physician
Trans		Access	Read	Understand	Write	Interact	Produce	Collaborate		Communicate
New Media	Multitask	Transmedia navigation	Judgment	Simulation	Play, performance	Distributed cognition	Appropriate	Collective intelligence, negotiation		Networking
ICT	Define	Access	Evaluate		Manage	Integrate	Create	Communicate		
Fluency	Sustained reasoning	Manage complexity	Evaluate	Think Abstractly	Test a solution; expect the unexpected	Manage problems	Anticipate changing technologies	Collaborate	Communicate	

The first section, "Discrete Literacies," describes seven separate literacies in relation to information literacy: media literacy, digital literacy, cyberliteracy, visual literacy, mobile literacy, critical information literacy, and health literacy. In the second section, "Combined Literacies," we discuss four models that integrate multiple modalities as part of each definition: transliteracy, new media literacy, ICT literacy, and information fluency. While this is not an all-encompassing analysis of related literacies, it does provide a starting point to demonstrate how elements of information literacy are still relevant in social media environments. There is some overlap between discrete and combined literacies, but for the most part this is an accurate differentiation that supports the connections between information literacy and each literacy type.

The definition of these integrated characteristics, within a metaliteracy model, has direct impact on how we define the learning objectives for this new model. Initially, we outlined seven assertions in our first article on this topic, "Reframing Information Literacy as a Metaliteracy" that defined the original set of objectives. Our work in this area has continued to develop, in partnership with colleagues as part of a grant-funded project at SUNY to establish a Metaliteracy Learning Collaborative. We will close this chapter with the section "Metaliteracy Learning Goals and Objectives" to review the original objectives and describe how this work has evolved through our partnership with colleagues. This section will discuss the expanded metaliteracy learning goals and objectives, describe the integration of the four domains of metaliteracy, and present a visual representation of the metaliterate learner (figure 3.1). In chapter 4 we discuss this reinvention of information literacy further with a review of prominent literacy constructs worldwide, showing rapid changes in how the term is being redefined internationally.

RELATED LITERACIES

This section provides an analysis of several related literacies (see table 3.1) in our integrated model. We show how the core characteristics of the standard information literacy definition (determine, access, evaluate, understand, use, and incorporate) provide a foundation for related literacies. We expand the traditional definition of information literacy to include key elements needed for social media interaction (produce, collaborate, participate, and share). For instance, a review of the Metaliteracy and Related Literacies table (table 3.1) shows that the ability to "determine the extent of information needed" as defined by the original ACRL (2000) *Information Literacy Competency Standards for Higher Education* is not a common characteristic among the related literacies (p. 2). The only other literacy that explicitly uses this competency is visual literacy, although new media literacy, ICT literacy, and information fluency address skills that are similar. We argue that determination is a unique characteristic of information literacy that has a metacognitive dimension.

When scanning across the Metaliteracy and Related Literacies table, we see that the abilities to *access, evaluate, understand,* and *use* information are clearly articulated in most of the related literacy types. This supports our view that information literacy informs many other literacy formats, while providing a unifying construct for information-related competencies. The ability to *incorporate* information is not as explicitly stated in other literacies, but these formats include comparable characteristics. Further, the expanded set of terms, including *produce, collaborate, participate,* and *share,* are clearly evident in the other literacies in this model, supporting the need to reinvent the original definition of information literacy. This example shows how related literacies influence information literacy as well. These interactive terms in particular represent the significant changes we describe in this book and align well with many other literacy formats, such as transliteracy, visual literacy, and new media literacy. As we will see, this exploration of metaliteracy in relation to other literacies supports a unified model that prepares learners for an increasingly complex social world. The reference point for our comparison of related literacies with the standard definition of information literacy is the ACRL (2000) *Information Literacy Competency Standards for Higher Education.* Definitions of information have expanded since 2000, and this ACRL document does not go far enough to describe a new metaliteracy, but it offers a useful reference point when exploring connected and emergent literacy terms.

DISCRETE LITERACIES

The discrete literacy types we analyze in this section are usually defined as separate literacies with unique characteristics based on a technology format or topical issue. Our discussion of each literacy focuses on specific elements that relate to the metaliteracy framework. We define each literacy type based on prominent sources and then compare the term to the standard ACRL information literacy definition. This shows the inherent relationship among literacies while identifying the potential for further influence and overlap within a metaliteracy model.

Media Literacy

According to the Center for Media Literacy (CML, 2012), media literacy "provides a framework to access, analyze, evaluate, create and participate with messages in a variety of forms—from print to video to the Internet." This definition considers resources beyond print, including video and the Internet, with an emphasis on critical thinking. The ability to access, analyze, and evaluate is similar to the standard definition of information literacy to access, evaluate, and understand (see table 3.1). In addition, the capacity to create and participate demonstrates the need to expand information literacy beyond using and incorporating information to explicitly producing it. This is an important distinction not only for the redefinition of information literacy as a metaliteracy but also for how we apply this change in our teaching practices. Participation is central to media literacy because it promotes a democratic process of active engagement. The CML further states, "Media literacy builds an understanding of the role of media in society as well as essential skills of inquiry and self-expression necessary for citizens of a democracy." These are critically important elements of an active and decentralized social media space and are supported as well by metaliteracy through the collaborative production and sharing of ideas.

ACRL (2000) identified a changing information environment with multiple media types and asserted, "Information is available through libraries, community resources, special interest organizations, media, and the Internet —and increasingly, information comes to individuals in unfiltered formats, raising questions about its authenticity, validity, and reliability" (p. 3). This early document recognized that media formats varied and that the emerging Internet was having an influence on how we process information. *Standard One* mentions multimedia as part of an outcome related to the determination of an information need because a learner: "Identifies the value and differences of potential resources in a variety of formats (e.g., multimedia, database, website, data set, audio/visual, book)" (p. 8). This supports our assertion that information literacy provides many of the foundation elements of an expanded metaliteracy, but the information environment has changed so drastically since 2000 that we need a more explicit reference to multimedia and social media than offered in the ACRL definition. Media literacy is overtly focused on, not only recognizing multimedia among a range of resources for the determination of use, but also critically understanding multimedia content as consumer, producer, and distributor of these materials. Within a metaliteracy framework, then, information literacy provides the overarching framework for literacy but is equally influenced by significant characteristics found in related literacy types, such as multimedia creation in media literacy, that contribute to the overall structure of this approach. This critical perspective informs how learners analyze and understand a variety of media resources, while preparing them to become effective creators of multimedia content.

Digital Literacy

Paul Gilster (1997) defines digital literacy as "the ability to access networked computer resources and use them" (p. 1). He also argues that "digital literacy is the ability to understand and use information in multiple formats from a wide range of sources when it is presented via computers" (p. 1). These capabilities relate to the *access, use,* and *understand* dimensions of information literacy with an emphasis on the evaluation of online content and gaining critical-thinking skills for the Internet (see table 3.1). Gilster's initial definition of digital literacy was grounded in his experience with the Internet of the late 1990s, with e-mail, nascent search, and the emerging multimedia features of the web, including digital images, audio, and video. Although prior to the era of social media, Gilster's discussion of digital literacy recognizes the networked dimension of the Internet because "literacy in the digital age—digital literacy—is partly about awareness of other people and our expanded ability to contact them to discuss issues and get help" (p. 33). Gilster acknowledges the collaborative and participatory dimension of the web, even at a time when this took place through static web pages, hypertext links, and e-mail, and online discussions. He also identifies the two-fold nature of this medium as both readable and publishable. According to Gilster, "The Internet provides us with new capabilities for using older media but it also *creates* content, and that content is interactive and demanding" (p. 34). For Gilster, this ability to freely publish also raises questions about the reliability of online content and the need for evaluation skills. The ability to share in these contexts is implicit in Gilster's definition because he recognizes the Internet as "a publishing medium in the most democratic sense" (p. 35). This continues to be an essential consideration in social networks as well. In some informal settings the term *digital literacy* is often used interchangeably with other concepts such as computer literacy and even information literacy, but the formal definition relates directly to the critical evaluation of Internet content in many forms.

The only overt reference to anything digital in the ACRL definition of information literacy is found in an outcome for *Standard Four* in which an information literate individual "Manipulates digital text, images, and data, as needed, transferring them from their original locations and formats to a new context" (ACRL, 2000, p. 14). While the digital information environment is implicit in this original document, and different forms of digital content are briefly mentioned here, this definition is based entirely on a basic transference model that addresses how digital information is simply moved from one source to another. This is a limited construct based on the assumption that research activity takes place when learners search and retrieve information for evaluation only. It fails to recognize that research also involves the creative production and distribution of a vast array of materials, including digital images, graphs, tables, multimedia, and presentation technologies. This updated approach requires learners to understand more than how to transfer one information type to another format, and instead involves proficiency with diverse modalities and knowledge about how the technologies may impact our interpretation of the information itself. Digital literacy is essential to a unified metaliteracy framework that encourages learners to reflect on digital content in all forms, including original digital media produced and shared by individuals and collaborators within a networked environment.

Cyberliteracy

In her book *Cyberliteracy: Navigating the Internet with Awareness*, Laura J. Gurak (2001) presents a series of case studies to support a definition of literacy based on how we understood cyberspace in the early 21st century. According to Gurak, "Cyberliteracy recognizes that on the Internet, communication is a blend of oral, written, and visual information: the technology, like many before it, shapes our social spaces, replacing the slower methods of handwriting and typing with the speed and frenzy of digitized text" (p. 21). Gurak argues that because of this multimodal and networked social environment "cyberliteracy requires a special form of critical thinking" (p. 14). From the author's perspective this radically different medium requires the development of a critical stance to actively engage with others and to understand how the Internet transforms our sense of community, writing, and communication. According to Gurak, "cyberliteracy means voicing an opinion about what these technologies should become and being an active, not passive, participant" (p. 27). Similar to information literacy, cyberliteracy addresses the abilities to access, evaluate, and understand content as a critical reader (see table 3.1), but the emphasis is focused more directly on the Internet than the standard definitions of information literacy initially asserted. As with digital literacy, cyberliteracy emerged prior to Web 2.0, so the emphasis on sharing information is not as overt as today's social media environments require, but cyberliteracy is adaptable to cyber trends and does promote active participation, with a particular emphasis on writing, critique, and design in these social spaces. Gurak's case study approach effectively demonstrates how cyberliteracy is about more than gaining particular skills; it prepares learners to raise critical questions about online flaming, Internet hoaxes, online privacy, and intellectual property.

Cyberliteracy is similar to the way information literacy approaches intellectual property issues as a part of information competencies. For instance, in the ACRL *Standard Five*, "The information literate student understands many of the economic, legal, and social issues surrounding the use of information and accesses and uses information ethically and legally" (ACRL, 2000, p. 14). As with cyberliteracy, the standard definition of information literacy investigates the issue-oriented topics that emerge from web-based information environments. Based on one of the outcomes of the ACRL definition, an information literate individual "demonstrates an understanding of intellectual property, copyright, and fair use of copyrighted material" (ACRL, 2000, p. 14). These competencies are especially relevant in Web 2.0 and social media environments that promote the collaborative production of new knowledge in shared spaces. For instance, Wikipedia has revolutionized the concept of peer review because a community of online writers, editors, and proofreaders contributes to this global information source and monitor the space for accuracy. This open technology requires learners to understand traditional definitions of intellectual property, copyright, and information ethics, while gaining insights about emergent concepts such as Creative Commons licenses (http://creativecommons.org/licenses), OERs, and the evolution of knowledge produced within social networks. Metaliteracy addresses these concerns by emphasizing critical thinking, metacognitive reflection, and the original creation of digital information.

Visual Literacy

According to the International Visual Literacy Association (2012), John Debes first applied the term *visual literacy* in 1969 and defined it as "a group of vision-competencies a human being can develop by seeing and at the same time having and integrating other sensory experiences." Over time visual literacy became associated with a range of visual information including digital and web-based materials. In 2011, ACRL developed the *ACRL Visual Literacy Competency Standards for Higher Education*. While the term had existed for several decades, this was the first formal effort to identify specific competency standards, performance indicators, and learning outcomes for visual literacy. ACRL did so by connecting the new visual literacy standards to the *Information Literacy Competency Standards for Higher Education*, published in 2000. This alignment with the information literacy standards further illustrates the way that information literacy is a metaliteracy for related literacy types. The visual literacy characteristics are consistent with the information literacy standards: determine, find and access, interpret, analyze, evaluate, understand, and use. In addition, several new components support an expanded metaliteracy, such as create, design, participate, and share information (see table 3.1). By associating the visual literacy standards so closely with information literacy, the overarching information competencies inform the way we design learning activities and outcomes.

Visual literacy is based on how we apply visual information in multiple forms and how we prepare students to do more than search and retrieve visual information. According to the ACRL (2011) standards:

> Visual literacy skills equip a learner to understand and analyze the contextual, cultural, ethical, aesthetic, intellectual, and technical components involved in the production and use of visual materials. A visually literate individual is both a critical consumer of visual media and a competent contributor to a body of shared knowledge and culture.

This set of competencies extends far beyond skills acquisition to include an expanded understanding of one's world as a critical reader and producer of digital information. It supports a research process that moves beyond text to develop a critical understanding of how visuals are produced and shared in participatory environments. Further, it emphasizes the ability to "determine the nature and extent of the visual materials needed," which we see as a metacognitive ability to reflect and think carefully about what is needed in any particular research situation. As we mentioned in the first chapter, we do not see the ability to make a determination as simply a first step in the research process but rather as a high-level ability to know when information is needed based on the integration of multiple skills and to reflect effectively on how prepared one is to do so. The overall completeness of the ACRL *Visual Literacy Competency Standards for Higher Education*, and the intentional associations made to ACRL's *Information Literacy Competency Standards for Higher Education*, fully support a reinvention of information literacy as a metaliteracy, while providing an example of how we could develop a similar approach for other related literacies. The clarity provided by the new visual literacy standards creates an opportunity for instructors to incorporate visual literacy into courses and assignments, while offering a pathway for assessing this work.

Mobile Literacy

The term *mobile literacy* has been used to describe the capacity for using mobile devices, although it does not have a clear set of standards for doing so. At the same time, there are several aspects of mobility that relate to information literacy and easily map within an interconnected metaliteracy framework. According to David Parry (2011), "one of our obligations as educators is to consider how the mobile Internet changes not only how we teach, but what it means to be knowledgeable and educated in our culture" (p. 16). Parry identifies three pedagogical dimensions of mobile literacy, including "understanding information access," "understanding hyperconnectivity," and "understanding the new sense of space" (p. 16). He emphasizes how the speed of information access via mobile phones requires "credibility detection—a skill that will be useful throughout their lives regardless of what they choose to do professionally" (p. 16). He also discusses the importance of "hyperconnectivity" via mobile devices and provides an example of using Twitter for "collaborative note-taking," and for extending the classroom discussions to virtual spaces (p. 16). Since mobile devices expand access to information to portable locations, he also argues that one of his primary pedagogical goals is "to get students to begin to understand how one can use a mobile device to both create and access spatial information" (p. 18). Mobility allows for collaboration and the creation of digital materials based on geographic coordinates and access to multiple data sets of information. As Parry suggests, by preparing students to be literate in these spaces, we move beyond the view of portable devices as distractions in the classroom to recognizing them as powerful resources for accessing, creating, and sharing information in partnership with others.

The original ACRL definition of information literacy recognized that "information is available through multiple media, including graphical, aural, and textual, and these pose new challenges for individuals in evaluating and understanding it" (ACRL, 2000, p. 3). This is a broad recognition of a diverse information environment that is useful in many different contexts and many of today's portable devices integrate these very elements. At the same time, however, this document was too early to address the radical changes brought forth by mobile technologies. Mobility transforms our understanding of location and how we access, create, and share information from anyplace in the world, unencumbered by notions of fixed locations or wired technological devices. Metaliteracy expands the scope of information literacy to include a mobile dimension and to adapt to emerging changes over time. This requires active engagement with mobile technologies as portable writing devices, virtual classrooms, and networked libraries. It also promotes deep reflection about knowledge creation and interactive communications that can happen anywhere.

Critical Information Literacy

James Elmborg (2006) argues for "critical information literacy" as a theoretical construct based on critical pedagogy. This critical perspective radically alters our definition of information literacy as more than discrete skills to a broader conception of knowledge acquisition within disciplinary contexts. According to Elmborg, critical information literacy engages learners in collaborative problem solving and in the process of continually asking questions about all dimensions of the information environment, including the library itself. He argues that "critical information literacy involves developing a critical consciousness about information, learning to ask questions about the library's (and the academy's) role in structuring and presenting a single, knowable reality" (p. 198). This necessitates that learners do more than access and retrieve information; they must instead ask critical questions about how information is organized, presented, and understood in a range of societal and institutional contexts. According to Elmborg, "If literacy is the ability to read, interpret, and produce texts valued in a community, then academic information literacy is the ability to read, interpret, and produce information valued in academia—a skill that must be developed by all students during their college education. Information functions in very unique ways in higher education" (p. 196). As Elmborg argues, to accomplish this and function at such a complex level of thinking and action requires more than acquiring skills; "it involves the comprehension of an entire system of thought and the ways that information flows in that system" (p. 196).

Critical information literacy demonstrates the need for an expanded metaliteracy that promotes collaboration, community, and the acquisition of new knowledge because the standard definition of information literacy as currently configured fails to do so. For instance, critical information literacy is about more than information access because it strives for a "critical consciousness" among teachers and learners (Elmborg, 2006, p. 193). Through this approach, students gain the ability to "critically evaluate the system itself" and not just different pieces of information in a search, demonstrating a much broader awareness and ability than the traditional search and retrieve model provides (Elmborg, 2006, p. 196). Through this metacognitive action, learners gain an understanding of the discipline itself and use information "to solve these problems and to create their own understandings and identities" (Elmborg, 2006, p. 198). Further, the production of information is conducted within a community of peers, and sharing is an essential part of this process as participants share readings, interpretation, and the experience itself (Elmborg, 2006, p. 195).

Critical thinking is core to the original conception of information literacy. ACRL argued that higher education has an essential role to play in "ensuring that individuals have the intellectual abilities of reasoning and critical thinking, and by helping them construct a framework for learning how to learn" (ACRL, 2000, p. 4). Although not explicitly identified as a metacognitive ability, "learning how to learn" is a reflective process that provides the learner with a high-level perspective on the learning process itself. In addition, *Standard Three* of the ACRL standard definition states, "The information literate student evaluates information and its sources critically and incorporates selected information into his or her knowledge base and value system" (ACRL, 2000, p. 11). Critical thinking is central to all information literacy endeavors, but in practice the prevalent one-shot library sessions are unable to provide the metacognitive perspective for learners to gain the self-reflective critical awareness about their own literacy. This reflective process takes place over time and within disciplinary and interdisciplinary contexts that make the learning meaningful. Metaliteracy promotes the inclusion of this critical element into an expanded and interconnected framework that unifies related characteristics.

Health Literacy

The Patient Protection and Affordable Care Act of 2010 defines health literacy as "the degree to which an individual has the capacity to obtain, communicate, process, and understand health information and services in order to make appropriate health decisions." This definition has been adopted by the Centers for Disease Control and Prevention and the National Network of Libraries of Medicine (NN/LM). Health literacy features several similar competencies to the standard definition of information literacy but with a particular emphasis on health information and services. The NN/LM (2012) applies this definition in specific ways to support patients in navigating complex health information, including "the ability to understand instructions on prescription drug bottles, appointment slips, medical education brochures, doctor's directions and consent forms, and the ability to negotiate complex health care systems." This definition emphasizes the ability to evaluate health care information and to make decisions about health services. The importance of accessing and evaluating information in these contexts is focused on "evaluating information for credibility and quality" and "analyzing relative risks and benefits" as well as "calculating dosages" and "interpreting test results" (NN/LM, 2012). In addition, health literacy recognizes the role of community organizations and that health care decisions take place "in an age of shared responsibility between physician and patient" (NN/LM, 2012). Further, it is important to note that the NN/LM identified connections to other literacy types, including visual, computer, information, numerical, and computational literacy. This approach is similar to metaliteracy since core information literacy competencies are identified, shared knowledge through communities is valued, and relevant multimodal literacies are foregrounded.

COMBINED LITERACIES

The combined literacy formats discussed in this section generally integrate multiple characteristics in one framework. This is similar to metaliteracy because we are also arguing for a combined model that builds on the strength of multiple perspectives. At the same time, however, we see metaliteracy as distinct from these other approaches because we identify information literacy as a foundation concept at the center of this combined method. Metaliteracy expands the core elements of information literacy and also includes the most influential characteristics of related and emerging literacies. This is an ever-evolving model that adapts and changes over time based on the needs of the learner.

Transliteracy

As we described in the first chapter, transliteracy offers a broad definition of literacy that covers the ability to engage with multiple modalities from print and orality to traditional mass media (television, radio, and film) and social networking. So far transliteracy has avoided any discussion of discrete skills because it is a fairly open and flexible conceptual model. This approach makes it difficult to map transliteracy within the metaliteracy model, but we identify some of the key elements of transliteracy that relate to metaliteracy and other literacy types (see table 3.1). As Sue Thomas and colleagues (2007) argue, "it offers a wider analysis of reading, writing and interacting across a range of platforms, tools, media and cultures." Based on this description, transliteracy may be similar to metaliteracy because it prepares learners for a range of technology formats, although for us information literacy is central to the metaliteracy model. Transliteracy emerged quite separate from information literacy. It does not build on the information literacy definition and instead proposes a new approach based on the ability to navigate multiple technologies. According to Tom Ipri (2010), transliteracy continues to develop while placing an important emphasis on social spaces and supporting several key elements of information literacy:

> As more research is created in the field, librarians can incorporate these new ideas into the ways they assist patrons with accessing, understanding, and producing information. The social aspects of transliteracy can enhance the workplace by creating robust systems of knowledge sharing and can enhance user experience by granting them a role in the construction of information.

By combining the Thomas (Thomas et al., 2007) and Ipri (2010) definitions of transliteracy, we identify several common characteristics within metaliteracy, although we realize that transliteracy is not usually segmented in this way (see table 3.1). For instance, transliteracy promotes the integrated ability to access, read, and understand all forms of information across multiple modalities. It also supports creating new information through writing, interacting, and producing in a variety of formats. This is a transformational experience mediated by effective collaboration and communication. While transliteracy may not explicitly identify concrete competencies in relation to information literacy, such a clear assertion to the obvious connections (as evident in table 3.1) would allow for the evolution of combined literacies in social environments, both on site and online.

New Media Literacy

The term *new media literacy* has been used in a variety of contexts and is often related to digital literacy and ICT literacy. Henry Jenkins and colleagues (2006) describe new media literacy as a part of his theory related to participatory culture. Jenkins (2006) uses the plural "literacies" and identifies a strong connection to the social and collaborative aspects of the term: "The new literacies almost all involve social skills developed through collaboration and networking" (p. 4). He also acknowledges connections to other literacy formats: "These skills build on the foundation of traditional literacy, research skills, technical skills, and critical analysis skills taught in the classroom" (p. 4). As with other media-related literacies, information literacy is not overtly discussed or recognized in any way, although the emphasis on the evolving information environment and critical thinking justifies a more direct link than we have seen to date.

In 2006, Henry Jenkins formalized his approach to literacy education through the publication of *Confronting the Challenges of Participatory Culture: Media Education for the 21st Century* with support from The John D. and Catherine T. MacArthur Foundation. This project validated his theory of "participatory culture" that he initially envisioned for television in 1992 within the contemporary context of social media (Jenkins, 1992). Jenkins and colleagues (2006) argue for a new set of skills based on participation and interactivity, including: "play, performance, simulation, appropriation, multitasking, distributed cognition, collective intelligence, judgment, transmedia navigation, networking, and negotiation" (2006, p. 4). While these skills are strikingly different from the standard information literacy language with a particular emphasis on collaboration and participation, the competencies are easily adapted to an expanded metaliteracy model (see table 3.1). As with metaliteracy, the new media framework promoted by Jenkins and colleagues also builds on critical thinking and research competencies, although information literacy itself is not mentioned as a primary influence. Each approach, however, reflects the changing dynamics of new media by providing learners with social skills to be actively engaged in these spaces.

We identify several opportunities for integration when mapping these skills to the standard ACRL definitions and to an expanded metaliteracy framework in practice. The purpose of doing so is not to subsume another literacy but rather to inform the evolution of a comprehensive framework for all literacies. For instance, *multitasking* is defined as "the ability to scan one's environment and shift focus as needed to salient details" (Jenkins, 2006, p. 4). This requires reading, evaluation, and critical-thinking skills, but it also aligns well with ACRL *Standard One* in which the "information literate student determines the nature and extent of the information needed" (ACRL, 2000, p. 9). In both contexts, learners need to balance multiple sources of information, make decisions about how to apply appropriate resources, and when to quickly shift gears to other formats. In addition, *transmedia navigation* is defined as "the ability to follow the flow of stories and information across multiple modalities" (Jenkins, 2006, p. 4). This approach is similar to how students use and incorporate information and it is consistent with ACRL *Standard Two* in which "the information literate student accesses needed information effectively and efficiently" (ACRL, 2000, p. 9).

In New Media Literacy, *transmedia navigation* involves how learners search, access, and connect different kinds of information in a variety of media formats In other examples, *judgment* is consistent with the *evaluation* of information, *simulation* includes interpretation and construction elements that are comparable to how we *understand* and create information, and *play* has a problem-solving component that aligns with how we evaluate and incorporate information (see table 3.1). In addition, *distributed cognition,* which is defined as "the ability to interact meaningfully with tools that expand mental capacities" (Jenkins, 2006, p. 4) would benefit from ACRL *Standard Three* because *incorporating* information encompasses different technologies while synthesizing "main ideas to construct new concepts" (ACRL, 2000, p. 11). Further, *performance* is defined as "the ability to adopt alternative identities for the purpose of improvisation" (Jenkins, 2006, p. 4) and relates to ACRL *Standard Four* because effectively using information includes "planning and creation of a particular product or performance" (ACRL, 2000, p. 13).

New media literacies are grounded in the idea that today's social media are collaborative and participatory. Many of the new media competencies that require teamwork and participation would relate more effectively to an expanded metaliteracy model than the standard information literacy definition. For instance, *appropriation* is "the ability to meaningfully sample and remix media content" (Jenkins, 2006, p. 4) and requires an emphasis on the production of information in a social media environment of mash-ups, multimedia, crowdsourcing, and participatory YouTube videos. This competency would benefit from ACRL *Standard Five* in which "the information literate student understands many of the ethical, legal and socio-economic issues surrounding information and information technology" (ACRL, 2000, 14). The *appropriation* of content requires individuals to understand how to use information in legal and ethical ways. In addition, with an expanded focus on OERs, Creative Commons, and the collaborative production of repurposed content, an expanded metaliteracy model would account for the dynamic changes in open learning. According to the new media literacy framework, *collective intelligence* is "the ability to pool knowledge and compare notes with others toward a common goal" and *negotiation* is "the ability to travel across diverse communities, discerning and respecting multiple perspectives, and grasping and following alternative norms" (Jenkins, 2006, p. 4). Both competencies clearly support the need for a metaliteracy that encourages cooperation as a core value. Further, *networking* is "the ability to search for, synthesize, and disseminate information" (Jenkins, 2006, p. 4), which supports the ACRL standard definition to access and evaluate information, while prioritizing the dissemination of new knowledge through a shared network. New media literacy is ideal for today's participatory culture with several relevant associations to a redefined vision for information literacy.

ICT Literacy

UNESCO asserts that ICT literacy provides an all-encompassing vision for opening education worldwide. In addition, Katz and Macklin (2007) define ICT literacy as the ability to "to solve problems and think critically about information" and argue that "researching and communicating information via digital environments are as important as reading and writing were in earlier centuries" (p. 50). The authors describe a web-based research instrument developed by the Educational Testing Service (ETS) to assess ICT literacy skills. As part of this research they refer to a set of skills originally identified by ETS, including the ability to *define, access, manage, integrate, evaluate, create*, and *communicate* information (Katz & Macklin, 2007, p. 51). As we can see in table 3.1, the ICT literacy skills align closely with the information literacy competencies identified in our expanded metaliteracy model. For instance, ICT literacy includes the ability to determine, access, and evaluate information, similar to the standard information literacy definition. ICT literacy also promotes the ability to manage, integrate, create, and communicate information. While ICT literacy may not push the bounds of the collaborative production of information in multiple modalities in the same way as transliteracy or new media literacy, it is still a relevant concept that provides a conceptual beacon for advancing global open education. Several key aspects of ICT literacy align well with our metaliteracy model as well as the MIL framework currently promoted by UNESCO.

Information Fluency

The term *information fluency* has become a part of our literacy nomenclature and was first formalized in 1999 in *Being Fluent with Information Technology*, developed by the Committee on Information Technology Literacy for the National Research Council. Information fluency shares some of the critical-thinking objectives with information literacy and was similarly devised as an alternative to basic computer literacy, but it presented a much stronger emphasis on computing and technology than has been traditionally envisioned for information literacy. Fluency with information technology (or FITness, as abbreviated in the founding document) "requires that persons understand information technology broadly enough to be able to apply it productively at work and in their everyday lives, to recognize when information technology would assist or impede the achievement of a goal, and to continually adapt to the changes in and advancement of information technology" (p. 16). This definition is for educational and occupational environments and includes three key components: intellectual capabilities, information technology concepts, and information technology skills (p. 4). For the purpose of this analysis within our metaliteracy model, we will focus on the intellectual capabilities of information fluency (see table 3.1).

Several of the intellectual capabilities identified as central to information fluency support an expanded metaliteracy framework, while others require further analysis for complementarity. For instance, the capabilities to *evaluate*, *communicate*, and *collaborate* with information technology match the same goals of metaliteracy. If we dig deeper than these obvious connections, we identify other similarities as well. The first capability of information fluency is to "engage in sustained reasoning," and according to the definition, "sustained reasoning starts with defining and clarifying a problem" (Committee on Information Technology Literacy, 1999, p. 21), which is comparable to the metacognitive ability of information literacy to "determine the extent of information needed" (ACRL, 2000, p. 2). While fluency may focus on technology and information literacy may focus on content, the abilities to determine or define an information or technology need are relevant in both contexts and are united concerns in today's social media environment. In addition, the capability to *manage complexity* requires individuals to "plan a project, design a solution, integrate the components, respond to unexpected interactions, and diagnose what is needed from each task" (Committee on Information Technology Literacy, 1999, p. 21). This is similar in some ways to the balancing act required when accessing information and making decisions about "the quantity, quality, and relevance of the search results to determine whether alternative information retrieval systems or investigative methods should be utilized" (ACRL, 2000, p. 10). In each case, the active participant in the process is investigating multiple options in an effort to make decisions that lead to project planning and completion. In another example, the capabilities to *test a solution* and to *expect the unexpected* work well in information technology environments but would also prepare metaliterate individuals to effectively use information. For instance, information fluency emphasizes testing that informs design decisions and takes "into account that most systems will be used in ways that were not intended, as well as in expected ways" (Committee on Information Technology Literacy, 1999, p. 22).

In turn, gaining the ability to *expect the unexpected* recognizes that technological "use may still have unexpected consequences, because the system is embedded in a larger social and technological context that may not have been properly anticipated" (Committee on Information Technology Literacy, 1999, p. 25). Related considerations play out in the design and use of information in a range of media formats and through the research process. These abilities improve in comprehensive ways when addressing information and technology together. For instance, the design of a multimedia or social media project may take unexpected pathways as multiple participants contribute to the work and as different resources are utilized. In addition, an individual or collaborative search strategy is bound to change over time through multiple iterations of the research process and based on findings that vary or offer unexpected surprises or discoveries. Further, different search engines will also impact the research process. For example, a freely available but commercial resource such as Google will provide access to a specific set of resources that will be significantly different from a library search engine associated with a particular institution. The researcher must have an awareness of the technology considerations as well as the search process itself to effectively pursue knowledge.

These are just a few examples of the complementarity found when looking at information fluency and information literacy in a relational framework (see table 3.1). We recognize other similarities with the abilities to *think abstractly* and *understand* information; *manage problems* and *incorporate* information; as well as *anticipate changing technologies* and how we *produce* information. This is not to suggest that information fluency and information literacy are the same because the emphasis of each construct has been different, but our learners would benefit from a model that is interrelated in nature. While the official definitions of information fluency were outlined in 1999, most of the terms are still relevant for how we use and understand information technology. In today's online and mobile spaces we expand the ideas further in relation to digital content in many forms to address the interactive and communal dynamics of social media and social networking.

As we have seen in this analysis of related literacies (table 3.1), metaliteracy expands the foundation elements of information literacy while linking to a number of relevant formats. Metaliteracy provides us with a conceptual bridge from the standard information literacy definition to an integrated and comprehensive model. Rather than consider each new literacy type as a replacement to previous models, or perhaps as competing concepts, this perspective allows us to find common ground and to advance a thorough approach to learning. At the same time, this analysis offers a way to think through an ever-evolving conception of information literacy that will necessarily transform beyond this current iteration. We recognize, for instance, that some of the standard terms will and should evolve into something else entirely as the social media landscape continues to shift and as cognate literacies influence this new framework. As part of this reinvention, metaliteracy should be continuously adaptable to the changing information environment and in response to the needs of our learners.

METALITERACY LEARNING GOALS AND OBJECTIVES

So far this chapter has focused on the characteristics of different literacies, all of which have some relationship to information literacy. Each unique literacy form enumerates the abilities that it values, with varying degrees of specificity and effectiveness. As such, the essential elements of each literacy type delineate the learning objectives required to successfully teach these concepts. The connections between related literacy types and information literacy are often understated in the literature. This prevents an all-encompassing view of information literacy to be fully realized since the objectives we teach with do not always adapt to innovative trends. As a result, the extent to which we have been able to benefit from new ideas that emerge from related literacies is limited by traditional notions of what information literacy could or should be. Additionally, information literacy models and standards are not always nimble because of the bureaucracy or slowness of the procedures involved in developing them. In just one example, the information literacy outcomes, as described in the ACRL (2000) *Information Literacy Competency Standards for Higher Education* are insufficient for the expanded metaliteracy model we propose. But this process is about more than responding to the ACRL document from 2000, especially since work has been underway to revise the original standards. We also need to rethink our conceptions of information literacy in our teaching and learning practices, given the considerable changes we continue to experience in the information environment.

As an overarching metaliteracy that informs and is influenced by key aspects of other literacies, this comprehensive model requires renewed objectives as well. Metaliteracy is an integrated framework that is metacognitive and promotes empowerment through the collaborative production and sharing of information. Traditional information literacy outcomes do not go far enough to support this approach. While metaliteracy asserts many unique characteristics, related to metacognition especially, it is an open framework that evolves with the visual, digital, new media, mobile, and critical perspective of other literacy types. Rather than see information literacy as a separate concern, we envision it as central to how all of these emerging literacies advance in relation to a metaliteracy model.

This next section will outline the essential learning objectives that develop metaliterate learners. These ideas were originally presented in the authors' article on metaliteracy in *College & Research Libraries* (Mackey & Jacobson, 2011) and in another essay for *Communications in Information Literacy* titled "Proposing a Metaliteracy Model to Redefine Information Literacy" (Jacobson & Mackey, 2013). Initially, we outlined seven learning objectives that constitute metaliteracy in practice. While these continue to develop and expand, the original objectives:

1. Understand Format Type and Delivery Mode
2. Evaluate User Feedback as Active Researcher
3. Create a Context for User-generated Information
4. Evaluate Dynamic Content Critically
5. Produce Original Content in Multiple Media Formats
6. Understand Personal Privacy, Information Ethics and Intellectual Property Issues
7. Share Information in Participatory Environments

(Mackey & Jacobson, 2011, pp. 70–76)

Since we first described these objectives in 2011, we collaborated with a team of colleagues in a grant-funded project to develop the ideas further. In 2012 we received an Innovative Instruction Technology Grant (IITG) supported by SUNY to create a Transliteracy Learning Collaborative to rethink information competencies throughout the SUNY system. As the project played out, the work of this team aligned more closely with metaliteracy than transliteracy and we developed a set of objectives as part of a Metaliteracy Learning Collaborative that expanded the core assertions we made in our original article. This partnership among SUNY colleagues led to the collaborative design of an expanded set of objectives, the design of a badging system to support the objectives, and the creation of a blog at Metaliteracy.org to gain additional input about the objectives and to publish ongoing changes to the extended document. All of this activity has allowed us to expand our initial ideas about how to effectively apply metaliteracy in practice. We will briefly describe the four primary goals and domains in relation to the expanded metaliteracy learning objectives.

Based on a suggestion by Project Manager Emer O'Keeffe, the original metaliteracy learning objectives are now organized into four domains: behavioral, cognitive, affective, and metacognitive. As we note in the introduction to the objectives at Metaliteracy.org:

> Metaliteracy learning falls into four domains: behavioral (what students should be able to do upon successful completion of learning

activities—skills, competencies), cognitive (what students should know upon successful completion of learning activities—comprehension, organization, application, evaluation), affective (changes in learners' emotions or attitudes through engagement with learning activities), and metacognitive (what learners think about their own thinking—a reflective understanding of how and why they learn, what they do and do not know, their preconceptions, and how to continue to learn) (http://metaliteracy.org/learning-objectives).

Information literacy models and standards tend to include both skills-based, behavioral aspects of learning, such as how to search a database, and cognitive elements, such as how to parse a topic and develop an effective search strategy. However, practices in the field, primarily the omnipresent one-shot library sessions, allow little time for a full exploration of the range of both behavioral and cognitive elements. Instead, behavioral objectives may take precedence, reinforcing the development of discrete skills only within clearly defined information contexts, such as library databases or search engines. Metaliteracy changes this perspective considerably by incorporating affective and metacognitive dimensions of literacy development, while expanding the cognitive and behavioral components involved in information literacy. For instance, the cognitive aspect of metaliteracy supports the abilities to evaluate, comprehend, and apply the effective use and production of information in a variety of social contexts, such as new media and open learning environments. The affective component focuses on how learners think or feel about a particular information-related situation, including an information search or the creation of a media project shared online. This domain connects to the fourth metacognitive area as well, because the way learners think or feel about something allows for a metacognitive experience. By doing so, learners are critically engaged and take the time to carefully and continuously reflect on their own thinking. This open framework moves beyond a single emphasis on skills-development and instead integrates all four dimensions: behavioral, cognitive, affective and metacognitive. In order to achieve this united model, our collaborative team increased the number of objectives within four over-arching goals:

1. Evaluate content critically, including dynamic, online content that changes and evolves, such as article preprints, blogs, and wikis
2. Understand personal privacy, information ethics, and intellectual property issues in changing technology environments
3. Share information and collaborate in a variety of participatory environments
4. Demonstrate ability to connect learning and research strategies with lifelong learning processes and personal, academic, and professional goals

(http://metaliteracy.org/learning-objectives)

All four goals are informed by the original assertions we made in the first metaliteracy article and each goal includes several specific objectives that also open out the ideas in specificity and scope. We will refer to this framework as a way to organize our discussion of the expanded objectives.

GOAL 1

Evaluate content critically, including dynamic, online content that changes and evolves, such as article preprints, blogs, and wikis.

This first goal includes several objectives that are primarily behavioral, cognitive, and affective. This goal builds on three of the original objectives, *Understand Format Type and Delivery Mode, Evaluate Dynamic Content Critically* and *Evaluate User Feedback as Active Researcher*. For instance, one of the expanded objectives within this goal includes *Evaluate user response as an active researcher; understand the differing natures of feedback mechanisms and context in traditional and social media platforms* (http://metaliteracy.org/learning-objectives).

Prior to the development of digital documents, format type and delivery mode were easily categorized. For instance, all of the resources that were initially defined as scholarly or popular, in a book or journal, were, most often, in print. The current situation, with dynamic digital documents accessible from anywhere in the world through a range of devices, is of course far more nuanced, more ambiguous, and demanding of increased awareness and discernment. Included in this goal is the need to be able to determine the scope of the research required to meet one's needs, and the importance of continually reassessing what is still missing.

Although traditional forms of research, with their attendant scholarly review mechanisms continue to exist, they are increasingly overtaken by the amount of information found in newer and less structured formats. The resources available through social media deserve consideration when seeking information, but the combination of dynamic social tools, in conjunction with the vigorous nature of user participation itself, requires an informed, inquisitive investigation. Metaliterate learners must understand the differing natures of the feedback mechanisms, as seen in blogs, wikis, and other social tools, and be aware of the context when deciding upon sources to utilize. Evaluation is a component common to many of the objectives within this goal and the overall framework. Given the open nature of publishing, for example, it is incumbent on information seekers to evaluate the sources that they find. Information is frequently fluid in such format types as blog postings, tweets, and user-generated content in a wide variety of social media spaces. Even more traditional sources, such as scholarly articles, may first appear as preprints, and then change slightly once officially published. Additionally, scholars request online feedback on their writings, and then make revisions for the next version. Individuals need to be able to recognize information for what it is, and be able to synthesize disparate information formats to effectively meet their needs.

GOAL 2

Understand personal privacy, information ethics, and intellectual property issues in changing technology environments.

This second goal includes several objectives that are mostly behavioral, cognitive, and affective. It is closely aligned with the original objective *Understand Personal Privacy, Information Ethics and Intellectual Property Issues.* The expanded goal and related objectives support the overall intention of metaliteracy to prepare learners to be active creators and distributors of information in open and online environments. Two of the new objectives within this goal include: *Differentiate between the production of original information and remixing or re-purposing open resources* and *Apply copyright and Creative Commons licensing as appropriate to the creation of original or repurposed information* (http://metaliteracy.org/learning-objectives).

In order to participate in today's open age of social media, it is incumbent upon individuals to be responsible global citizens. This requires being knowledgeable about the world and to understand how to effectively interact and contribute to an international network. Metaliterate learners must gain knowledge about copyright laws and ways to license original and repurposed work through the Creative Commons. As we stated in our original article, "This requires an ongoing exploration of the legal, economic, political, and social issues that mediate our access to technology and often define the types of documents we evaluate and use" (Mackey & Jacobson, 2011, p. 75). In addition, the ethical and personal privacy dimensions continue to be important as users share more about themselves in these spaces than previous technologies enabled. Increasingly, this component also intersects with the need to know more about information security issues and how to protect oneself and one's digital resources in these interconnected spaces. It also requires metaliterate learners to be aware of their digital footprint and how their contributions to social media spaces may be permanent representations of their thoughts and actions at specific moments in their lifetime. While this environment may seem transient and mutable, it is also fixed, searchable, and archival, requiring participants to be aware of how they represent themselves at any given time through a range of devices and platforms.

GOAL 3

Share information and collaborate in a variety of participatory environments.

The third goal in this framework includes several new objectives that represent all four domains: behavioral, cognitive, affective, and metacognitive. This goal supports the collaborative and sharing aspects of metaliteracy as well as the emphasis on producing information in open and online communities. It is informed by the original objectives to *Produce Original Content in Multiple Media Formats*, to *Share Information in Participatory Environments*, and to *Create a Context for User-Generated Information*. Two of the objectives within this goal include *Describe the potential impact of online resources for sharing information (text, images, video, and other media) in collaboration with others* and *Produce original content appropriate to specific needs in multiple media formats; transfer knowledge gained to new formats in unpredictable and evolving environments* (http://metaliteracy.org/learning-objectives).

Today's information seeker is generally also an information producer. Information can be published in a wide variety of formats, from a lengthy scholarly article to a 140-character tweet. Content might be traditional text, or a dramatically innovative remix of word, image, and sound. Metaliterate individuals must be aware of the possibilities of repurposed content, understand that the tools and environment will change, and actively seek out and explore new options. Additionally, there has been a significant change in the ways in which information might be shared with others. Metaliterate individuals will take advantage of the possibilities open to them, and will participate responsibly and ethically in sharing information with others. Within this user-generated environment, it is vital that learners place the information they find from other producers within a context that includes identifying the author, the author's expertise, and the reason for the publication of the information, in whatever format. In the cases where such markers are missing, incomplete, or equivocal (such as entries within Wikipedia), metaliterate individuals will be able to identify other cues in order to ascertain the value of the material for any particular situation.

This third goal and related learning objectives encompass a variety of translation-related activities as well. This includes synthesizing and adapting information so that it effectively moves from one format (scholarly article, for example) to another (blog posting) in order to reach a wider, or different, audience. This process might involve using one's ability to translate personal experiences using web-based resources to inform and assist others. For instance, an online contributor may create a media slide show using original digital images from a local event to raise the profile of a nonprofit community organization. This translation of static images to a dynamic presentation impacts viewer perceptions and promotes the goals of the local organization, while increasing the potential audience for the group online. It also expands the understanding of the media maker about the translation and adaptation of ideas across multiple formats and artistic expressions. Ideally, as the metaliterate learner contributes to this social space, and reflects on their own thinking as a knowledgeable and collaborative participant, the learner becomes a teacher of others. The participatory, open web environment encourages this translation of ideas and transformation from learner to teacher. Knowledge gleaned from active information seeking, evaluation, use, collaboration, and production prepares for this transition in roles, which is entirely aligned with the objective to share information in participatory environments.

GOAL 4

Demonstrate ability to connect learning and research strategies with lifelong learning processes and personal, academic, and professional goals.

The fourth learning goal in this model includes several related objectives based on domains that are primarily cognitive and metacognitive. For instance, it includes cognitive learning objectives such as *Determine scope of the question or task required to meet one's needs* and *Reevaluate needs and next steps throughout the process* (http://metaliteracy.org/learning-objectives). Two of the metacognitive objectives include *Use self-reflection to assess one's own learning and knowledge of the learning process* and *Demonstrate the ability to think critically in context and to transfer critical thinking to new learning* (http://metaliteracy.org/learning-objectives). This goal in particular demonstrates how the metacognitive dimension of metaliteracy has advanced since our first article on this topic introduced the idea.

As we argue in this book, metacognition, the willingness to think about one's own thinking and to engage in this process without prompting, is a key attribute of metaliterate learners. Metacognition is critical to determining what one does as an active reflective learner and helps to identify and challenge preconceptions one might have that hinder growth. For instance, critical reflection on a failed search strategy should result in new approaches to seeking information while blogging about media projects will lead to insights about the creative process and potentially inform practice. Metacognition allows for ongoing critical thinking that builds on previous experience so that learners adapt to new information situations. The metacognitive dimension of metaliteracy also reinforces related characteristics such as adaptability and flexibility. For instance, the need to stay aware of continually shifting digital resources requires adaptability. As technologies and format types change, so must our abilities to recognize and respond to the transitions. In addition, the willingness to learn from the mistakes that come with new learning illustrates the kind of flexibility that guards against complacency. Rather than seeing the search process as linear and fixed, for instance, metaliterate learners are encouraged to understand the changing nature of circuitous information environments that require alternative methods in response to any given situation. Further, curiosity and creativity promote informed, self-directed learning, which is critical in a world where change is a given. Curiosity encourages individuals to expand their worldview through the global reach of today's information technology and creativity generates new ideas for producing and sharing information.

Integrating the Four Domains

Although we did not discuss every learning objective developed with our colleagues in the Metaliteracy Learning Collaborative, we have outlined the four main goals associated with our original assertions related to praxis. We have also added another layer to consider because in this extended framework we identified four domains: behavioral, cognitive, affective, and metacognitive. From our viewpoint, the behavioral objectives allow metaliterate learners to actively participate in connective social media by preparing them with concrete abilities for navigating and contributing to this space. At the same time, the cognitive objectives encourage learners to stay ahead of the evolving information environment by cultivating habits of mind. The cognitive domain supports continued knowledge acquisition in collaborative social networks. In addition, the affective objectives consider how one thinks and feels about a range of dynamic information situations, supporting the contemplation and reflection that occurs within the metacognitive domain.

The Metaliterate Learner

As we see in figure 3.1, the metaliterate learner, the four domains support a learner-centered framework for metaliteracy. At the center of this figure is the metaliterate learner, surrounded by each domain: metacognitive, cognitive, behavioral, and affective. The domains are fluid, representing a comprehensive and interrelated set of goals and learning objectives that lead to empowering roles. The outer sphere illustrates many of the dynamic parts played by the learner as a result of applying the metaliteracy model. Through the support of the four domains and goals, as well as the connected learning objectives, the metaliterate learner is an active *participant* who is an effective *communicator* and *translator* of information. The metaliterate learner is an *author* of information in many forms, including web documents, visual and aural materials, essays, presentations, annotations, and interactive communications. In addition, this figure illustrates the transformation of learner to *teacher* because the learning objectives support the self-empowering transfer of knowledge to others. The metaliterate learner is an effective *collaborator* within this context and works individually and in teams as *producer* and *publisher* of information. Ultimately, this approach prepares the metaliterate learner to be a critically

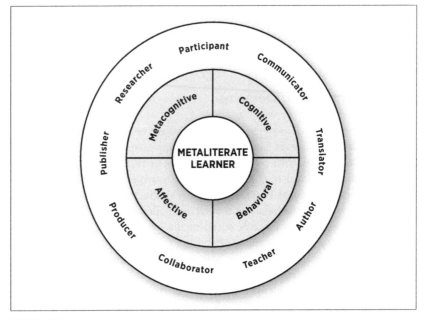

FIGURE 3.1
The Metaliterate Learner

engaged and active *researcher* capable of differentiating among a multitude of document types and modalities, while identifying critical questions and making an informed contribution to the scholarly discourse.

Readers who would like to apply principles of the metaliteracy model in practice will find that the objectives can be met in a variety of different ways, depending on the learning context. The teacher, facilitator, or individual intent on developing his or her own metacognitive perspective will find that the flexibility so often found in real-world situations fits easily within this framework. The core learning objectives will be examined further in the last two chapters in the book, where two courses that focus on metaliteracy are described. It is important to note that throughout the book we use the term "learners," often interchangeably with "students," because we envisage metaliterate individuals as constant and adaptable lifelong learners. Indeed, this is a necessity, given the evolving information landscape.

CONCLUSION

As we demonstrate in this chapter, all of the core characteristics of information literacy still have value, and based on our Metaliteracy and Related

Literacies table (table 3.1), the key characteristics share something in common with other literacies. At the heart of the model is a critical perspective on how we access, locate, evaluate, and use information in various digital forms. Many differences exist among the new literacies as well. In particular, the ways in which we participate, collaborate, create, and share information vary somewhat among the different literacies, but there is a clear recognition that these are the necessary competencies for an open social network. The contrast in definition and description allows us to introduce new elements to an integrated metaliteracy framework that further support a democratic process of collaboration and participation. In addition, metaliteracy provides an overt recognition of interactive systems and the need to consider how learners adapt to continuous technological change. The ability to look up and compile text information for later synthesis in a research essay does not go far enough in encapsulating the competencies required for a socially constructed multimedia system. We also need opportunities for self-reflection and collaboration in a learner-centered environment that values the contributions of all participants. This approach does not take place in one-shot library sessions or lectures but instead is encouraged through active engagement with contemporary media. Through an expansion of the original information literacy definition, and a mapping of key characteristics to related literacy types, we argue for a comprehensive metaliteracy that meets the needs of technology-mediated and socially immersed learners.

This new interconnected model emphasizes the original production of digital documents by metacognitive learners who are aware of new media formats and their ability to adapt to these changing environments. They effectively respond to change and are open to learning by participating in social media spaces. To be metaliterate requires critical reflection about individual and collaborative learning and active engagement in the production of new knowledge. The metaliterate learner reflects internally while opening up externally to collaborative partnerships with peers and distant connections in a global network. Metaliteracy shifts the emphasis from a set of discrete skills one learns in an information session to an iterative process of reflection and interactivity.

The theory of metaliteracy must be grounded in praxis and to do so requires a reimagining of learning goals and objectives to support the new model. We expanded our original seven learning objectives by working closely with the Metaliteracy Learning Collaborative. This process itself demonstrated metaliteracy in action and informed our own thinking on this topic. Through a grant-funded project, we opened the framework to colleagues and accomplished a great deal of the writing and editing of the renewed objectives using a wiki, and then further extended this work to a larger community via Metaliteracy.org. This partnership enhanced the experience and the ideas and led to a revised set of objectives within four primary learning goals. This group also allowed us to define the larger domains at play within each of the objectives as behavioral, cognitive, affective, and metacognitive. This collaborative work continues to advance, and will shape the future direction of the metaliteracy learning goals and objectives over time.

As we will see in the next chapter, the fundamental changes we have identified in the information environment are a global concern and have already had impact on how information literacy is defined around the world.

REFERENCES

Association of College and Research Libraries (ACRL). (2000). *Information literacy competency standards for higher education*. American Library Association. www.ala.org/ala/mgrps/divs/acrl/standards/standards.pdf

ACRL. (2011, October 27). *ACRL visual literacy competency standards for higher education*. American Library Association. Document ID: 4d02961f-23ff-b874 -7d6d-9f8d0b87e7c2. www.ala.org/acrl/standards/visualliteracy

Center for Media Literacy. (2012). *Media literacy: A definition and more.* www.medialit.org/media-literacy-definition-and-more

Centers for Disease Control and Prevention. (2014). Health literacy: Accurate, accessible and actionable health information for all. www.cdc.gov/healthliteracy

Committee on Information Technology Literacy, National Research Council. (1999). *Being fluent with information technology*. Washington, DC: National Academy Press.

Creative Commons. (n.d.). About the licenses. http://creativecommons.org/licenses

Elmborg, James. (2006). Critical information literacy: Implications for instructional practice. *Journal of Academic Librarianship, 32*(2), 192–199.

Forte, Michele, Jacobson, Trudi, Mackey, Tom, O'Keeffe, Emer, & Stone, Kathleen. (2013). Learning Objectives. Developing Metaliterate Learners. http:// metaliteracy.org/learning-objectives

Gilster, Paul. (1997). *Digital literacy*. New York, NY: Wiley.

Gurak, Laura J. (2001). *Cyberliteracy: Navigating the Internet with awareness*. New Haven, CT: Yale University Press.

International Telecommunication Union. (2012). *The world in 2011: ICT facts and figures*. www.itu.int/ITU-D/ict/facts/2011/material/ICTFactsFigures2011.pdf

International Visual Literacy Association. (2012). *What is visual literacy?* www.ivla .org/org_what_vis_lit.htm

Ipri, Tom. (2010, November). Introducing transliteracy: What does it mean to academic libraries? *College and Research Library News, 71*, 532–567. http://crln .acrl.org/content/71/10/532.full.pdf+html

Jacobson, Trudi E., & Mackey, Thomas P. (2013). Proposing a metaliteracy model to redefine information literacy. *Communications in Information Literacy*.

Jenkins, Henry. (1992). *Textual poachers: Television fans & participatory culture*. London, England: Routledge, Chapman, and Hall.

Jenkins, Henry. (2006). *Convergence culture: Where old and new media collide*. New York, NY: New York University Press.

Jenkins, Henry, with Clinton, Katie, Purushotma, Ravi, Robison, Alice J., & Weigel, Margaret. (2006). *Confronting the challenges of participatory culture: Media education for the 21st century*. The John D. and Catherine T. MacArthur Foundation. http://digitallearning.macfound.org/atf/cf/%7BE45C7E0-A3E0-4B89-AC9C-E807E1B0AE4E%7D/JENKINS_WHITE_PAPER.PDF

Katz, Irvin R., & Smith Macklin, Alexius. (2007). Information and communication technology (ICT) literacy: Integration and assessment in higher education. *Systemics, Cybernetics and Informatics, 5*(4), 50–55. www.iiisci.org/journal/sci/Contents.asp?var=&Previous=ISS5626

Literacy. (2012). In *Oxford English dictionary (OED) online*. Oxford University Press. www.oed.com/view/Entry/109054?p=emailAca24wNhiFpOw&d=109054

Mackey, Thomas P., & Jacobson, Trudi E. (2011). Reframing information literacy as a metaliteracy. *College & Research Libraries, 72*(1), 62–78.

National Network of Libraries of Medicine. (2012). Health literacy. http://nnlm.gov/outreach/consumer/hlthlit.html

Parry, David. (2011). Mobile perspectives: On teaching mobile literacy. *Educause Review*. www.educause.edu/ero/article/mobile-perspectives-teaching-mobile-literacy

The Patient Protection and Affordable Care Act of 2010, H.R. 3590, 108th Cong. 2010. U.S. Government Printing Office: www.gpo.gov/fdsys/pkg/BILLS-111hr3590enr/pdf/BILLS-111hr3590enr.pdf

Thomas, Sue, Joseph, Chris, Laccetti, Jess, Mason, Bruce, Mills, Simon, Perril, Simon, & Pullinger, Kate. (2007). Transliteracy: Crossing divides. *First Monday* 12(12). www.uic.edu/htbin/cgiwrap/bin/ojs/index.php/fm/article/view/2060/1908

United Nations Educational, Scientific and Cultural Organization (UNESCO). (2012a). Communication and information: Open educational resources. www.unesco.org/new/en/communication-and-information/access-to-knowledge/open-educational-resources

UNESCO. (2012b). ICT in education: UNESCO mobile learning week produces tangible results. www.unesco.org/new/en/unesco/themes/icts/single-view/news/unesco_mobile_learning_week_produces_tangible_results

UNESCO. (2012c). 2012 Paris OER Declaration. 2012 World Open Educational Resources (OER) Congress UNESCO, Paris, June 20–22. www.unesco.org/new/fileadmin/MULTIMEDIA/HQ/CI/CI/pdf/Events/Paris%20OER%20Declaration_01.pdf

West, Mark. (2012). Turning on mobile learning: Global themes. UNESCO. www.unesco.org/new/en/unesco/themes/icts/m4ed/mobile-learning-resources/unescomobilelearningseries/.

Wilson, Carolyn, Grizzle, Alton, Tuazon, Ramon, Akyempong, Kwame, & Cheung, Chi-Kim. (2011). UNESCO. *Media and information literacy curriculum for teachers*. www.unesco.org/new/en/communication-and-information/resources/publications-and-communication-materials/publications/full-list/media-and-information-literacy-curriculum-for-teachers

4

Global Trends in
Emerging Literacies

THE RADICAL CHANGES IN EMERGING TECHNOLOGY AND THE attendant social and educational ramifications discussed in the initial chapters in this book are a global phenomenon. The exponential growth in personal devices and methods of interacting with others is taking place throughout the world. Indeed, the transformation in some developing countries is dramatic due to a rapid jump from limited information technology to a widespread mobile presence. The convergence of these factors has led to an increasing awareness of the critical need for individuals to be information literate in the broadest sense in order to participate fully as citizens. While information and technology infrastructures differ from one country to another, people who are able to access, use, evaluate, create, and share information effectively through emerging technologies will have great economic, intellectual, social, and political advantages. The relevance of these abilities in today's networked global society was especially evident in the Arab Spring movement of 2011. In these contexts, the informal sharing of information takes place through portable social technologies and the potential impact on social change at the local level continues to increase around the globe. The creation and distribution of information has become democratized, emphasizing the critical need for a broad conception of information literacy as a metaliteracy. Information no longer emanates from the top down, despite the best effort of some regimes to have it do so. Further, how we observe and analyze such movements from a distance, through social media, rather than traditional news sources only, requires a metaliteracy that supports self-reflection and critical thinking. In a decentered social network, news travels quickly and is often unfiltered without the editorial review and analysis of traditional news organizations.

This chapter will examine global trends in information technology and emerging literacy frameworks. We begin with "International Trends in Open Education" to identify the enhanced conceptions of information literacy from around the world. This section is followed by "Literacy Initiatives from International Organizations" and provides a spotlight on global efforts that fully conceptualize what it means to be information literate. Recent initiatives by UNESCO and IFLA illustrate progress in this arena. The European effort to harmonize education across countries provides fertile ground for new models of information literacy, as explored in "The Bologna Process and the Tuning Project." Then, in "Evolving Information Literacy Frameworks" we feature two specific models emanating from the United Kingdom and Hong Kong. This review of information literacy in a global context will illustrate that we all share similar challenges in how we understand and teach information competencies in an era of social media. It will also demonstrate the need for metaliteracy as a persuasive pedagogical response to understanding information and communication through networked social technologies.

INTERNATIONAL TRENDS IN OPEN EDUCATION

Being metaliterate in today's social media age involves interacting with a network of users and interfaces in a constantly changing information environment. The emergence of OERs as a global phenomenon provides an opportunity for individuals to expand their knowledge through freely available and reusable content in a variety of formats. OERs offer a shared approach to knowledge that advances lifelong learning and provides opportunities for educators from around the world to collaborate at a distance and dialogue about open praxis. OERs present teachers, librarians, and learners with a new context for understanding information as something that is easily accessible and available for reuse in a networked environment. John Robertson (2010), in his presentation at the Open Ed conference in 2010 about the role of academic libraries and OERs, noted that an important role for libraries is to assist those who would benefit from OERs in this quest to expand knowledge. He stated that selecting and using OERs require enhanced information literacy skills, exactly those abilities that an individual might be seeking to continuously update as a lifelong learner:

> One of the ways in which libraries might be involved with OERs (and more widely in Open Education) would be through extending some of the work they already often do in the provision of information literacy classes to encompass supporting students in selecting and evaluating OERs. This isn't to suggest a new thing called "OER Literacy" but rather to place the discovery and use of OERs within an existing framework— as the skills needed to find and use OERs draw on a number of recognised skills relating to information literacy, to study skills, and the promotion of self regulated learning. (Robertson, 2010, p. 5)

Robertson identified a clear role for libraries in addressing OERs as valuable global information sources with unique attributes (as open and reusable entities). He also suggested that OERs be brought into existing information literacy practices that build on established skills related to the access and evaluation of information. In addition, Robertson argued, "Discovering, selecting, and using OERs should, on some level, also consider with [sic] the design of materials and required study skills" (p. 6). While it is important to build on existing information literacy practices, the relationship to "discovery" and "design of materials" suggests a broader and expanded framework that extends beyond traditional information literacy instruction. OERs require an understanding of information in open environments that extend beyond traditional library websites and databases. This requires users to gain critical-thinking abilities and knowledge about changing technologies that mediate these spaces. In order to achieve the "self regulation" that Robertson mentioned in his proceedings paper, learners would benefit from an expanded metaliteracy framework that emphasizes self-reflection about one's learning (p. 5).

According to Sir John Daniel and David Killion (2012), OERs offer great promise for bridging educational divides internationally while serving as a catalyst for economic development and growth. They argue, "As policymakers struggle to apply traditional fiscal and monetary tools to mend world markets restrained by weak purchasing power, accelerated learning based on OERs could do more to stimulate global economic demand and growth than all the world's tax holidays combined—then multiplied ten-fold." The authors suggest that OER initiatives such as the $2 billion grant program announced by President Obama in 2011 titled *Trade Adjustment Assistance Community College and Career Training* support higher education while creating closer alliances with industry. Timothy Vollmer (2011) argued that this program in particular supports "President Obama's goal of having the highest proportion of college graduates in the world by 2020 by helping to increase the number of workers who attain degrees, certificates, and other industry-recognized credentials."

Sir John Daniel and David Killion (2012) state that this OER initiative and others "are working closely with industry to create credentials earned from

OER that are linked to specific occupations or job openings." This supports accelerated open learning through shared resources while preparing learners for today's work environment based on precise feedback from business partners. The authors wrote:

> OERs can be used to create a better trained, more flexible global workforce for the 21st century. Imagine what our global economy will look like when the estimated 90% or more of earth's inhabitants currently locked out of high-quality post-secondary education and job training opportunities finally get a fair shot. And what happens when we can finally start matching curricula to the changing employer needs?

The continued development of OERs will inform how education is understood and practiced internationally, as a shared enterprise that has the potential to unite educators, learners, and industry partners globally. According to Sir John Daniel and David Killion (2012) governments also have a central role to play in this process because "Governments are by far the biggest suppliers of education worldwide. They have the most to contribute to the OER movement and the most to gain in terms of cost savings and economic growth." This "call to action" by Daniel and Killion (2012) is supported by the *2012 Paris OER Declaration* that states: "Governments/competent authorities can create substantial benefits for their citizens by ensuring that educational materials developed with public funds be made available under open licenses (with any restrictions they deem necessary) in order to maximize the impact of the investment." As OERs continue to develop as a global resource for transforming education and lifelong learning, this work must be supported at every level, including institutions of higher education, potential industry partners, and governments worldwide. Sharing information requires a shared responsibility to promote widespread access and to take full advantage of collaborative opportunities in formal and informal settings. We see it as essential to include OERs in literacy education, and from our perspective, this is why OERs are an integral part of our expanded metaliteracy model (see figure 1.1).

The next section of the chapter will examine how UNESCO and IFLA are engaging with issues connected to information literacy. These developments will demonstrate that seeking an expanded approach to information literacy is an international pursuit.

LITERACY INITIATIVES FROM INTERNATIONAL ORGANIZATIONS

International organizations, including UNESCO and the International Federation of Library Associations and Institutions (IFLA), are focusing on the issue of information-related competencies needed in today's networked world. National as well as international organizations understand the necessity of highlighting metaliteracy-related abilities and are revising or developing frameworks that embrace the new realities of how information is produced and used.

UNESCO

The more inclusive conception of information literacy is obvious in the stated interests of UNESCO. The convergence of information literacy and media literacy, as well as the increasing importance of OERs, characterizes the focus of this influential organization. UNESCO is a member of the United Nations family and shares its goals: "peace and security, justice and human rights, promotion of economic and social progress and better standard of living" (UNESCO, 2008). UNESCO has 195 member states and 8 associate states (UNESCO, 2011a).

UNESCO's Media and Information Literacy

UNESCO's Communication and Information Sector, whose goals include "Empowering people through the free flow of ideas and by access to information and knowledge," identifies MIL as a capacity-building theme of interest. The sector's website includes this statement: "Empowerment of people through information and media literacy is an important prerequisite for fostering equitable access to information and knowledge, and building inclusive knowledge societies." This assertion broadens the concept of information literacy to include media literacy as part of a combined construct that is concerned with access, knowledge acquisition, and empowerment. The statement continues: "Information and media literacy enables people to interpret and make informed judgments as users of information and media, as well as to become skillful creators and producers of information and media messages in their own right" (UNESCO, 2011c). This approach acknowledges both the critical consumption and proficient production of digital information in media enhanced environments. When UNESCO published its model Media and Information Literacy Curriculum for Teachers, the press release further explained UNESCO's evolving vision of the combination of MIL through the lens of the curriculum:

> It is forward thinking, drawing on present trends toward the convergence of radio, television, Internet, newspapers, books, digital archives and libraries into one platform—thereby, for the first time, presenting MIL in a holistic manner. (UNESCO, 2011e)

UNESCO's definition accords well with envisioning information literacy as a metaliteracy by acknowledging the importance of multiple literacy types and the need for critical evaluation of sources. The definition also addresses the inclination and skill for attending to the increasingly broad scope of information formats and the ability to use available tools to create and produce information, which will then be shared with others.

UNESCO is focusing its efforts on "encouraging the development of national information and media literacy policies." As a UNESCO initiative, this focus on the development of media literacy recognizes the international dimension of this concern and the role policy development plays in this process. Through this work, UNESCO is placing an emphasis on educational policies and "on training teachers to sensitize them to the importance of information and media literacy in the education process, enable them to integrate information and media literacy into their teaching and provide them with appropriate pedagogical methods and curricula" (UNESCO, 2011c). This emphasis recognizes the interrelated nature of information and media literacy and the need for appropriate training and resources to support teachers around the globe. In addition, UNESCO envisions libraries as a key partner in the endeavor of promoting MIL through their mission to provide free access to both the resources and the services that allow people to learn at their own pace throughout their lives (UNESCO, 2011c).

The seriousness of UNESCO's intent in this arena was demonstrated by its co-sponsorship of the First International Forum on Media and Information Literacy, held in Fez, Morocco, in June 2011.

> This Forum was the first of its kind at the international level to examine media and information literacy as a combined set of competencies (knowledge, skills and attitudes). Issues relating to importance of media, Internet and other information providers and their impact on learning, cultures and public opinion, as well as the empowering effect of MIL practices and global Internet governance were among the main topics discussed at the Forum. (UNESCO, 2011b)

The forum, organized under the auspices of Adbellah University in Fez and UNESCO, with other partners, including the Islamic Educational, Scientific and Cultural Organization, the Arab Bureau of Education for the Gulf States, and the United Nations Alliance of Civilizations, issued a declaration affirming eight tenets based on the social, personal, economic, and cultural importance of MIL (First International Forum on Media and Information Literacy, 2011). The first five of these relate more immediately to issues addressed in this volume:

1. Reaffirming the conviction that MIL is a fundamental human right, particularly in the digital age of explosion of information and convergence of communication technologies;

2. Considering that MIL enhances the quality of human life and sustainable development and citizenship;

3. Emphasizing the importance of MIL for social, economic and cultural development;

4. Noting that the main obstacle for MIL comprehensive development is the current unawareness of its empowering capacities;

5. Believing that MIL is key to engage all citizens, men and women, with particular focus on the youth, in active participation in society;

(First International Forum on Media and Information Literacy, 2011)

Participants at the forum encourage others to share their concerns over these issues, including heads of state, the United Nations and UNESCO in particular, international and regional organizations, educators, media and information professionals, and others. There are 11 action steps contained in the declaration. The first asks stakeholders to "reaffirm their commitment to initiatives relating to MIL for All." Several revolve around issues connected to education, including the importance of integrating MIL into formal curricula and informal educational initiatives. The declaration asserts that only information- and media-literate citizens will build knowledge societies. In order to identify and fulfill educational gaps, research is needed to determine the status of MIL in different countries. Outreach and continuing meetings to address MIL-related research and issues are recommended, as is an MIL institute to operate in Fez. One step that is of particular interest, as seen through the lens of metaliteracy, is "Include the production and distribution of user generated content, particularly youth-produced media, as part of the overall framework of MIL" (First International Forum on Media and Information Literacy, 2011). UNESCO recognizes the importance of participatory social media as a means for producing and sharing original content. This point also acknowledges the democratization of new media in youth culture. Similarly, metaliteracy expands traditional information literacy definitions to include the collaborative production and distribution of dynamic materials through emerging social technologies.

UNESCO provides online a collection of practical resources related to international initiatives that support MIL. The UNESCO Media and Information Literacy page (www.unesco.org/new/en/communication-and-information/media-development/media-literacy/mil-as-composite-concept) links to information literacy news and events throughout the world. Some of those items have included a collaboration between UNESCO and the University of Pretoria to improve the information literacy of teachers, workshops in Latin America on ICT literacy, training in South Africa on information literacy for rural teachers that is being supported by UNESCO, and a publication by UNESCO Bangkok on ICT literacy in the Asia-Pacific region. The breadth of literacies included in the list of the events, which span several years, provides evidence that this international organization emphasizes the need for a broad conception of information literacy. Particularly noteworthy, at the time of this writing, were details about the International Conference on Media and Information Literacy in Knowledge Societies, held in June 2012 in Moscow. UNESCO's information page for this conference reaffirms its commitment to MIL:

> UNESCO recognizes that today's society in general needs to apply a new notion of literacy, plural, dynamic and situational, which relates not only to basic writing and numeracy skills, but also the competencies to identify, understand, create, communicate and compute information and other contents through any media or platform. It is also equally important to critically interpret media messages and produce own content [sic] sharing it through diverse communication and information tools and channels. It means that individuals, communities and nations require for new competencies based on new notion of literacy [sic]. (UNESCO, 2012a)

This description supports the expansion of global literacy education beyond reading, writing, and arithmetic to include the broader range of interactive media proficiencies required for today's social media environment. UNESCO advances this work through its leadership in promoting and developing OERs, bringing international thought leaders together to develop open education policies, and sponsoring conferences and meetings that unite participants from around the world.

The collective statements documented in this section prove that UNESCO, through its advocacy for MIL, is fully cognizant of the need for an all-encompassing approach to this vital competency. The organization recognizes the important role of social media, the expanded scope of information producers, and the need to consider and evaluate all information sources holistically. Given the worldwide reach of UNESCO's influence and assistance, the organization has the potential to be a driving force in raising awareness and providing educational opportunities for individuals to become full participants in the evolving information age.

OERs

As we have discussed previously, another theme that is evident in the UNESCO vision, and connected to the scope of this book, is that of OERs. Teaching and learning materials that are either in the public domain or that have been made freely available will not only help to improve the quality of education but will also have further benefits. According to UNESCO, "universal access to high quality education is key to the building of peace, sustainable social and economic development, and intercultural dialogue" (UNESCO, 2011). The goals of open learning align well with the overall vision of UNESCO itself as an international organization that promotes peace and literacy for all. Central to this vision is the empowerment of individuals through open access to information and the tools for communication. Accordingly, UNESCO argues that "OERs provide member states with a strong opportunity to increase the quality and access to education and facilitates knowledge sharing, dialogue, and capacity building" (UNESCO, 2011). Within this context, openness extends beyond access itself to include an interactive and collaborative dialogue about education and related policy concerns that promote knowledge acquisition.

UNESCO is developing an OER platform that not only provides access to selected UNESCO publications but also encourages and facilitates the sharing and adaptation of education resources by teachers, learners, and researchers. The platform launched in November 2011 with a UNESCO document, UNESCO Model Curricula for Journalism Education. In conjunction with this inaugural item, two universities in Namibia will make available their adaptations of these curricula. Plans have been made for the Media and Information Literacy Curricula and the General History of Africa Curricula to follow (UNESCO, 2011).

Nancy Graham and Jane Secker (2012) published the results of a survey co-sponsored by UNESCO and the Chartered Institute of Library and Information Professionals Information Literacy Group about the use of OERs by information literacy librarians. The survey, titled "Librarians, Information Literacy and Open Educational Resources: Report of a Survey," emerged from the Developing Educators Learning and Information Literacies for Accreditation (DELILA) project that looked at digital and information literacy OERs. The two most common OERs used by librarians were Jorum, a UK-based OER repository, and Google search, while others included YouTube, Slideshare, MERLOT, Flickr, and Creative Commons (pp. 6–7). According to Graham and Secker (2012), "responses give a picture of an active community willing to share, but one that lacks confidence, skills and knowledge of technicalities such as Creative Commons licences and uploading to national learning repositories to be participating fully in sharing openly" (p. 6). The awareness of OERs among librarians continues to increase, but a great deal of work still needs to be done in order to integrate information literacy OERs into teaching and learning practices. For instance, it would be interesting to know what faculty members and others involved in teaching students metaliteracy-related concepts are doing in this regard. This would be a leap beyond what the Graham and Secker survey considered and would recognize a holistic approach to teaching information literacy. Further, we need more specialized OERs that go beyond information literacy competencies to include the wider range of knowledge acquisition supported by the metaliteracy framework.

The Prague Declaration: Anticipating Later MIL Initiatives

Although UNESCO has been a strong proponent for an inclusive conception of MIL in recent years, it has been active in this domain for some time. An early meeting, in 2003, led to a report that can be seen as a precursor to more recent documents, declarations, publications, and other products. UNESCO provided support for the Information Literacy Meeting of Experts, held in September 2003 in Prague, Czech Republic. It was attended by representatives of 23 countries, under the auspices of the US National Commission on Library and Information Science and the National Forum on Information Literacy, with the aforementioned support from UNESCO. Participants identified basic information literacy principles that address:

- its importance for social, cultural, and economic development,
- its role in promoting tolerance and understanding while reducing disparities among peoples,
- the need for governments to reduce the digital divide for the health of the society,
- the importance of tailoring information literacy based on individual situations, and
- the need to include information literacy in Education for All movement.

(The Prague Declaration: "Towards an Information Literate Society," 2003)

One of the principles of the declaration addresses the core competencies of an information literate individual: "knowledge of one's information concerns and needs, and the ability to identify, locate, evaluate, organize and effectively create, use and communicate information to address issues or problems at hand; it is a prerequisite for participating effectively in the Information Society, and is part of the basic human right of life long learning" (The Prague Declaration, 2003, p. 18). Thus, as early as 2003, there was a nascent expansion of traditional information literacy competencies to include a focus on the creation and use of information as a part of lifelong learning in a global society.

While the Prague Declaration predates the explosion of social media and online communities, it does specifically note the importance of "information and communication technologies" as key components of information literacy in playing "a leading role in reducing the inequities within and among countries and peoples, and in promoting tolerance and mutual understanding through information use in multicultural and multilingual contexts" (The Prague Declaration, 2003). The intent behind the declaration is evident in the inclusiveness of the issues that UNESCO currently embraces and supports, such as the conferences in Morocco and Moscow. The declaration also supports the need for an integrated approach to information literacy that considers the inter-relationships between information, communication, and technology. As with the UNESCO vision the overarching principles are related to access, equity, and empowerment as fundamental human rights. Considering the integrated nature of the concerns and the ever-changing technology environments inter-nationally, a metaliteracy approach to information supports this vision as a means for promoting the production and sharing of new knowledge through evolving social technologies.

UNESCO is not the only international organization that is working to raise the awareness of new conceptions of information literacy. However, what sets it apart from the one to be considered in the next section is that it is not an organization composed of librarians. It is significant that the issue has expanded beyond the purview of those who have long been concerned with individuals' ability to interact effectively with information.

IFLA

Members of IFLA are also concerned with information literacy. This emphasis is manifested both through IFLA's own statements and in materials written by IFLA members from a number of countries. Therefore, there are numerous conceptions of the term. The following discussion addresses the association's own view of what information literacy is, as well as one taken from Colombia's country report, which together provide a particularly forward-thinking reflec-tion on the changing nature of the competencies needed in today's informa-tion environment.

IFLA was founded in 1927 and describes itself as "the leading interna-tional body representing the interests of library and information services and their users. It is the global voice of the library and information profession" (IFLA, 2011). IFLA contains an active Information Literacy Section, whose goal is to "foster international cooperation in the development of information literacy education in all types of libraries and information institutions" (IFLA, 2010). The Information Literacy Section's "About" page includes two quotes, one from the American Library Association:

> To be information literate, a person must be able to recognize when in-formation is needed and have the ability to locate, evaluate and use effec-tively the needed information. (American Library Association, 1989)

This definition reflects one of the core elements of information literacy because it emphasizes the ability to determine when information is needed. As stated earlier in this book, this ability is a metacognitive aspect of metalit-eracy because users must self-reflect on their own literacy and know if they have the critical-thinking ability to evaluate a need for information. While this determination of information need is often one of the first steps in an information literacy framework, this ability develops over time as experience with research and searching online takes place. The second quote is from Johnston and Webber:

> Information literacy is the adoption of appropriate information behaviour to identify, through whatever channel or medium, information well fitted to information needs, leading to wise and ethical use of information in society. (Johnston & Webber, 2003, p. 336)

While neither definition specifically addresses information literacy as conceived as a metaliteracy, the importance of these proficiencies across multiple platforms is recognized. Johnston and Webber's definition was developed to broaden the focus beyond library skills and IT literacy. For instance, the authors argue, "Information literacy can be seen more positively as a response to the cultural, social and economic developments associated with the information society" (Johnston & Webber, 2003, p. 336). This view would certainly allow for expanding the repertoire of an information literate individual to encompass a wider range of literacies and the need to be an effective producer of information. This particular focus, however, does not address the information and technology changes in a networked web environment. The revolution in social media since 2003 requires a further development of ideas beyond the traditional information literacy framework.

The Information Literacy Section of IFLA includes an official statement on its website, IFLA Media and Information Literacy Recommendations. Endorsed by the IFLA Governing Board in December 2011, this statement addresses the importance of information to individuals, communities, and nations; describes MIL as "a basic human right in an increasingly digital, interdependent, and global world" and urges governments and organizations to take a number of enumerated steps that would lead to "policies and programs that advocate for and promote Media and Information Literacy and Lifelong Learning for all" (IFLA, 2012). This document includes a more up-to-date description than appears on the section's homepage. It acknowledges the range of information formats to be considered and mentions that communication is a component, although it does not specifically address the interrelationship of the dual roles of information consumer and information producer:

> Media and Information Literacy consists of the knowledge, the attitudes, and the sum of the skills needed to know when and what information is needed; where and how to obtain that information; how to evaluate it critically and organize it once it is found; and how to use

it in an ethical way. The concept extends beyond communication and information technologies to encompass learning, critical thinking, and interpretative skills across and beyond professional and educational boundaries. Media and Information Literacy includes all types of information resources: oral, print, and digital. (IFLA, 2012)

The Information Literacy Section of IFLA's website also includes an array of reports that provide overviews of information literacy in a number of countries: Colombia, the United Kingdom, Nordic countries, France, Italy, Poland, Russia, and Germany. These reports reflect a range of circumstances, from an emerging emphasis on information literacy instruction to environmental scans that reveal flourishing activity. These reports, therefore, are not designed to provide nationally accepted definitions of information literacy. However, they provide insight into the direction that information literacy professionals and initiatives are taking. For example, in the English-language report on the state of the art of information literacy in Colombia, the authors use this quite extensive definition of information literacy:

The teaching-learning process designed for an individual or group of persons, under the professional leadership and guidance of an educational or library institution, using different teaching strategies and learning environments (classroom, mixed-blended learning or "virtual"/ E-INFOLIT), to be able to achieve the competences (knowledge, skills and attitudes) in computing, communications and information that would enable and empower them, after identifying and recognizing their information needs, and applying different formats, media and physical, electronic or digital resources, to locate, select, retrieve, organize, evaluate, produce, share and disseminate in an efficient and effective way, as well as with a critical and ethical approach (Information Behavior) the information that best satisfies those needs, building upon their potentialities (cognitive, practical and emotional) and previous knowledge (multiple literacies: reading and writing, functional, visual, media, digital) and to achieve an appropriate interaction with other individuals and groups (cultural practices-social inclusion), according to the different roles and contexts involved (educational levels, research, job-training) . . . (Uribe Tirado & Machett's Penagos, 2010, p. 4)

Before moving to the second part of the definition, reflection on this first section highlights its all-encompassing realm, from method of the instruction, to format of information resources, to the knowledge and abilities called upon, to the contexts involved, and to the social and dissemination aspects involved in the pursuit and use of information. One item in the first sentence of the definition is, however, somewhat limiting, in envisioning information literacy as a process that occurs under supervision, particularly given the emphasis on lifelong learning, as outlined in the last part of the definition:

> . . . for finally with all this process, to get and share new knowledge as well as the foundations for lifelong learning (to which every citizen has the right) in order to facilitate the decision-making for personal, organizational, community and social benefits in view of the everyday and long-term demands (opportunities and threats) in the current information society. (Uribe Tirado & Machett's Penagos, 2010, p. 5)

This definition fully acknowledges the pan-information literacy skills that recognize the need for a metaliteracy. The characterization above, drawn from the work of Uribe Tirado, recognizes information literacy as a comprehensive framework, acknowledges the diversity of information formats with which individuals will engage, and certainly encompasses metaliteracy's provision of "an integrated and all-inclusive core for engaging with individuals and ideas in the digital information environments" (Mackey & Jacobson, 2011, p. 70). Individuals are seen as creators of information who share what they produce. This definition also elucidates the needs of the lifelong learner and the importance of a variety of types of learning opportunities. The metacognitive component of metaliteracy is not explicitly mentioned, yet attitudes and empowerment are. The willingness to reflect upon one's needs, knowledge, and abilities connected to information is an attitude that is essential to metaliteracy, and one that leads to empowerment, because a self-aware information seeker will search out what is needed to succeed.

The report goes on to state the challenges faced in Colombia in connection with information literacy instruction. The use of this definition, with some adjustment to the first sentence to allow for other venues, would provide an expansive framework in which to grapple with the information-related issues that the country faces.

While IFLA and UNESCO are fundamentally different types of organizations, their interests overlap in the evolving MIL environment. IFLA is composed of librarians from around the globe, while UNESCO represents, among others, teachers, educators more generally, librarians, and additional groups who have a strong stake in teaching students and citizens to become fully conversant with information sources, communication methods, avenues for information creation and dissemination, and, in general, the broad impact of technology on today's information environment. Together, they represent the interests of the vast majority of countries. The range of information, technology, and education scenarios in this array of nations allows them to engage in broad-ranging discussions about issues connected with metaliteracy, hence expanding the stakeholders and the scope of the issues. At the heart of this book is the assertion that traditional definitions of information literacy are no longer adequate. The work of both UNESCO and IFLA support this idea and extend the concerns to a global community.

The next section of this chapter describes a continent-wide initiative that offers great potential for expanding the scope of the information literacy discussion, both in regard to the participants and the shape of the competencies needed.

The Bologna Process and the Tuning Project

The Bologna Process is a method to harmonize higher education across Europe. In 1999 in the city of Bologna, ministers of education from 29 European countries signed the Bologna Declaration, from which emerged the Bologna Process. As of the end of 2012, 47 countries are participating. The ultimate goal of the Bologna Process is to create a European Higher Education Area, which involves the restructuring of education and degree cycles to enhance mobility and employability as well as acknowledging the importance of lifelong learning (Bologna Process, 2010a). Pechar provides a concise summary of the objectives of the Bologna Process:

> [T]he objectives of the Bologna Process include the creation of a common framework of internationally understandable and comparable degrees, undergraduate and graduate levels of study in all countries, a European approach to quality assurance, and a European Credit Transfer System (ECTS). The overarching aim is to create a coherent and transparent European Higher Education Area with compatible a/nd high quality systems that will make European higher education more attractive to the rest of the world. (Pechar, 2007, p. 113)

The Bologna Process does not specifically mention information literacy, but it has provided avenues for dialogue as educational institutions work to align themselves with the Process's tenets. The Tuning Project was developed as a way to effect this realignment of degrees and programs across the signatory countries. The methodology provided a number of steps to take when instituting a degree or program of study. Several of these steps are potential entry points for information literacy instruction:

- Describe the objectives and learning outcomes of the program in terms of knowledge, understanding, skills, and abilities.
- Identify generic and subject-related competencies for the program.
- Translate educational units into activities to achieve the learning outcomes.

(Holliday, 2011, p. 192)

Tuning has emphasized the importance of "the development of generic competences or transferable skills. This last component is becoming more and more relevant for preparing students well for their future role in society in terms of employability and citizenship" (Tuning, n.d.). The elements of metaliteracy related to metacognition and critical thinking fall solidly within Tuning's category of instrumental competencies, which include cognitive, methodological, technological, and linguistic abilities. For instance, metaliteracy requires us to think about knowledge acquisition within social media environments and the relationship to basic skills development. In addition, the ability to "Identify generic and subject-related competencies" is a part of curriculum planning and would benefit from a metacognitive approach that allows students to reflect on their abilities to differentiate between generic and subject specific resources (Holliday, 2011, p. 192). Lastly, as with information literacy, a metaliteracy framework requires a clear articulation of outcomes and a plan for assessment of learning. A metaliteracy approach would take this a step further by encouraging opportunities for students to self-reflect and self-assess their own learning and to actively engage in collaborative problem solving.

Holliday points out that the Tuning Project process "capitalizes on collaboration with faculty, students, and external stakeholders to generate learning outcomes. These outcomes...are expressed in the language of faculty and avoid the pitfall of library and information literacy jargon....Information literacy, in this process, becomes something defined and owned by faculty..." (Holliday, 2011, p. 193). Beyond this faculty ownership, the input of employers and graduates speaks to needs that must be addressed. For example, in phase one of Tuning, "a large scale consultation was organized among graduates, employers and academics to identify the most important generic competences for each of the academic fields involved." While different fields identified slightly different generic competencies as the most important, there was consensus on which were critical, such as "capacity for analysis and synthesis, the capacity to learn, and problem solving." Others were identified by graduates and employers as necessary for employability, and these included "the capacity to adopt [sic] to new situations,...information management skills,...and oral and written communication skills" (Tuning, n.d.). These abilities to effectively communicate, manage information, and adapt to changing situations are components of metaliteracy. The recognition of their importance within the Tuning framework provides the opportunity for the conversation to extend beyond traditional participants and gain traction in a continent-wide higher education initiative.

Therefore, while neither traditional information literacy components nor those that characterize metaliteracy are explicitly stated with the Bologna Process itself, the discussions and decisions resulting from the Tuning Project open the door for recognition of the importance of metaliteracy components within disciplines. This supports a metaliteracy approach to learning throughout the curriculum and in a multitude of global educational contexts.

This is a complex situation: there is no explicit mention of information literacy within the Bologna Process, yet a door has been opened for some recognition of this theme through other elements and language. This state of affairs has been noted by librarians in some of the countries that are involved in this movement. For example, the significance of this development is described in a chapter about a national information literacy project in Finnish universities:

> When the project was launched in 2004, it was obvious that, in accordance with the Bologna Process, the impending changes in the university curriculum to be implemented by 2005 would require the university libraries to act together to emphasize the importance of information literacy skills training. Thus the Bologna Process was viewed as an opportunity to link information literacy more closely and coherently to the disciplines taught in the universities. (Juntunen, et al., 2008, p. 119)

Thomas Hapke (2008), in his description of the recent state of information literacy in Germany, describes a system in which networking among librarians nationwide has occurred, resulting in the development of a portal to communicate and share materials (www.informationskompetenz.de). However, there is no national set of standards or set of directives concerning information literacy in Germany. The responsibility for education is held by the governments of the Federal States, and thus there are varying standards, statements, and information literacy working groups in the various states. Beyond these existing differences, there is another important distinction. The Bologna Process has emphasized each library's connection with its parent organization. Hapke acknowledges the need to work within not only the strictures of the Bologna Process but also the varying university environments: "Accreditation offices force university administrations to include more courses in key qualifications into the curricula. Nevertheless the universities can decide themselves to which [sic] extent and how key competencies will be implemented" (Hapke, 2008, p. 170). Those librarians who have worked with faculty members over a variety of disciplines to address the information literacy needs of students will recognize the diversity of potential responses and the ensuing challenge. While there may be some agreement about the recognition of qualifications, the implementation of competencies across diverse institutional contexts varies considerably. If we could agree on another level of understanding, through a metacognitive framework such as metaliteracy, we would strengthen the overall learning goals and objectives at the local level while unifying diverse approaches internationally.

Given the linking of learning outcomes with the needs of different disciplines, a one-size-fits-all information literacy model or definition will not, indeed should not, be the result. However, the issue of ownership is critical, and both the organic development and the resulting buy-in by faculty members will enhance the strength and impact of the varied outcomes. This will lead to particular elements of the metaliteracy or information literacy model being highlighted by different disciplines. Some may be willing to accept and find ways to incorporate the complete structure, while others will select those components that are seen as most critical for their discipline. It will require those who are advocating for information literacy to do so strongly, while remaining sensitive to the unique needs of each department or program of study.

A second aspect of the Bologna Process, lifelong learning, also offers potential for recognition of information literacy as an evolving knowledge set. Lifelong learning is recognized as an important, overarching part of the Bologna Process. This aspect of learning is enhanced by

- improving the recognition of prior learning, including non formal and informal learning;
- creating more flexible, student-centred modes of delivery;
- and widening access to higher education.
- National qualifications frameworks are also an important tool in supporting lifelong learning.

(Bologna Process, 2010b)

Open learning opportunities and respect for nontraditional methods of learning are highlighted by these components. In addition, the qualifications frameworks emphasize the real-life needs of learners. Together, these elements provide a fertile ground for enhanced opportunities to stress the importance of an expanded metaliteracy framework, and for faculty members and librarians to collaborate to include multimodel instruction focused on evolving information literacy needs. For instance, recognition of prior learning assessment fits nicely into a metaliteracy framework that promotes multiple ways of knowing through collaboration and the sharing of knowledge in participatory environments. The metaliteracy model is a flexible and permeable one that prepares learners to adapt to multiple platforms.

It will be interesting to review the effect of the Bologna Process in a decade to see what impact it has had upon both the evolving definition of information literacy and the content and types of instruction that are developed in accordance with its guidelines. While it is to be expected that there will be the usual combination of noteworthy breakthroughs and successes, as well as more limited or even negligible progress in other situations, the potential exists for groundbreaking work that will serve as exemplars.

EVOLVING INFORMATION LITERACY FRAMEWORKS

The radical developments connected to information—ease of publication, availability, formats, modes of access, and all the attendant knowledge needed to traverse this shifting landscape—have precipitated the need to examine and revise standards, guidelines, and frameworks focusing on information literacy. New ones are created, such as ACRL's 2011 *Visual Literacy Competency Standards for Higher Education,* in order to address these changing boundaries. It became evident that one key document, the *ACRL Information Literacy Competency Standards for Higher Education,* written in 2000, needed to be updated. The impact of factors such as mobile technologies and social media, along with the rapidly evolving formats in which information is found, was unknown to the authors of the original version of this iconic document. As this chapter is being written, a new ACRL task force was constituted in 2013 to re-envision the Standards and their purpose. A diverse group of librarians and non-library educators will work to craft a flexible framework that will speak to the needs of both constituencies.

The following segment will examine two information literacy documents sufficiently recent enough to have incorporated some of the changes. They were developed in the United Kingdom and Hong Kong since the burgeoning of the World Wide Web as an information source, although six years apart. The goal of this section is to determine whether aspects of metaliteracy are included within those documents. Obviously, the changes from 2005 to 2011 will affect how directly these elements are identified. In terms of information and the technological access to it, even a 2005 document may seem dated.

United Kingdom:
Seven Pillars of Information Literacy

The Seven Pillars of Information Literacy (Society of College, National and University Libraries, 2011) offers a concise, current, and adaptable information literacy framework. The Society of College, National and University Libraries (SCONUL) published their original Seven Pillars of Information Literacy model in 1999, with a redesign in 2004 (SCONUL, 2008) and a 2007 expansion by Sheila Webber (Webber, 2007). The 2011 version is the only document examined in this section of the chapter that fully reflects the information environment at the time of this writing.

The original version, first presented in a position paper written by the Information Skill Task Force on behalf of SCONUL, was fairly basic, particularly when compared to the 2011 model. These were the original seven skills:

1. Recognise information need
2. Distinguish ways of addressing gap
3. Construct strategies for locating
4. Locate and access
5. Compare and evaluate

6. Organise, apply and communicate
7. Synthesise and create
(SCONUL, 2007)

The model has gone through several revisions since 1999. The 2004 model included the same sections, but the graphical representation was redesigned. "Basic Library Skills and IT Skills" evolved from their original portrayal as two separate building blocks to a single joint foundation. The graphic for the 2007 model includes the words "Information Literacy" prominently above the pillars themselves, but at their base is "Basic Library Skills and IT Skills," held over from the 2004 version (SCONUL, 2007). The 2011 version of the graphics refers to the "Information Literacy Landscape" and the "Information Literate Person." This change reflects how much the information environment has changed since the original inception of this framework. Libraries are now just one of many places that people seek information, and what were once specialized technology skills have now become *de rigueur* in our daily lives.

Sheila Webber's 2007 gloss provides an intermediate step between the earliest and latest versions. By that year, more experienced statements can be made regarding individuals' use of ubiquitous information technologies. The mention of the web as an information repository in the original version has been supplanted by experienced recommendations to critically analyze information sources. RSS feeds, a tool on the way to Web 2.0, are explicitly mentioned. Webber also addresses the sharing of information, whether it is in the education or work setting or in one's personal life.

2011 SCONUL Seven Pillars Model

The newest version of the Seven Pillars Model has changed in a number of ways from the 2007 version. It truly reflects the current dynamic and expansive information environment. Not only is the base layer of "Basic Library Skills and IT Skills" gone, but so too is the library-centric focus, acknowledging that today's information seeker has a far wider range of resources at hand.

Revised Pillars and Graphical Representation

The 2011 version also includes revised pillars:

- Manage
- Evaluate
- Identify
- Plan

- Present
- Gather
- Scope
(SCONUL, 2011)

Despite the common mental image of pillars lined up in a row, as was seen in the earlier graphic models, the new visual representation of the pillars arranges them circularly. This design discourages a linear view of the development of these information literacy skills and emphasizes that using these abilities when faced with an information need is not a rigidly sequential process. It is entirely possible, indeed usual, that students and other information seekers may develop expertise within some of the pillars simultaneously. Unlike ACRL's approach, for example, the Seven Pillars model, in all of its iterations, has highlighted the developmental nature of these skills: it is not simply a matter of being competent in one domain or not. One may be anywhere on the continuum from novice to expert (SCONUL, 2003). The 2011 model includes a twist on this developmental aspect. It acknowledges that people can move both up pillars, as they develop their knowledge and abilities, and down pillars, as they become less adept by not keeping up with evolutions in technology, a constant risk in today's ever-changing information environment.

Convergences between Metaliteracy and the Seven Pillar Models

The 2011 model includes an important component not delineated in the earlier versions: each of the seven areas is composed of a section of understandings about that domain, followed by abilities. For example, The Identify pillar is explained as the ability to "identify a personal need for information," and two of the four bullets for "Understands" are:

- That new information and data is constantly being produced and that there is always more to learn
- That being information literate involves developing a learning habit so new information is being actively sought all the time

This section is followed by seven bullets under "Is able to," two of which are:

- Identify a lack of knowledge in a subject area
- Recognise a need for information and data to achieve a specific end and define limits to that information need
  (SCONUL, 2011, p. 5)

All of these bullets are aspects of metacognition. The first two reflect a critical mindset that needs to be present, while the latter two are components that might be repeated at multiple stages when working on a project. A person who is effective at seeking, using, and producing information will be thinking about the process in a variety of ways as it evolves. This individual is also adept at using social technology to document the experience with posts, tweets, status updates, and communications that reflect on the creative process itself.

Another of the "Understands" bullets, in this case connected to identifying information, elucidates a component of metacognition: "That ideas and opportunities are created by investigating/seeking information" (SCONUL, 2011, p. 5). Only someone who is deliberating on the unfolding situation will understand how it fits into the broader picture. And one of the abilities in the

Evaluate pillar is "Know when to stop," which most certainly is important in accomplishing one's information-related task (SCONUL, 2011, p. 9).

This updated model very explicitly overlaps with metaliteracy in several regards. Certainly, elements that correspond to the second inner ring of the metaliteracy model are present (see figure 1.1). Determine aligns with Identify, Access aligns with Gather, and Evaluate is labeled identically in both. The Understand component of the metaliteracy model is spread widely in the Seven Pillars model, as each pillar contains a bulleted list with that exact label, while Understand has its own spot in the circular metaliteracy model in order to point out the lack of barriers between elements and the flow that would be occurring between components within a layer. Thus, the intent in regard to need for understanding within all components of both models is very similar, and it is only because of the difficulty of representing the intermingling nature in a two-dimensional figure that it may not seem so. The metaliteracy model has redefined several of the standard information literacy terms in a new way by integrating these competencies within an open framework that also emphasizes collaboration, production, and sharing. Many of these key terms are still relevant in a social media age but need to be expanded through a reinvention that incorporates the participatory nature of today's information environment. This redefinition of information literacy also aligns well with the SCONUL model.

A sampling of other components that overlap with metaliteracy include the following two clusters, which are both the understanding required and the ability to act upon that understanding:

- Understands how digital technologies are providing collaborative tools to create and share information (Gather)
- Is able to engage with their community to share information (Gather)
- Understands the risks involved in operating in a virtual world (Gather)

and

- Understands that individuals can take an active part in the creation of information through traditional publishing and digital technologies (e.g., blogs, wikis) (Present)
- Is able to develop a personal profile in the community using appropriate personal networks and digital technologies (e.g., discussion lists, social networking sites, blogs, etc.)

(SCONUL, 2011)

The overlap between the Seven Pillars and the metaliteracy models is due partly to their recent development, at a time when social media plays a significant role in connection with information. This overlap, however, is also indicative of an expansive view of information literacy, one that goes far beyond the original conception of information as being closely connected to libraries and other traditional sources. While each model has separate elements, they complement each other extremely well.

Adaptations via Lenses

The Seven Pillars model was explicitly designed to be adaptable. The core version is directed to higher education in general, but there is the ability to apply various focused lenses. The process has begun with a lens focused explicitly on research in higher education, and drafts are currently available for digital literacy and OERs. SCONUL encourages professionals to adapt the generic model to the population groups with whom they work (SCONUL, 2011, p. 3).

OERs are highlighted in the metaliteracy model as an important, though nontraditional, source of information. The Seven Pillars model as seen through the open content lens provides extensive guidelines for these materials. It indicates the need to:

- understand what this type of resource is,
- know where to find such information, recognizing that the systems containing such information vary in quality or access, and
- be able to evaluate it given its distinguishing characteristics

This provides a useful set of skills to apply when engaging with OERs. A consumer of open resources engages in a critical thinking process when trying to understand, recognize, and evaluate the source of information freely available through open systems. As an information producer, it is important to:

- understand what audience needs are,
- how the content might be structured and
- gain a critical perspective related to the whole gamut of issues connected with OERs

(SCONUL, 2012).

This set of proficiencies supports the effective creation of new information. A producer of open digital content should always understand audience considerations, while thinking about the structure of the information and applying a critical thinking perspective to the open format. These targeted lenses flesh out the basic Seven Pillars model extremely well, and the flexibility of creating new lenses, as needed, will help to maintain its relevance.

A second recent model, this one from Hong Kong, is described in the following section.

Hong Kong:
Information Literacy Framework
for Hong Kong Students

The Education and Manpower Bureau in Hong Kong published the *Information Literacy Framework for Hong Kong Students*, written under the auspices of the Information Literacy Framework Working Group. It addresses the needs of the 21st century, including the need for knowledge in order to be successful throughout life (Information Literacy Framework Working Group, 2005, p. 5). A section of the introduction points out the situation plainly and identifies the need for an encompassing understanding of information literacy:

> Very often, the information from the Internet comes to searchers in unfiltered formats through multimedia such as graphical, aural and textual. For many searchers who are at the beginner levels, to find relevant and accurate information involves only typing a word or two into a search engine. This raises the questions about its authenticity, validity and reliability because anyone can publish information on cyberspace without editorial or expert review as opposed to the traditional print reference materials. (Information Literacy Framework Working Group, 2005, p. 6)

The developers of this document examined standards articulated by a number of organizations and institutions in several countries: SUNY; Association of College and Research Libraries, American Association of School Librarians; Association for Educational Communications and Technology; Standing Conference of National and University Libraries from United Kingdom; Alaska Association of School Librarians; Washington Library Media Association; Australian and New Zealand Institute of Information Literacy; and Juarez University Libraries, Mexico. The authors classified the eleven standards in four categories: cognitive, meta-cognitive, affective, and socio-cultural. Noteworthy, given its 2005 publication date, is standard number one in the socio-cultural dimension, "An information literate person is able to contribute positively to the learning community in knowledge building" (Information Literacy Framework Working Group, 2005, p. 16). This standard contains two indicators labeled "Communal" that address the need to share knowledge and information with others and to collaborate effectively in groups to pursue and construct knowledge (Information Literacy Framework Working Group, 2005, p. 16). The specified anticipated learning outcomes for these two indicators reflect the information environment when the document was written, yet the core concept is present: these indicators address a key component vital to an understanding of an enhanced definition of information literacy.

This framework is also significant for including metacognition as one of the four categories, with three metacognitive standards:

M1 An information literate person is able to be aware that information processing is iterative, time-consuming and demands effort.

M2 An information literate person is able to plan and monitor the process of inquiry.

M3 An information literate person is able to reflect upon and regulate the process of inquiry.

(Information Literacy Framework Working Group, 2005, p. 15)

Each category indicates what individuals are able to do in order to successfully meet the standard. Although developed for students in Hong Kong, this model emphasizes the need for lifelong learning, and anyone engaged in that pursuit would find these standards equally applicable. These categories recognize the importance of self-awareness, self-monitoring, and self-reflection in the research process. While these metacognitive abilities are individual rather than collaborative, this work leads to the development of critical thinkers who will be able to actively engage with a social network as informed lifelong learners. The inclusion of a metacognitive dimension supports the need to fully realize information literacy as a metaliteracy for the social media age. By doing so we have the opportunity to build on information literacy research and practice to date, while moving it in a new direction that reflects the revolutionary changes we have seen in social technologies and social interactions online.

CONCLUSION

As we have seen in this chapter on global perspectives, the continued progression and transformation of information literacy is an international concern. We have presented the most significant global perspectives that have emerged over the last decade, including initiatives from UNESCO and IFLA, as well as the Bologna Process, the Seven Pillars model (SCONUL), and international trends in open education. In addition, we have examined standards emanating from the United Kingdom and Hong Kong. This chapter has shown us that significant changes are taking place in our conception of information literacy and technology. We have seen a blurring of the line between information literacy and technology competencies because today's social media environment necessitates a collaborative and integrated framework for understanding information and all of its environments. The changes we have identified internationally support our assertion that the foundation elements of information literacy are still relevant today, intersect with related literacy types, but require a new metacognitive model. The various information competencies that have been identified around the globe would benefit from a unified metaliteracy model that emphasizes collaboration and participation.

Now that we have established a global perspective that supports the need to reconfigure information literacy, the next chapter will discuss an initial metaliteracy survey with faculty and librarian respondents at colleges and universities from many international locations. Through this research study we identify the related literacy types considered most relevant by the participants, the perception of technology infrastructure at different institutions, reasons some instructors may not include related literacy types in instruction, forms of emerging technologies currently used, and how instructors learn about new technologies and approaches to information literacy instruction.

While information systems are constantly evolving, we do not seek to overemphasize any particular technology format. But we have witnessed a significant and revolutionary shift in how people communicate and create using collaborative social media environments. This has been an international phenomenon that we need to better understand as we prepare our students to be global citizens in a world that continues to get smaller and yet more complex than we have ever known.

REFERENCES

American Library Association. (1989). *Presidential committee on information literacy: Final Report.* www.ala.org/acrl/publications/whitepapers/presidential

Association of College and Research Libraries. (2011). *Visual Literacy Competency Standards for Higher Education.* www.ala.org/acrl/standards/visualliteracy

Bologna Process. (2010a). About the Bologna Process. www.ond.vlaanderen.be/hogeronderwijs/bologna/about

Bologna Process. (2010b). Lifelong learning. www.ond.vlaanderen.be/hogeronderwijs/bologna/actionlines/LLL.htm

Daniel, Sir John, & Killion, David. (2012, July 4). Are open educational resources the key to global economic growth? *The Guardian.* www.guardian.co.uk/higher-education-network/blog/2012/jul/04/open-educational-resources-and-economic-growth

First International Forum on Media and Information Literacy. (2011). Fez declaration of media and information literacy. *UNESCO Communication and Information Resources.* www.unesco.org/new/fileadmin/MULTIMEDIA/HQ/CI/CI/pdf/news/Fez%20Declaration.pdf

Graham, Nancy, & Secker, Jane. (2012). Librarians, information literacy and open educational resources: Report of a survey. http://delilaopen.files.wordpress .com/2012/04/findingsharingoers_reportfinal1.pdf

Graham, Nancy, & Secker, Jane. (2012). DELILA Project Blog. http://delilaopen .wordpress.com

Hapke, Thomas. (2008). Information literacy activities in Germany between the Bologna Process and the web 2.0. In Carla Basili (Ed.), *Information literacy at the crossroad of education and information policies in Europe* (pp. 165–183). Rome: Consiglio Nazionale delle Ricerche.

Holliday, Wendy. (2011). Harmonic convergence: Using the tuning process to build relationships and transform information literacy. *ACRL 2011 Conference Papers.* www.ala.org/acrl/sites/ala.org.acrl/files/content/conferences/confsandpreconfs/ national/2011/papers/harmonic_convergence.pdf

International Federation of Library Associations and Institutions (IFLA). (2010). About the information literacy section. www.ifla.org/en/about-information -literacy

IFLA. (2011). About IFLA. www.ifla.org/en/about

IFLA. (2012). IFLA Media and Information Literacy Recommendations. www.ifla.org/ en/publications/ifla-media-and-information-literacy-recommendations

Information Literacy Framework Working Group. (2005). *Information Literacy Framework for Hong Kong Students: Building the Capacity of Learning to Learn in the Information Age.* Hong Kong: Education and Manpower Bureau www.edb.gov.hk/ FileManager/EN/Content_1619/il_eng.pdf

Johnston, Bill, & Webber, Sheila. (2003). Information literacy in higher education: A review and case study. *Studies in higher education, 28*(3), 335–352.

Juntunen, Arja, Lehto, Anne, Saarti, Jarmo, & Tevaniemi, Johanna. (2008). Supporting information literacy learning in finnish universities: Standards, projects, and online education. In Jesús Lau (Ed.), *Information literacy: International perspectives* (pp. 117–132). Munich: K. G. Saur.

Mackey, Thomas P., & Jacobson, Trudi E. (2011). Reframing information literacy as a metaliteracy. *College & Research Libraries, 72*(1), 62–78.

Pechar, Hans. (2007). "The Bologna process" A European response to global competition in higher education. *Canadian Journal of Higher Education, 37*(3), 109–125.

The Prague declaration "Towards an information literate society." (2003). *UNISIST Newsletter 31*(2), 18.

Robertson, R. John. (2010). *What do academic libraries have to do with open educational resources?* http://openaccess.uoc.edu/webapps/o2/bitstream/10609/4847/6/ Roberston.pdf

Society of College, National and University Libraries (SCONUL). (2003). *Information skills in higher education: A SCONUL position paper.* www.sconul.ac.uk/groups/ information_literacy/papers/Seven_pillars.html

SCONUL. (2007). The seven pillars of information literacy model. www.sconul.ac.uk/ groups/information_literacy/sp/sp/spportcol.pdf

SCONUL. (2008). The seven pillars of information literacy model. www.sconul.ac.uk/ groups/information_literacy/sp/model.html

SCONUL. (2011). The SCONUL seven pillars of information literacy, core model for higher education. www.sconul.ac.uk/sites/default/files/documents/coremodel .pdf

SCONUL. (2012). Seven pillars of information literacy. www.sconul.ac.uk/groups/ information_literacy/seven_pillars.html

Tuning: Educational Structures in Europe. (n.d.) Competences. www.unideusto.org/ tuningeu/competences.html

United Nations Educational, Scientific and Cultural Organization (UNESCO). (2008). Communities. United Nations system. http://portal.unesco.org/en/ev.php-URL _ID=32248&URL_DO=DO_TOPIC&URL_SECTION=201.html

UNESCO. (2011a). Communities. Member states. http://portal.unesco.org/en/ ev.php-URL_ID=11170&URL_DO=DO_TOPIC&URL_SECTION=201.html

UNESCO. (2011b). Launch of the UNESCO open educational resources platform. *UNESCO Communication and Information.* www.unesco.org/new/en/ communication-and-information/resources/news-and-in-focus-articles/all -news/news/launch_of_the_unesco_open_educational_resources_platform

UNESCO. (2011c). Media and information literacy. http://portal.unesco.org/ci/en/ ev.php-URL_ID=15886&URL_DO=DO_TOPIC&URL_SECTION=201.html

UNESCO. (2011d). News. Declaration on media and information literacy adopted by Fez International Forum. http://portal.unesco.org/ci/en/ev.php-URL _ID=31456&URL_DO=DO_TOPIC&URL_SECTION=201.html

UNESCO. (2011e). UNESCO launched model media and information literacy curriculum for teachers. *News: Communication and Information Sector's News Service.* http://portal.unesco.org/ci/en/ev.php-URL_ID=31461&URL_DO=DO _TOPIC&URL_SECTION=201.html

UNESCO. (2012a). International Conference on Media and Information Literacy in Knowledge Societies. www.unesco.org/new/en/communication-and -information/resources/news-and-in-focus-articles/all-news/news/ international_conference_on_media_and_information_literacy_in_knowledge _societies

UNESCO. (2012b). Paris OER Declaration. 2012 World Open Educational Resources (OER) Congress UNESCO, Paris, June 20–22. www.unesco.org/new/fileadmin/ MULTIMEDIA/HQ/CI/CI/pdf/Events/Paris%20OER%20Declaration_01.pdf

Uribe Tirado, Alejandro, & Penagos, Leonardo Machett's. (2010). Information literacy in Colombia: Report of the state of the art 2010. *IFLA Information Literacy State of the Art Reports*. www.ifla.org/files/information-literacy/publications/il-report/colombia-2010-en.pdf

Vollmer, Timothy. (2011). New federal education fund makes available $2 billion to create OER resources in community colleges. *Creative Commons News*. http://creativecommons.org/weblog/entry/26100

Webber, Sheila. (2007). The seven headline skills expanded. Society of College, National and University Libraries. www.sconul.ac.uk/groups/information_literacy/headline_skills.html

5
Survey of the Field

From Theoretical Frameworks to Praxis

T HE FIRST PART OF THIS BOOK FOCUSED ON THE COMPREHEN-
sive nature of metaliteracy. We outlined the reasons why it is imperative
to examine information literacy in this new light and explored the impact of
the open age of social media and its role in shaping a new metaliteracy model.
We also identified related literacies and multiple nomenclatures that are a
part of the conversation and discussed the changing conceptions of literacy
due to the profound global educational and social effects of emerging technologies. Additionally, we outlined the evolving metaliteracy learning objectives
that will be analyzed further in the two case studies following this chapter.
The second half of this book, as shown in these final three chapters, moves
the conversation beyond theoretical frameworks and factors related to the
educational and information environment to the lens of practice.

In this chapter, we describe research we undertook in 2012, using a survey instrument titled Information Literacy as a Metaliteracy (appendix 5.1).
We explore the questions we were endeavoring to answer and describe the
research methods used. The resulting data is provided, as is an in-depth analysis that focuses on the key elements of the research instrument. This survey

was exploratory and limited in scope, so we offer a number of avenues for further exploration of the issue in this chapter.

The survey of the field reported on in this chapter explored current and changing understandings of information literacy while supporting the need for a reinvention of long-held conceptions of both theory and practice. We found that respondents were familiar with the changing landscape of literacies and recognized such emergent terms as transliteracy and metaliteracy. The survey also showed that librarians are using different forms of technology in their teaching but need more time and institutional support to incorporate new approaches into instruction. While new technologies are being explored in information literacy sessions and collaboration is promoted by many instructors in current teaching situations, much more can be done to further support these essential aspects of a comprehensive and unifying metaliteracy.

RESEARCH QUESTIONS

In developing this preliminary survey, we reflected upon our own attempts to adjust to the rapid changes in the information environment. We also considered the work of our colleagues and our unique institutional settings. Naturally, adaptations varied, from slower or reserved acceptance of new approaches to teaching and learning to early adoption through innovative transformation of personal, professional, and teaching behaviors. We were interested in learning more broadly about how teachers of information literacy, be they librarians or educators in other disciplines, were addressing the continuously evolving nature of information gathering and usage. Beyond the curiosity surrounding this particular issue, we knew it was important to gain greater insight into those who teach information literacy, whether as a stand-alone discipline or as a component of a subject-based discipline. As part of this inquiry, we sought to obtain preliminary answers to the following research questions:

- Which specific literacy types do respondents view as related to information literacy?
- Do respondents recognize emerging literacy frameworks such as metaliteracy and transliteracy?
- How do instructors learn new technologies and information literacy-related concepts that will impact their teaching?
- What are some of the challenges in teaching new literacy frameworks (or new information and technology competencies)?
- Is age a factor in the responses?
- Do national differences affect instructors' responses?
- Do those who self-identify as librarians respond significantly differently than other populations?

In order to explore these questions, we developed a preliminary survey, Information Literacy as a Metaliteracy.

METHODS

Survey Design

This survey, created by the authors, was tested on half a dozen information literacy librarians, underwent minor revisions based on their comments, and was then placed in SurveyMonkey. The final version contained 26 questions, five of which collected respondents' demographic data (see appendix 5.1 for the Information Literacy as a Metaliteracy survey). In the design of the survey, the response type for each question varied. A few of the questions included Likert scale options (highly effective, effective, neutral, ineffective, highly ineffective) while most of the questions included specific response selections and in many cases the option to choose all relevant responses that pertain. The survey received approval from the Institutional Review Board (IRB) at the University at Albany. While the survey design is somewhat limited, this preliminary effort provided us with a useful starting point to gain a better understanding of this first set of research questions. It also provides a basis for future research in this area.

Distribution Method

We set out to distribute the survey widely to faculty, librarians, and instructional designers internationally. Announcements about the survey were made on a number of professional distribution lists, including instructional, regional, and international ones for librarians, as well as information science-targeted ones. Twitter and LinkedIn were also used to distribute an announcement. Respondents were self-selected.

RESULTS

Response Rate

Based on an analysis of the results, the survey was started by 551 people. Overall, a total of 361 people (65.5%) completed the survey between January 9 and February 22, 2012. The survey included 21 questions in the main section, followed by five additional demographic questions, with multiple response types to consider and open-ended options for most of the questions. Due to the design of the instrument, completing the survey was a fairly extensive process, but one benefit of including an open-ended selection in the survey questions is that we gained unique insights from respondents that would not have been possible with an instrument that included multiple choice or Likert scale options only. The authors hypothesized that the overall length of the survey and varied question type may have been responsible for the number of people who chose not to complete the survey. In addition, since respondents were not required to complete all of the questions, they may have focused on those areas that interested them the most or skipped questions they were unsure of.

Demographics

The demographic section required respondents to identify the specific country in which they teach. There were 352 responses to this question. A majority (246, 70%) indicated that they teach in the United States, followed by the United Kingdom (58, 16%), Canada (14, 3%), Germany (6, 1%), Australia (4, 1%), and Ireland (3, < 1%). One or two people responded from each of the following countries: Belgium, Botswana, Brazil, Chile, China, Croatia, Czech Republic, Egypt, Finland, Greece, Iran, Israel, New Zealand, Norway, Portugal, South Africa, and Vietnam.

About a third of the 367 respondents for this survey item were between 30–39 years of age (113, 30.8%), followed by 40–49 (93, 25.3%), 50–59 (77, 21%), 60 or older (46, 12.5%), and 21–29 (34, 9.3%). One individual self-identified his or her age as 17 or younger.

A large majority of respondents were librarians (313, 85.5%, n=366). There were a small number of discipline faculty (18, 4.9%) and administrators (11, 3%). There were also 24 (6.6%) who indicated that they had a position not represented by the three choices. Based on the descriptions of these positions, at least nine more (2%) had strong librarian components. There were also archivists, instructional designers, a student, combined library and discipline faculty members, and several others that were too ambiguous to classify.

Almost all who responded to the survey indicated that they teach undergraduate students (153, 41.6%, n=368) or both undergraduate and graduate students (174, 47.3%). Only 13 (3.5%) teach just graduate students, five do not teach at all (1.4%), and 24 (6.3%) selected "other." Within this last category, those who teach secondary or elementary school students were most prominent (8, 2%).

Respondents indicated that they work at a research university (133, 36.2%, n=368), four-year college (118, 32.2%), or two-year college (67, 18.3%). A large number (49, 13.4%) selected "other." Based on the write-in comments, a number of the institutions are in countries that do not use this tripartite classification. The majority of the 49 who responded "other" teach either at a non-research university (17, 5%) or at a secondary school or K–12 institution (9, 2%).

Survey Results

Teaching Background

The first three survey questions were designed to elicit background information about respondents' specific contexts for teaching information literacy. The instrument included questions about the type of instruction provided, and a majority of those answering, 65.4% (n=541), teach course-related information sessions. Just under half (46.2%) teach stand-alone classes, while 32.3% teach information literacy as a component of discipline-based courses. Just about one-fifth of those who answered the question, 21.3%, teach credit-bearing courses. Twenty-five people selected "other." Many of the situations reported in the write-in responses fit into the course-related category. Congruent with the responses to this first question, when asked about the number of credits attached to their information literacy courses, 109 (43.1%, n=253) responded zero, 66 (26.1%) said one, 26 (10.3%) said two, 27 (10.7%) teach a three-credit course, and 7 (2.8%) teach a four-credit course. The 31 (12.3%) who marked "other" indicated that they teach in a system that uses a different credit system, teach in high school, or said that this question doesn't apply. The last basic question about teaching asked about the form that teaching takes, with most doing so face to face (411, 77%, n=534). Others teach in a blended situation (202, 37.8%), fully online (70, 13.1%), and "other" (24, 4.5%). The comments indicate that these "other" responses primarily describe situations where more than one type of instruction is offered.

Technology Infrastructure and Support

The next two questions (Q4 and Q5) asked about technology infrastructure and support at the respondent's school. A majority indicated that the infrastructure is effective (317, 59.1%, n=536), followed by neither effective nor ineffective (113, 21.1%), highly effective (66, 12.3%), ineffective (35, 6.5%), and highly ineffective (5, 0.9%). The responses to the technology support question were similar: effective (290, 53.9%, n=538), neither effective nor ineffective (124, 23%), highly effective (64, 11.9%), ineffective (55, 10.2%), and highly ineffective (5, 0.9%).

Knowledge of Literacies and Literacy Frameworks

Questions 6 through 9 probed knowledge of a range of literacies and information literacy frameworks and their relationships to information literacy. The first of these questions (Q6) provided a list of seven literacies, with brief definitions of each type to find out which ones respondents were familiar with, as well as an open-ended "other" response for direct input of different types. Digital literacy was familiar to the largest number (85.3%), followed closely by media literacy (81.3%). Critical literacy (69%), cyberliteracy (68.5%), and visual literacy (62.9%) were all known by more than half the respondents, while health literacy (48.7%) and mobile literacy (43.8%) were recognized by fewer than half. There were 48 "other" responses, many of which mentioned a different literacy framework not available in the list of choices. Information literacy was included in the "other" responses, as were scientific, mathematical, statistical, financial, environmental, cultural, disciplinary, and generic (reading) literacy.

Question 7 asked which literacies are components of information literacy, and the same selection of choices from the previous question were presented as options. In response to this question, all of the listed literacies were mentioned by more than half of the respondents, with digital literacy (88.3%) closely followed by media literacy (88.1%) and critical literacy (84.7%). Health literacy, at 54.2%, was selected least often. A wide variety of comments were left in the "other" category. Some of the literacies mentioned include those written in for question 6, and also academic literacy, transliteracy, social media literacy, print literacy, systems thinking literacy, aural literacy, and health literacy.

The next two questions (8 and 9) asked about familiarity with literacy frameworks, rather than discrete literacies, and expanded the selections beyond the original list to include metaliteracy, transliteracy, new media literacy, ICT, and information fluency. The purpose of this expanded list of options was to identify literacy frameworks that integrated related literacy types or competencies in some way, beyond those literacies that have a single focus (such a digital literacy). The open-ended "other" option, with a direct input field, was available for these questions as well. Question 8 asked respondents to identify the literacy frameworks they are most familiar with. As with the literacy types, the frameworks were briefly defined within the survey. Information fluency, the conceptual understanding of and ability to adapt to changing information technologies, was familiar to 71.7%, followed by transliteracy (69%), ICT (65.6%), metaliteracy (47.7%), and new media literacy (47.5%).

Question 9 asked about which of these frameworks were related to information literacy. Information fluency was also the framework most selected as related to information literacy (87.1%), followed by transliteracy (80.7%), ICT (76.8%), metaliteracy (75.2%), and new media literacy (72.6%).

Components of Information Literacy Teaching

The following two questions (10 and 11) asked which of the literacies are important to include in information literacy instruction, and what reasons might be given for not including them. Question 10 asked specifically about which literacy types are important to include in information literacy instruction. We returned to the original list of options as selections for this question, and an "other" selection. Critical literacy, with an emphasis on gaining a critical thinking perspective, was selected by 80.6% as important to include, followed by digital literacy (78.2%), media literacy (74.8%), cyberliteracy (61.4%), visual literacy (51.2%), mobile literacy (37.5%), and health literacy (26%). Many of the "other" responses indicated that the literacy selected is dependent on the context for teaching, and that many, if not all, might be appropriate at one time or another. A number of them also pointed out that it would not be possible to include all of these literacies in a single instruction session.

Question 11 asked respondents to identify reasons for not including related literacies in information literacy instruction. We offered a number of options to choose from based on our own expectations but also offered an open-ended response selection to identify those reasons we may not have considered. The response selected by the largest number of survey takers for not including them was, "I do not have enough classroom time to teach related literacies" (71.1%). All the other responses were chosen by much smaller numbers, from "I am not interested in teaching related literacies" at 3.7%, to "Lack of interest on the part of students" at 12.1%, to "I lack expertise" at 40.3% (figure 5.1). As with question 10, time, context, and appropriateness were all mentioned by a number of respondents. The open-ended response option garnered a variety of opinions:

- Librarians should select one field of expertise; they cannot be experts on every aspect of every form of literacy.
- Technology instruction is a separate skill from information literacy and should be taught as such.
- It is important to teach the basic concepts of information literacy so that they can be applied to other literacies.
- I teach one shots, and not all literacies may be specifically relevant to the discipline or skills that I am focusing on.
- Perhaps I lack expertise, but I think a lot of these components are not "related literacies," but part of information literacy.

Questions 12 through 15 ask about actual elements of each respondent's instruction. The first question of this group (12) asks which technologies they require their students to learn as a part of the information literacy instruction. We offered a range of selections to choose from based on current trends,

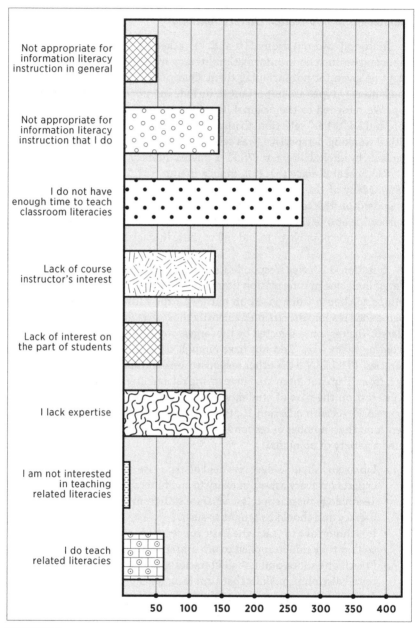

FIGURE 5.1

Which of the following are reasons for not including related literacies in information literacy instruction?

including blogs, wikis, Facebook, multimedia, Twitter, social bookmarking, presentation technology, and Second Life (as well as an open-ended option). Based on the responses to this question, presentation technology was selected the most, but by just 45.4%, multimedia followed (40.6%), as did blog technology (35.9%), wiki (29.5%), social bookmarking (23.9%), Twitter (18.3%), and Facebook (13.5%), with Second Life trailing: a mere 2.8% require students to learn it. However, only 251 survey takers responded to this question; 200 did not. "Other" responses included web navigation, databases, citation software, and course management systems, depending upon need. One respondent mentioned, "None. I don't believe IL instruction should be tied to any technology, ideally. Only one needed for my specific environment is using a browser." Another points out the limitations of one-shot instruction sessions: "I can't require my students to learn anything. I just present what the library has to offer. It doesn't include any of those, tho I use them all myself and often talk about them informally with students and faculty." And a third says, "Nothing is 'required' but it is all encouraged. Each semester all students choose different platforms to communicate. I have learned as much as I have taught."

Question 13 moved from specific technologies to ask each respondent to identify the distinct information literacy skills they include in instruction. Many of these skills are taken directly from the ACRL *Information Literacy Competency Standards for Higher Education* (2000), but we also included "share information" as an option, which is more of a metaliteracy element than an information literacy characteristic (as traditionally defined). Based on a review of responses, every listed item was selected by more than half completing the survey: access information (98%), evaluate information (97.7%), determine information need (91%), organize information (74.4%), understand information (73.1%), use information (69.6%), incorporate information (59.1%), and share information (53.2%). Included in the "other" responses were curating information, making connections between unrelated topics, information ethics, and the social life of information.

Questions 14 and 15 addressed student collaboration and whether it is built into the respondent's information literacy instruction. Question 14 asked directly if collaboration was built into information literacy instruction, and included a yes or no response. Of the 360 who responded to this question, 56.7% selected yes, while 43.3% said no. The next item (Q15) was open-ended and asked respondents to describe the types of collaborations they built into instruction and how much they typically do so. Only about a third of all those who began the survey answered this item, 181 out of 551. The responses varied from a question about the use of the term "collaboration" to descriptions of particular projects that use collaboration, to actual methods of teaching such as team-based learning and the Socratic method.

Changing Information Environment

Questions 16 to 21 centered on changes in the information environment. Question 16 asked respondents how they learn about new technology-related material that they would like to begin teaching. Multiple response options were possible, and 361 people answered this question. Clustered as the most frequently used methods were readings (87.1%), workshops (73.1%), conferences (72.3%), and instruction from knowledgeable colleagues (70.9%). Less frequently selected methods were online tutorials (53.2%), and instruction from knowledgeable students (31.9%). Methods that were frequently cited as a response to the "other" option include experimentation and play, blogs, and electronic mailing lists.

Question 17 asked a similar question, but concerning information literacy-related concepts. The 362 responses were similar to question 16, though workshops and conferences switch position: readings (89.2%), conferences (76.5%), workshops (69.6%), and instruction from knowledgeable colleagues (63.8%). Less frequently selected methods were online tutorials (43.6%) and instruction from knowledgeable students (15.5%). Blogs, Twitter, the web, and networking were mentioned by a number of respondents to the "other" option.

Respondents were asked in question 18 whether a lack of knowledge or skills keep them from teaching items they'd like to include, and 360 people answered this question. More said no (201, 55.8%) than yes (159, 44.2%). Many mentioned a lack of time, support, and faculty interest as barriers. Those who were able to overcome these obstacles noted that if they felt something was important, they made the time to learn it.

Question 19 asked how prepared respondents feel to include new technology-related material or information literacy concepts in their instruction. The largest group of respondents said they felt well prepared to teach new material or technologies. However, this group comprised just 45.9% of the respondents (169, n=368). The second largest group said they felt neither prepared nor unprepared (31.5%, 116). Those who felt unprepared (11.4%) slightly outnumbered those who felt very well prepared (10.3%). Fewer than 1% of those who completed the survey felt very unprepared. Ninety-six people expanded on their responses in question 20. Most of the comments fell into several categories pertaining to: method of preparation to remain up to date; difficulty of keeping abreast of changes and determining which new tools to concentrate on; and curriculum, time, or financial constraints connected to learning and teaching new concepts and applications.

The last question, 21, asked for an open-ended response to the question, "What do you consider the single most important change you have made in the last 2–4 years in your teaching due to the current information environment?" There were 263 responses to this question, 48% of those who started the survey and 73% of those who finished it. The strong response for this open-ended question clearly struck a chord, compared to the question about the types and uses of collaboration. The responses to this question address an enormous scope of changes. Themes include increased active learning and student-center learning experiences, the need or desire to incorporate social media tools and strategies into the covered content, more emphasis on critical analysis, increased availability and use of technologies in the classroom, the shift to online courses, and augmented assessment.

DATA ANALYSIS

The data were analyzed with crosstabulations in SurveyMonkey. As noted at the SurveyMonkey website, "Crosstabulated data is useful for showing a side by side comparison of two or more survey questions to determine how they are interrelated" (http://help.surveymonkey.com/articles/en_US/kb/What -are-Crosstabs). Crosstabs were run on the pairs of questions that would answer the original research questions:

- Did age affect which specific related literacy types are seen as related to information literacy?
- Did the choice of these literacy types affect decisions about what information literacy elements were taught to students?
- Did perceived preparation for teaching new technology-related material or information literacy concepts have an impact on what was taught?

The results are analyzed below. Examination of two areas of interest was not possible in the way the authors intended:

- Did differences vary by country?
- Did those who self-identified as librarians respond significantly differently than other populations?

While 31% of the responses came from individuals outside the United States, they were widely scattered. Only those from the United Kingdom, at 16%, comprised more than a small number of respondents, and the next largest contingent of respondents were from Canada, at only 3% of the total.

The imbalance between librarian and non-librarian was more marked than differences based on country. Based on the results, only 7.9% of those who took the survey self-identified as being either discipline faculty or administrators. It was difficult to categorize those who answered "Other," but it was clear that a number of these individuals are librarians, and, indeed, it is possible that some of those who self-identified as "administrator" might actually be library administrators.

Age

Age (Q23) was cross tabulated with **familiarity with various literacies** (Q6), before examining which ones should be taught as components of information literacy. Figure 5.2 indicates the results of this cross-tabulation. Across survey respondents as a whole, digital literacy was the one with which most respondents were familiar with (314, n=363), followed closely by media literacy (301). The recognition of digital literacy over media literacy was slightly more pronounced in the 30–39 age group. For those in other age groups, awareness of media literacy and digital literacy were in close contention. The variation in responses based on age was not noteworthy.

Age was also cross tabulated with Q7: **literacies seen as components of information literacy**, Q8: **literacy frameworks familiar with**, and Q9: **literacy frameworks related to information literacy**. Again, responses between age categories were similar. These relationships are represented in figures 5.3, 5.4, and 5.5.

When **Age** was cross tabulated with **literacies important to include in information literacy instruction** (Q10), it became clear that respondents in most age categories felt that critical literacy was most important, although for those aged 21–29, it tied with media literacy, and those aged 40–49 selected digital literacy as most important. (Since there was only one respondent aged 17 or younger, that age category saw little variation.) Health literacy was selected least frequently in all age categories. See table 5.1.

Literacies to Include
in Information Literacy Instruction

The authors examined the correlation between those literacies identified as a component of information literacy (Q7) and those chosen as important to include in information literacy instruction (Q10). It must be remembered that respondents were able to select as many responses as desired. The strongest such correspondence involved critical literacy: 88% of those who thought it a component of information literacy felt it was important to include in instruction. The weakest correlation involved mobile literacy: only 52.2% of those who considered it a component of information literacy felt it was important to include in instruction. See table 5.2 for a complete listing of these correspondences.

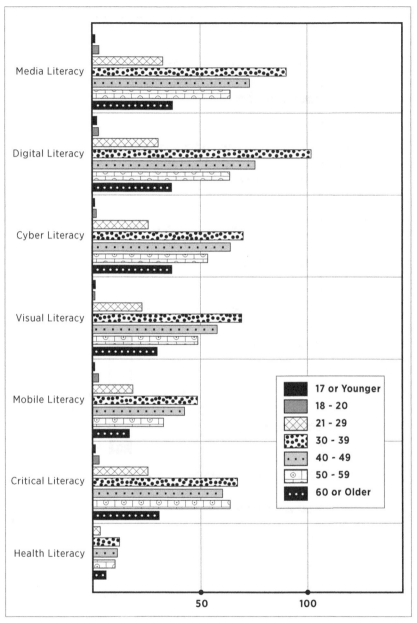

FIGURE 5.2

Which of the following literacies are you familiar with?

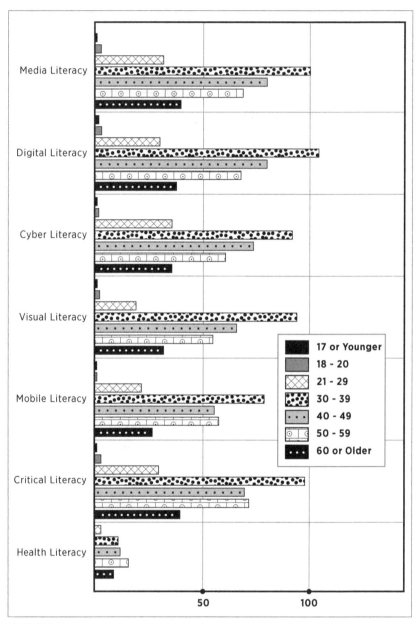

FIGURE 5.3

Which of the following literacies do you think are components
of information literacy?

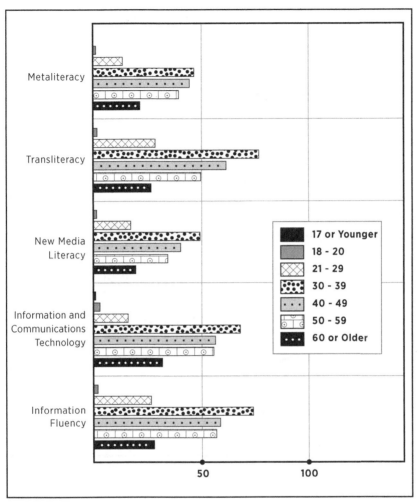

FIGURE 5.4

Which of the following literacy frameworks are you familiar with?

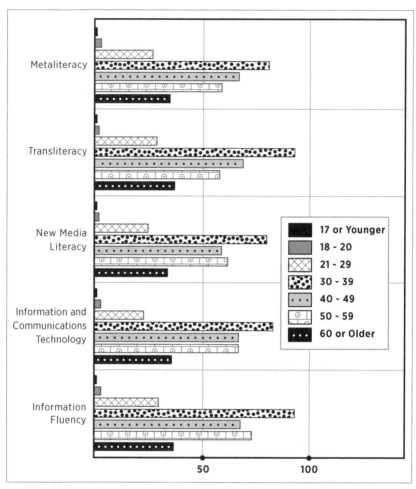

FIGURE 5.5

Which of the following literacy frameworks do you think are related
to information literacy?

TABLE 5.1

Literacies important to include in information literacy instruction by age

Literacies important to include in information literacy instruction by age							
Age Category	Which of the following literacies are important to include in information literacy instruction? (select all that apply)						
Answer Options	Media literacy	Digital literacy	Cyber-literacy	Visual literacy	Mobile literacy	Critical literacy	Health literacy
17 or younger	1	1	1	1	1	1	0
Row percentage	16.67%	16.67%	16.67%	16.67%	16.67%	16.67%	0%
18-20	2	2	1	1	1	3	0
	20%	20%	10%	10%	10%	30%	0%
21-29	28	26	20	13	14	28	6
	20.74%	19.26%	14.81%	9.63%	10.37%	20.74%	4.44%
30-39	78	85	72	52	29	88	25
	18.18%	19.81%	16.78%	12.12%	6.76%	20.51%	5.83%
40-49	69	74	57	53	34	66	25
	18.25%	19.58%	15.08%	14.02%	8.99%	17.46%	6.61%
50-59	57	59	47	40	41	65	26
	17.01%	17.61%	14.03%	11.94%	12.24%	19.40%	7.76%
60 or older	34	33	26	22	18	39	11
	18.58%	18.03%	14.21%	12.02%	9.84%	21.31%	6.01%
							answered question 353

Preparation Levels and Required Technologies

The authors compared responses to **how well prepared do you feel to teach new technology-related material or information literacy concepts (Q19)** to the question about **which technologies do you require your students to learn as a part of your information literacy instruction (Q12)**. A number of responders to the latter question pointed out that, as a librarian providing course-related instruction, they are not able to require anything, it is up to the instructor of record. However, it was very interesting to see that the instructor's level of preparation did not necessarily translate into students being required to learn a particular technology. Although the low number of responses may be influencing the percentages reported here, those who felt well prepared required these technologies more than those who

TABLE 5.2

Components of information literacy compared to inclusion
in information literacy instruction

Components of IL	Which of the following literacies do you think are components of information literacy? (select all that apply)						
Answer Options	Media literacy	Digital literacy	Cyber-literacy	Visual literacy	Mobile literacy	Critical literacy	Health literacy
Media literacy	274	274	218	187	135	279	91
Digital literacy	261	282	222	183	137	276	87
Cyberliteracy	235	244	224	167	132	249	85
Visual literacy	219	219	182	183	116	226	78
Mobile literacy	189	197	176	142	129	203	75
Critical literacy	246	258	212	174	126	287	87
Health literacy	162	160	138	116	87	169	89

answered question 353

labeled themselves as very well prepared. Based on this analysis, those respondents who considered themselves neither prepared nor unprepared required Twitter and presentation technology more than those who felt very prepared. Only multimedia, social bookmarking, and Second Life were most used by those who felt very well prepared. See table 5.3.

DISCUSSION AND IMPLICATIONS FOR FURTHER RESEARCH

Populations

While the authors were pleased with the large number of responses to this preliminary survey overall, they did not meet their goal of reaching as many international and non-librarian respondents as they had hoped. While the survey was specifically announced in several international venues, an additional effort will be needed to obtain an adequate response that will allow crosstabulations based on country. Without this perspective, it is not possible to judge what the perceived information literacy competencies are in regions that have information environments similar to that in the United States, or in those environments that differ radically. With the increasing focus on

TABLE 5.3

Technologies students are required to learn compared
to preparation level

Technologies students are required to learn compared to preparation level					
Technologies students learn as part of IL	How well prepared do you feel to teach new technology-related material or information literacy concepts?				
Answer Options	Very well prepared	Well prepared	Neither prepared nor unprepared	Unprepared	Very unprepared
Blog	10	48	26	2	0
Wiki	10	41	17	2	0
Facebook	4	19	8	2	0
Multimedia	15	44	31	5	0
Twitter	6	22	14	3	0
Social bookmarking	9	31	17	1	0
Presentation technology	13	55	34	8	0
Second Life	3	2	1	0	0
					answered question 236

metaliteracy, transliteracy and UNESCO's MIL, obtaining increased responses from a range of countries should be possible at some future point. This initial survey at least helps us to identify the need for further work in this area.

A second group of respondents that the authors hoped to reach were teaching faculty in a variety of disciplines. According to the Middle States Commission on Higher Education (2003), faculty members and librarians should share the teaching of information literacy competencies. What conceptions does this population hold about information literacy? Are these conceptions, as the authors hypothesize, based on traditional research skills connected to finding appropriate sources, particularly scholarly sources? Perhaps discipline faculty are keenly aware of what they would like their students to be able to do concerning information, but they have not put names to these abilities nor are they aware that there is a field of study and practice that might assist them. Thus, responding to the survey would not only provide data for research, but might also serve as an alert for educators who have a significant role to play in the teaching of these new literacies.

Although the original survey was not targeted to K–12 educators, it would be productive to learn more about their understanding of the topics under discussion. School administrators, teachers, and librarians are cognizant of the changing nature of information and how it impacts their students' use of that information. Data gained from such a study would prove useful as secondary schools and institutions of higher education align educational goals.

Increased Awareness of Evolving Literacies

Metaliteracy, transliteracy, and MIL are gaining prominence in the field of education, particularly with librarians. In a *College & Research Libraries* email of March 6, 2013, the authors' 2011 *C&RL* article (Mackey & Jacobson) was noted as one of the top five most read articles from the journal's archives in 2012. The Transliteracy, Technology and Teaching conference held its third annual conference in March 2013. Developed by librarians in the SUNY system, it increasingly attracts speakers and attendees from far beyond the state's boundaries. Sue Thomas, the British originator of the concept of transliteracy, was the keynote speaker at the 2013 conference. Based on national survey results, the Educause Learning Initiative (ELI) includes "digital and information literacies" as a "content anchor" for the year (2013). It is notable that this theme moved up on the list from 9 in 2012 to 4 in 2013. As a content anchor for 2014, "digital and information literacies" is featured in the 2014 ELI Conference (2013). Other significant venues such as the Sloan Consortium International Conference on Online Learning often include presentations on topics related to emerging literacies. In addition, we have seen continued conversations about emerging literacy frameworks in social media (through blog postings and tweets) and regional conferences that have taken on these issues as central concerns. The dialogue has continued in scholarly articles as well.

We hypothesize that awareness of new models of information literacy will increase dramatically in the next year or two, particularly as professional associations and international organizations either re-examine dated standards or increase their participation in outreach efforts. For example, the work of the ACRL Information Literacy Competency Standards for Higher Education Task Force to review and rethink the original ACRL competency standards (2000) demonstrates a significant shift in how the field of library and information science is responding to these fundamental changes.

Efforts by UNESCO to promote MIL through a variety of avenues should also affect awareness throughout the world. For example, UNESCO announced, at the end of 2012, that it would offer an online course in MIL and intercultural dialogue. The course was targeted to policy makers, teachers, and professionals and was offered from February through May 2013 by the Queensland University of Technology (UNESCO, 2012).

In 2013, the United Nations published *Conceptual Relationship of Information Literacy and Media Literacy*, a series of research papers by authors from China, Mexico, the United States, and the Russian Federation. These papers, published in conjunction with the World Summit on the Information Society, discuss the evolving competencies needed for individuals to be fully informed citizens, participating in knowledge societies, and also explore new models, both independent literacies (such as media) and compound literacy concepts, including metaliteracy.

The Executive Summary preceding the first paper, Literacy and Competencies Required to Participate in Knowledge Societies, explains the importance of staying abreast in the new social and technological environment:

> The globe is under the influence of three major world trends: the revolutionary development of information and communication technologies, the transition to a knowledge society and the new learning mode of the Net Generation. These trends have generated a shift in the educational paradigm, giving rise to the need to cultivate new competencies for citizens in knowledge societies. (Lee, 2013, p. 4)

The remarkable effect of mobile phone use on worldwide access to information is one example provided. UNESCO's strong emphasis on 21st-century literacies and the accompanying educational changes have dramatic implications for awareness of these issues. That, in conjunction with the wide range of countries represented in the survey responses, led the authors to believe that it would be illuminating to administer an updated version of the current study in several years and compare the findings.

The State of the Literature/The State of Awareness

A separate study focusing on the emergence of published material related to metaliteracy and transliteracy might shed light on the changing awareness and applications of these terms and concepts. In addition, other models or approaches may emerge that share key values with metaliteracy and transliteracy, so it would also be productive to review articles, books, and other sources in the fields of education and information studies that do not explicitly mention either.

Traditional information sources would be one area to explore and would inform what is being written for scholars and practitioners. Yet there are also information and initiatives directed to the general public. While a broad sweep of the resources in this realm is far too massive, individual projects might yield interesting observations about how the general public is dealing with the changes that have created the need for the suite of metaliteracy-related abilities in order to effectively interact with information in all its guises.

CONCLUSION

The study reported in this chapter was exploratory, probing respondents' conceptions of the changing nature of information literacy, their use of a limited number of web-based technologies, and their preparation for evolving instructional components. While the survey did not answer questions connected to particular populations and their relationships to evolving information literacy, it did successfully provide a snapshot of the range of the knowledge, perceptions, teaching, and learning practices connected to emerging literacies as reflected by a number of primarily English-speaking librarians. Yet the number and diversity of countries represented attest that the issues are global ones. Librarians teaching information literacy competencies are in many cases already incorporating elements such as new participatory technologies, new collaborative endeavors, and components of the metacognitive aspects of metaliteracy.

Survey results indicate that strides have been made in providing effective technology infrastructure and support at many institutions while some respondents are still struggling with ineffective resources. Respondents are familiar with many of the related literacy types that we see as connected to metaliteracy in a comprehensive framework. They also identified a number of terms, related to quantitative literacy especially, that would fit within this expanded model and could be examined in future research. A majority of respondents agreed that the related literacies we identified in our model are components of information literacy, and a number of responses provided additional formats that we did not mention, such as print literacy and systems thinking literacy. This contribution of additional literacies supports our overall assertion that, rather than address multiple and disconnected formats, we need a comprehensive model that identifies relevant connections within a metaliteracy framework. The survey shows that many of the models that combine multiple literacies are also familiar to respondents and that metaliteracy is emerging as one of those recognizable terms. Respondents identified digital literacy and media literacy as the two most recognizable approaches within the discrete category, while information fluency and transliteracy are the two most familiar terms within the combined category.

This survey indicates that we have a few barriers to overcome in order to transform current information literacy practices into a metaliteracy. Most respondents identified with the assertion that they do not have enough time to teach related literacies while a smaller group indicated lack of expertise in these other elements. Some respondents do not see a connection to technology instruction and information literacy while others are limited by the constraints of one-shot library sessions. At the same time, however, we are encouraged that many of the respondents are already using a number of technologies in their instruction, with a particular emphasis on presentation applications. The survey demonstrates that the traditional characteristics of information literacy are being addressed in instruction, and that sharing information, which is a key element of metaliteracy, is often covered as well. In addition, more than half of the respondents are incorporating some level of collaboration into instruction. These are encouraging findings, but if we are going to reinvent information literacy as a metaliteracy, we will need to continuously increase the use of technology, with a focus on producing and sharing information in collaborative contexts. Since a majority of respondents learn about new technology and literacy concepts through readings, workshops, conferences, and colleagues, we need to renew the conversation in all of these arenas and provide the necessary institutional support to advance professional development for both faculty and librarians. This will present us with an opportunity to further support faculty and librarian collaboration in this enterprise and to expand metaliteracy beyond traditional information literacy instruction.

Given the rapid pace of technological change, and the concomitant emphasis on new models of education globally, further research related to metaliteracy might return different results in a fairly short time. Further, this survey sets the stage for additional research using quantitative and qualitative methods for identifying relationships among literacies within a metaliteracy framework, testing the evolving metaliteracy learning objectives in association with student learning, and developing effective teaching practices that support this model. We see considerable potential in research efforts that involve K–12 settings as well. As metaliteracy advances in higher education, it will be useful to return to this preliminary survey to see if perceptions of the terminology identified and the overall results change over time. We also need to move beyond the survey format as the primary instrument and enhance future research with expanded methods including individual interviews and focus groups.

In the next two chapters we will provide ideas for situating oneself, as a teacher, within this new construct. Chapters 6 and 7 will examine the metaliteracy-related aspects of two undergraduate learning experiences, one an information literacy course at the University at Albany, the other an online digital storytelling course at Empire State College that lends itself well to metaliteracy elements. Circumstances will differ for each teaching situation, but we are confident that readers will be reassured by both examples and the insights provided by practitioners grappling with this evolving field. The accounts of the two courses will encourage further inquiry about the ways in which instructors and instructional designers can adapt to diverse teaching and learning settings.

REFERENCES

Association of College and Research Libraries. (2000). *Information literacy competency standards for higher education*. American Library Association. www.ala.org/acrl/ standards/informationliteracycompetency

Educause Learning Initiative. (2013). Content anchors. www.educause.edu/eli/ programs/seeking-evidence-impact/content-anchors

Lee, Alice. (2013). Literacy and competencies required to participate in knowledge societies. In *Conceptual relationship of information literacy and media literacy* (pp. 3–75). UNESCO World Summit on the Information Society.

Mackey, Thomas P., & Jacobson, Trudi E. (2011). Reframing information literacy as a metaliteracy. *College & Research Libraries, 72*(1), 62–78.

Middle States Commission on Higher Education. (2003). Developing research and communication skills: Guidelines for information literacy in the curriculum. www.msche.org/publications/Developing-Skills080111151714.pdf

Sloan Consortium. (2013). Sloan-C International Conference on Online Learning. http://sloanconsortium.org/conference/2013/aln/welcome

UNESCO. (2012). Communication and information sector. www.unesco.org/new/en/ media-services/single-view/news/unesco_launches_online_course_in_media _and_information_literacy_and_intercultural_dialogue

Information Literacy as a Metaliteracy

Thank you very much for taking this survey. We are interested in finding out via our research if the current Web environment has had an impact on your teaching of information literacy. We will initially share the results of the research through a forthcoming book to be published by Neal-Schuman.

Trudi Jacobson, MLS, MA
Head of Information Literacy
University Libraries
University at Albany

Tom Mackey, PhD
Dean
Center for Distance Learning
SUNY Empire State College

This project has been approved by the University at Albany Institutional Review Board.

Approval of this project only signifies that the procedures adequately protect the rights and welfare of the participants. Please note that absolute confidentiality cannot be guaranteed due to the limited protections of Internet access. Please be sure to close your browser when finished so no one will be able to see what you have been doing.

Your participation in this survey is voluntary. You may choose not to answer any questions and may exit from the survey at any time.

1. Do you teach information literacy as:

    ☐ Credit-bearing information literacy-specific courses

    ☐ Courserelated information literacy sessions

    ☐ Stand-alone information literacy sessions

    ☐ A component of discipline-based courses

    ☐ Other (*please specify*)

2. If you teach information literacy-specific courses, how many credits are they?

    ☐ 0 credits   ☐ 3 credits

    ☐ 1 credit   ☐ 4 credits

    ☐ 2 credits   ☐ Other (*please specify*)

3. How would you describe the format your information literacy instruction takes?

    ☐ Face to face

    ☐ Blended (combining face to face and online)

    ☐ Fully online

    ☐ Other (*please specify*)

4. How would you describe the technology infrastructure at your school?
   - ☐ Highly effective
   - ☐ Effective
   - ☐ Neither effective nor ineffective
   - ☐ Ineffective
   - ☐ Highly ineffective

5. How would you describe the technology support at your school?
   - ☐ Highly effective
   - ☐ Effective
   - ☐ Neither effective nor ineffective
   - ☐ Ineffective
   - ☐ Highly ineffective

6. Which of the following literacies are you familiar with? (*select all that apply*)
   - ☐ Media literacy (critical evaluation, creation, and participation with media content)
   - ☐ Digital literacy (use of digital technology to evaluate and create information)
   - ☐ Cyberliteracy (ability to actively participate via the Internet and Web)
   - ☐ Visual literacy (competencies based on visual design and communication)
   - ☐ Mobile literacy (understanding how to access and communicate information via mobile devices)
   - ☐ Critical literacy (gaining a critical perspective about information through critical pedagogy)
   - ☐ Health literacy (ability to critically understand health information)
   - ☐ Other (*please specify*)

7. Which of the following literacies do you think are components of information literacy? (*select all that apply*)
   - ☐ Media literacy
   - ☐ Digital literacy
   - ☐ Cyberliteracy
   - ☐ Visual literacy
   - ☐ Mobile literacy
   - ☐ Critical literacy
   - ☐ Health literacy
   - ☐ Other (*please specify*)

8. Which of the following literacy frameworks are you familiar with? (*select all that apply*)
   - ☐ Metaliteracy (framework for related literacies with focus on producing and sharing information)

☐ Transliteracy (ability to read, write, and interact across multiple media platforms)

☐ New Media Literacy (ability to evaluate and participate via new media environments)

☐ Information and Communications Technology (ICT) (combining information and communications technology skills)

☐ Information Fluency (conceptual understanding of and ability to adapt to changing information technologies)

☐ Other (*please specify*)

9. Which of the following literacy frameworks do you think are related to information literacy? (*select all that apply*)

☐ Metaliteracy

☐ Transliteracy

☐ New Media Literacy

☐ Information and Communications Technology (ICT)

☐ Information Fluency

☐ Other (*please specify*)

10. Which of the following literacies are important to include in information literacy instruction? (*select all that apply*)

☐ Media literacy   ☐ Mobile literacy

☐ Digital literacy   ☐ Critical literacy

☐ Cyberliteracy   ☐ Health literacy

☐ Visual literacy   ☐ Other (*please specify*)

11. Which of the following are reasons for not including related literacies in information literacy instruction? (*select all that apply*)

☐ Not appropriate for information literacy instruction in general

☐ Not appropriate for information literacy instruction that I do

☐ I do not have enough classroom time to teach related literacies

☐ Lack of course instructor's interest

☐ Lack of interest on the part of students

☐ I lack expertise

☐ I am not interested in teaching related literacies

☐ I do teach related literacies

☐ Other (*please specify*)

12. Which of the following technologies do you require your students to learn as a part of your information literacy instruction? (*select all that apply*)

☐ Blog   ☐ Social bookmarking
☐ Wiki   ☐ Presentation technology
☐ Facebook   ☐ Second Life
☐ Multimedia   ☐ Other (*please specify*)
☐ Twitter

13. Which of the following information literacy skills do you include in your information literacy instruction? (*select all that apply*)

☐ Determine information need
☐ Access information
☐ Evaluate information
☐ Understand information
☐ Incorporate information
☐ Organize information
☐ Use information
☐ Share information
☐ Other (*please specify*)

14. Do you build student collaboration into your information literacy instruction?

☐ Yes   ☐ No

15. Please describe the types of collaborations and how much you typically use them.

16. How do you learn about new technology-related material you would like to begin teaching? (*select all that apply*)

☐ Workshops
☐ Conferences
☐ Readings
☐ Online tutorials
☐ Instruction from knowledgeable colleagues
☐ Instruction from knowledgeable students
☐ Other (*please specify*)

17. How do you learn about other new information literacy-related concepts you would like to begin teaching? (*select all that apply*)
    - ☐ Workshops
    - ☐ Conferences
    - ☐ Readings
    - ☐ Online tutorials
    - ☐ Instruction from knowledgeable colleagues
    - ☐ Instruction from knowledgeable students
    - ☐ Other (*please specify*)

18. Does lack of knowledge or skills keep you from teaching items you would like to include?
    ☐ Yes   ☐ No

    Please explain

19. How well prepared do you feel to teach new technology-related material or information literacy concepts?
    - ☐ Very well prepared
    - ☐ Well prepared
    - ☐ Neither prepared nor unprepared
    - ☐ Unprepared
    - ☐ Very unprepared

20. Please use this box to expand upon your response to question 19, if you choose to.

21. What do you consider the single most important change you have made in the last 2–4 years in your teaching due to the current information environment?

22. Please list the country in which you teach.

23. Which category below includes your age?

☐ 17 or younger   ☐ 40–49

☐ 18–20   ☐ 50–59

☐ 21–29   ☐ 60 or older

☐ 30–39

24. Which best describes your current position?

☐ Librarian

☐ Discipline faculty

☐ Administrator

☐ Other (*please specify*)

25. Do you teach undergraduate students or graduate students?

☐ Undergraduate students

☐ Graduate students

☐ Both undergraduate and graduate students

☐ I do not teach

☐ Other (*please specify*)

26. Which best describes your school?

☐ Two-year college

☐ Four-year college

☐ Research university

☐ Other (*please specify*)

Thank you for participating in this survey.

6

The Evolution of a Dedicated Information Literacy Course toward Metaliteracy

IN THE FIRST THREE CHAPTERS OF THIS BOOK WE ESTABLISH A theoretical framework for metaliteracy by expanding the traditional definitions of information literacy to include pathways to cognate literacies and competencies for collaborative participation in open and online communities. In Chapter 4 we examine global trends in information literacy, including several recent models from UNESCO, the United Kingdom, and Hong Kong. Chapter 5 reports on a survey of the field that shifts from a theoretical perspective to a pragmatic one and from a macro to a micro view. The last two chapters in this book now examine the real-world practice of metaliteracy in teaching and learning, illustrating how face-to-face, blended, and online instruction are improved through a comprehensive and integrated model for related literacy types and an emphasis on emergent social technologies. These last two chapters present case studies that show how metaliteracy encourages positive changes in learning design in ways that challenge our own assumptions about information literacy pedagogy in a social media age.

At the turn of the 21st century, both authors of this book taught at the University at Albany during a period of significant change in technology from print to web in classroom and library environments. This was also a time when the university adopted a general education requirement for information literacy and Web 2.0 emerged as a significant trend in popular culture and higher education. During this transition, Trudi E. Jacobson was involved in developing a university-wide course dedicated to information literacy and Tom Mackey taught a discipline-specific course in the undergraduate information science program that combined information literacy and web development (Mackey & Ho, 2005; Mackey, 2005; Mackey & Jacobson, 2005). The primary focus of this chapter will be on the evolution of the course-dedicated information literacy format taught by Jacobson and librarian colleagues at the University at Albany. The chapter also includes a section authored by Gregory Bobish, associate librarian at the University Libraries, who currently teaches a version of the same dedicated information literacy course model with expanded Web 2.0 and social media resources.

The changes we observed in our own learning environments at the start of the 21st century and the emergence of Web 2.0 and social media in 2005 informed our thinking about the limits of existing frameworks, leading to the development of a comprehensive metaliteracy model. Our own professional collaborations involved the design of teaching practices in support of the information literacy general education requirement. This work also influenced the case study in the next and final chapter in this book that focuses on a fully online course in digital storytelling at SUNY Empire State College. In that chapter we demonstrate how the metaliteracy framework informs teaching an interdisciplinary online course for students, to create original projects with Web 2.0 resources, but does not explicitly require information literacy. The last chapter in this book will be especially useful to instructors who want to incorporate metaliteracy approaches into blended and online course environments, whether or not that course meets a specific information literacy requirement. This approach will demonstrate the importance of integrating metaliteracy throughout the curriculum.

The academic librarian co-author of this volume (for the rest of this chapter, other than in Gregory Bobish's section, "the author" refers to Trudi Jacobson) has worked in the area of library instruction for long enough to see several dramatic changes in her area of specialization, both generally and in her position at the University at Albany, SUNY. Not only has the nomenclature changed from bibliographic instruction to information literacy instruction (with "user education" along the way) but the shape of the program has undergone some of the same types of transformations that have occurred in other academic libraries' instructional programs. Along this 20-plus year journey, new skills were required, and areas of expertise had to shift, often quickly, to meet the challenges of the changing information environment and the evolving needs of students. This is, of course, most appropriate, lest the program and the librarian stagnate. The transformations began to have a greater impact when the author's primary form of instruction transitioned from course-related instruction, which affected a very small percentage of students each year, to teaching an information literacy course within a larger program that meets the needs of thousands of students per year.

In 2000, a new information literacy general education requirement was instituted at the University at Albany. Librarians teach two of the courses that meet this requirement (UNL205x and UNL206x, the science version). Reflection on changes made to the course taught by the author provide an illuminating look at the increasing need for students to be information literate in a broad sense, as defined by the concept of information literacy as a metaliteracy.

EVOLVING INFORMATION LITERACY
GENERAL EDUCATION REQUIREMENT

The university's general education requirement stemmed from a designated competency, information management, which was included in a new general education program decreed by the Board of Trustees of SUNY. The University at Albany decided to require that students take a course with a demonstrated information literacy component (Jacobson, 2004). These courses might be taught by faculty members within their disciplines or by librarians. This integrated approach to information literacy led to a broad expansion of information literacy instruction in such disciplines as Women's Studies, English, Information Science, History, Computer Science, and East Asian Studies. In addition, a first year experience program and several courses aimed at freshmen also were certified as meeting the requirement. In 1996 a nascent approach to information literacy instruction in Project Renaissance, the first-year experience program at the university focused on the themes "human identity and technology," helped shape the direction of information literacy instruction and established the first collaborative endeavor for the two book authors. In 2000 a subcommittee of the General Education Committee was formed to provide guidance to faculty members interested in adapting courses to meet the requirement, to review syllabi and plans for implementation, and to assist those who had received approval. Two librarians, including Jacobson, served on the subcommittee, along with several faculty members whose own courses had been approved or who had an interest in the topic.

One of the author's most vivid memories, which highlights the contrast between what was considered critical at the turn of the 21st century, as compared to today, was the subcommittee's discussion about the need for students to be able to show their mastery of the knowledge and skills needed to retrieve a variety of types of information sources. In order to have a course certified to meet the new information literacy requirement, faculty members had to submit evidence that their course would meet designated learning objectives. This expectation was described in the information literacy requirement:

> Approved courses describe the processes of finding, organizing, using, producing and distributing information in a variety of media formats, including traditional print as well as computer databases. Students acquire experience with resources available on the internet and learn to evaluate the quality of information, to work ethically and professionally, and to adjust to rapidly changing technology tools. Students must complete this requirement within the freshman or sophomore year. (University at Albany, State University of New York, 2000)

The discussion revolved around the first item: locate, evaluate, synthesize, and use information *from a variety of media formats* (emphasis is the author's). Students needed to find a number of different types of sources: students would be challenged to extend their searches beyond items kept on reserve for a course and articles from scholarly journals. The librarians were adamant on this point. There was not much discussion about the finished product, which was generally assumed to be a traditional research paper or something similar, although this requirement was often interpreted by faculty in different ways. The extent to which instructors addressed "a variety of media formats" in information literacy instruction often depended on how often they used or addressed such resources in their teaching.

However, less than two years later, the tables had turned. Faculty members on the subcommittee, from disciplines such as geography and information science, argued that it was important to explicitly address the appropriateness of research projects that may not take the traditional form of paper-based, written products. At that time, some faculty were requiring student-centered web development in their courses and the adoption of the WebCT learning management system by the university was having an impact on how some instructors were starting to enhance their courses with online components. In the discipline-specific course The Information Environment (IST301X) taught by Mackey, for instance, students were required to create learner-centered web development projects, including web-based annotated bibliographies, hypertext research pages, and collaborative web pages on topical issues in information science, but this was not the standard interpretation of the information literacy requirement (Mackey & Jacobson, 2004). Changes in the library environment were also taking place with the adoption of electronic reserves (ERs), an ongoing expansion of web-based resources, including online information literacy tutorials, and the start of a transition from print to electronic scholarly journal articles. By 2002, approved criteria for information literacy courses had been added, and the third criterion explicitly addresses the concern:

Approved Criteria for Information Literacy Courses: Courses that satisfy the Information Literacy requirement will have three characteristics:

1. Classroom activities on finding, evaluating, citing, and using information in print and electronic sources from the University Libraries, World Wide Web, and other sources. Courses should address questions concerning the ethical use of information, copyrights, and other related issues that promote critical reflection.
2. Assignments, course work, or tutorials that make extensive use of the University Libraries, World Wide Web, and other information sources. Assignments should include finding, evaluating, and citing information sources.
3. At least one research project that requires students to find, evaluate, cite, and use information presented in diverse formats from multiple sources and to integrate this information within a single textual, visual, or digital document. (University at Albany, State University of New York, 2002)

This wording stood until fall 2014, when information literacy and three other competencies were moved in each major. For the period it was in use, it was particularly pertinent when thinking about information literacy in its broader metaliteracy construct. By expanding the technology formats from print to web, a few additional literacy types are implicitly recognized (textual, visual, digital), although this could be expanded further to be even more explicit in recognizing the expanded possibilities in a metaliteracy framework. Colleagues from other disciplines suggested visual and digital documents, and while they may be teaching information literacy courses within their own disciplines, librarians will be doing a service to their students to consider alternative formats within their own instruction.

Despite new criteria that explicitly broadened the playing field, the standard final product for all sections of the one-credit information literacy courses taught by librarians altered little. The original product was an annotated bibliography, to contain strictly defined information formats:

- One primary source
- One secondary source
- A book
- A reference source in book format
- A print article from a popular magazine or newspaper
- A print article from a scholarly journal
- A full-text article

- A popular Internet resource
- A scholarly Internet resource
- One additional resource from one of these categories: electronic reference source, government document, or multimedia source

The bibliography was a major element throughout the course. Each week, students would locate, cite, and critically annotate items that would appear in the final project for the course. They were thus able to receive feedback on their weekly assignments, which would afford them the opportunity to learn from errors and to excel on their completed bibliography. This approach, however, did not guarantee that all students would be engaged in critically evaluating the expanding array of web resources, and the evolution of the web from a static and expansive collection of interconnected documents to an active and participatory social environment. Mackey's course on the information environment integrated information literacy and web literacies and expanded over time to include collaborative blogs and wikis in 2006 and 2007, but this work was integral to the disciplinary themes of the information science program and was not a common expectation among other information literacy courses. This presented a challenge in how to reach more students across the curriculum and to engage them in information literacy within a rapidly evolving web that continued to have significant influence in popular culture, research, and educational environments.

TRANSFORMATIONS TO THE FINAL PROJECT IN THE INFORMATION LITERACY COURSE TAUGHT BY LIBRARIANS

While there were small adjustments in the required formats of sources in the information literacy courses taught by librarians over a decade (for example, the need for students to find articles in hard copy was dropped), the annotated bibliography and its components proved to be remarkably resilient. Several years after the campus-wide criteria changed, the librarians began to migrate to an enhanced final product, a research guide, which retained the annotated bibliography at its core. The more robust research guide's bibliography was supported by additional materials, such as a thesis statement and exposition tying key resources to that statement, as well as definitions of unfamiliar terms, and, in some instructors' versions, short biographies of several authors of entries in the bibliography. However, the various iterations as developed by different instructors still required students to use traditional information sources, and to compile their research guides in print format.

It was only about 2008 when one of the librarians began to assign students to work in groups and to develop their research guides as wikis (Zazzau,

2009). In her article, this UNL205x instructor discusses the students' unfamiliarity with wikis, other than Wikipedia, and the learning curves involved in forming students into groups to present their work via this medium. She also explains compelling reasons for using a wiki in a course:

> With wikis, students can work together in teams, learn from one another, and form their own conclusions regarding course subject matter. Teaching with wikis allows instructors to observe their students' processes with project construction and design in real time. This realtime function allows instructors to quickly recognize problems and remedy them. (Zazzau, 2009, p. 61)

The author of this chapter was also strongly influenced by an article she read in draft form, written by the book's co-author (Mackey, 2011). In the article, "Transparency as a Catalyst for Interaction and Participation in Open Learning Environments," Mackey described the importance of "transparent design" in the development of open learning in wikis, OERs, and mobile applications. The development of the "transparency" article was informed by several years of teaching with wikis at the University at Albany, in The Information Environment, and another class, Social and Community Informatics (Mackey & McLaughlin, 2007), as well as later courses taught at the Sage Colleges and SUNY Empire State College. The issues raised in the following excerpt were particularly motivational in her move to using a course wiki, given the situation described in the section Team-Based Learning and Its Effect on the Research Guide later in this chapter:

> Transparency encourages self-directed learning and multiple methods for producing, publishing and distributing content to the Web and via mobile applications. The collaborative aspects of Web 2.0 resources such as blogs and wikis, in which many users contribute to or edit the same page or pages, creates instant peer-to-peer opportunities for authorship, content management, critical thinking, and the visualization of ideas. The peer review process for creating and editing learner-generated content is supported by the ability to link to and comment on shared online resources. Similarly, the emergence of OERs as cooperative materials for producing and sharing knowledge in open spaces for access to everyone requires a collective commitment to the development of dynamic digital resources. (Mackey, 2011)

This portion of Mackey's article describes how extensively the web has evolved into a social media environment, opening up opportunities to engage learners in collaboration and peer review, which are critical to teaching information literacy today. It goes on to describe this shift and how important it is for instructors to change our pedagogical practices as well:

> Transparency promotes sharing and producing documents online in a seamless way rather than focusing on the mechanics of Web design with HTML code and Web editors. We have seen a significant change from the static Web that required HTML coding to produce and publish information online, to Web 2.0 formats with GUIs for the creation and distribution of content. This change has enhanced transparency by opening the logical or coding layer to users through informal interfaces. As a result, transparency of the user interface has opened up course time, in class and online, for the exploration of disciplinary and interdisciplinary studies, as well as emerging technologies, rather than how to code a Web page. Transparency shifts priorities from technical skills development to critical thinking and collaborative active learning. (Mackey, 2011)

While these ideas immediately engaged Jacobson from the perspective of a faculty-librarian teaching dedicated information literacy courses, it took the author time to decide whether to attempt to use a wiki in her classroom. The circumstances that compelled her to do so in practice are described in the next section.

Team-Based Learning and Its Effect on the Research Guide

The author made a significant change to her course in the fall of 2009 that eventually led her to explore student use of a wiki as well (Jacobson, 2011). She had learned about the team-based learning approach (TBL) pioneered by Larry Michaelsen in the late 1970s at the University of Oklahoma (Michaelsen, Knight, & Fink, 2004) through a workshop at her university's teaching center. TBL uses permanent teams as a key element for student learning, and is highly structured in order to shift the responsibility for learning from the instructor to the student. Committing to this transformative teaching method just a week before the start of a new section of the course, the author used TBL for all but those elements of the course connected to the students' own research guide topics. It did not initially appear problematic that the course had two tracks running at once, as TBL requires both team and individual accountability. However, the disconnection became increasingly obvious to the instructor. She then tried to reap the benefits of group energy and discussion by requiring teams to review the citations and annotations of each team member before they were submitted, in the expectation that they would learn together as mistakes were identified and rectified. However, this intended fix was overly optimistic. Teams usually split into pairs to accomplish the task, which meant that the full potential of the team was lost. The most advanced students within the team would often work together, and thus their advice was lost to students who were struggling. The author was frustrated, but unsure about how to proceed.

After having read Mackey's draft article with its strong support of the learning advantages of a course wiki, and recalling Vivien Zazzau's pioneering use of a wiki within UNL205x, the author introduced team topics for the research guide in spring 2011, which students would present via a wiki, rather than in paper format. She had two goals: to introduce students to evolving communication technologies that they will continue to encounter, and perhaps use, in daily life, and to leverage the benefits of TBL on this aspect of the course. It is important to emphasize that the adoption of the wiki was informed by pedagogical considerations not technological ones. The appeal of using a wiki was based on how it might foster TBL as a collaborative approach to information literacy, not simply to use a Web 2.0 technology in the course.

Topic Selection for Final Projects

Before further discussing the impact of this use of wikis in the course, the change in topic selection should be addressed. Previously, each student was able to select his or her own topic in order to have the opportunity to relate it to work being done in another course. Instructors of UNL205x and UNL206x use this as a way to engage students in the course content: students appreciate the chance to do research in this course that helps them prepare for a project or paper, often for a course within their major. Moving to team topics would eliminate this motivational factor. The hope was that selecting highly relevant or intriguing topics connected with information technology would continue to inspire students.

The author had long used newspaper articles about information and information technology for student engagement purposes. Students arriving early to the first day of class would be given such an article to read before class was underway, and many became absorbed in it. Starting a discussion on the topic during the class was fairly easy. Students were also asked to respond to articles the author posted about in a blog and, later, in Blackboard discussions. Additionally, they were assigned the task of finding articles themselves that related to the course, and engaging the class in the issues raised by the articles, again via electronic media. Expanding upon this element of the course for the final project seemed logical. In addition, it appeared that there was a good chance of successfully incorporating team-based elements with this changed focus.

Implementation of Wiki

Zazzau found that only one of her students had used a wiki, and indeed only seven of 44 had heard of a wiki (Zazzau, 2009, pp. 59–60). Taking into account that several years had passed since Zazzau taught her course, the author was curious to see if the students in her current section had wiki experience that went beyond the use of Wikipedia. As it turned out, none of the 21 students in Jacobson's section had done so. The class was composed of one sophomore, eight juniors, and 12 seniors. Fourteen students were majoring in social science disciplines (including one in information science), 13 in business, three in science, and one in humanities. It appeared that moving the research guide format to the wiki was already teaching students a new facility with a social media tool. This supported one of the key aspects of metaliteracy: to combine information technology and literacy and provide learners with the opportunity to adapt to new technologies. As we will see, it also created a collaborative learning experience for participants.

Incorporating the wiki into the course required new skills on the part of the author as teacher of this section. She used PBWorks, as it had been recommended to her by co-author Mackey. It was also the system used by Zazzau in her course (Zazzau, 2009). Setting up a wiki was not difficult. It was easy to invite students to register on the site, and most students had completed the process before the course began. Nor was it difficult to set up a linked page for each team.

The students seemed to be intrigued by the requirement to present their work on the wiki. While some students were not initially comfortable using it, each team had at least one person who quickly gained a measure of competence, and who then taught others on the team. In this context the practice supported the theory. This approach to TBL through the use of a wiki opened up opportunities for learners to share experiences and gain new knowledge in partnership with one another.

The new assignment, in summary, moved away from individual topics for a paper-based research guide to team topics presented via a wiki. Each team was given a newspaper article and asked to develop their topic from the theme of the article. So the teams were not directly assigned a topic and had some scope for creativity. The articles focused on:

- The use of social media in courtrooms
- Cyberstalking
- Plagiarism in the academic setting
- The need to evaluate information sources

The teams tackling the first three topics selected the focus that the instructor expected, while the fourth team added a twist to their topic: yellow journalism. Students found, cited, and annotated each of the nine sources required individually, and then the team selected one individual's entry for each category that was most appropriate to add to the wiki guide. The team that was researching the use of social media in courtrooms found that they had a difficult time trying to find the more traditional sources, such as a print reference book or other books. Their topic was very new and presented challenges. However, the team members showed a great deal of ingenuity in finding sources. As an example, one student found the *Federal Jury Practice and Instructions* (O'Malley, 2000) for the print reference book.

This process of team selection of sources not only increased the research skills of each team member but also enhanced the opportunity for evaluation and selection of a best source, accompanied by the need to correct or augment the citation and annotation.

The topics intrigued the students, so there was no resistance to the idea of using a preselected topic rather than choosing their own. Actually, students were very enthusiastic about the real-life nature of the topics, and the topics' relevance to the world in which these students live.

After having used the wiki format for three sections of the course at the time of writing, the author is able to make additional observations about the students' reaction to the unconventional final project format. Some students take the novelty in stride and start to play with the features of the platform shortly after being introduced to it. More students, however, are initially anxious or timid. However, after the first week, few showed any reluctance to engage with the tool, and by the end of each course, the author saw no evidence of student avoidance of using the wiki. This may be due to at least two factors: each member's accountability to the team, and increasing familiarity with the features of wikis in PBWorks. One of the features of PBWorks that has had a somewhat inhibiting effect on all team members jumping in and using the wiki is that only one person can edit a section at a time. Because most of the editing to the wiki is done during class, teams have to work out who will do what during this concentrated period of time, and delegate responsibility for the actual work on the site. The next section addresses the success of project revision, based on the author's aspirations.

GOALS FOR THE PROJECT REVISION

The author had a number of goals in mind for the new project format, some related to increased learning through team functioning and others connected to the metaliteracy conception of information literacy. Not only was the creation and sharing of information an important change, but the wiki allowed students to use formats not normally included in the strictly print-based earlier projects, including images that would enhance readers' understanding of the presented material. However, directly addressing literacies other than digital was not a key component of this revision. It was, however, an element that led to changes a semester later in the development of a new course, and that have now become an increasingly important component of the original information literacy course, as described later in this chapter.

The author observed mixed results from this new approach, with some expectations successfully met, but while others moved in the right direction, they were not as effective as the instructor hoped.

Team Functioning

Team spirit in the course in general. The inclusion of the team-based project, which involved some in-class hands-on work almost every time the class met, added to the scope of the teams' responsibilities.

Team cohesiveness in the review process. This goal was met. Each teammate had an equal stake in the final product, so the teams found ways that worked for them to select the items they thought were best for incorporation into the research guide.

Increased accuracy resulting from the review process. Based on knowledge of past research guides, and the ability to track changes on the wiki, students were somewhat more diligent about critiquing teammates' work. However, this issue was complicated by the fact that a new and comprehensive citation guide, CitationFox (http://library.albany .edu/usered/cite/index.html), debuted at the start of the quarter. CitationFox contains citation examples for both MLA and APA styles, and students used its extensive examples as models when writing their citations.

Metaliteracy Components

Enhanced student engagement in current information-related issues. This component of the course was very effectively strengthened. Social, political, and ethical issues related to the changing information world moved from an interesting but peripheral component of the course to its backbone. Student consciousness of important issues increased accordingly.

New wiki-related skills. Based on student feedback, active participation in a wiki was new to most, if not all, of the students in this section of UNL205x. While not all the students will contribute to wikis in the future, they have all had the opportunity to see the ease with which they were able to add material to this web-based communication forum. In addition, editing the work of others was unfamiliar to them. Given the participatory nature of the web, this was a very valuable experience for students.

Once the author had committed to the use of team-based learning, developing and enhancing the work of the teams through course elements was critical. Equally important to the author was enhancing students' information literacy skills for today's world. This section has reviewed how those elements fared in connection with the revised course project. But a third lens through which to examine the initiative is that of transparency, which will be examined in the next section.

Analysis of Wiki Project Based on Elements of Transparency

Mackey's article on the transparency of collaborative Web 2.0 learning environments includes a table (table 1) and ensuing discussion of the common elements of transparent design for open learning (Mackey, 2011). This section of the chapter will analyze the experience of using the wiki-based project over three sections of the course, based on these elements: flexibility, interactivity, fluidity, visualization, collaboration, production, and publishing and distribution. In doing so, the experiences and resulting insights will clarify where possible issues or disconnects may arise, and to plan for their resolution. Others planning to use transparent systems may find this information, which has only gradually become clear to the author, useful for consideration at the outset. Many of the following comments are based on concentrated team work done during the class period, which introduces components that others may not encounter.

Flexibility. Mackey's definition of flexibility indicates that flexibility and ease of use which encourage user participation are necessary for the transparency critical to open education. As already mentioned, the limitation of a PBWorks free wiki of one editor at a time within a group of pages has not fully supported flexibility when all members of a team are working on the wiki at once. This circumstance may not be applicable to others using a wiki with their students. And the ease of use rates much higher, as students generally only have to be shown a feature once, if that, to be able to use it successfully. In comparison, the author is familiar with another wiki system, used at her university, which is so rigid and seemingly impenetrable that those invited to use it refuse to do so, and look for alternatives.

Interactivity. According to Mackey, "transparent systems are highly interactive, enhancing communication and collaboration among users, building cooperation among participants and the sharing of information and ideas." The author has observed a great deal of interactivity in designing the wiki, but somewhat less on the elements that make up the content. This most likely is a result of assignments leading to the team wiki: each student must individually complete each assignment in order to demonstrate mastery of searching, citing, writing, and evaluation skills. Just as with the author's unfulfilled hope that students, when creating a paper-based project, would help to teach their teammates while editing their work, teams often do not critique the work mounted by individual members. This element highlights one of the few areas in which there is tension between the competing goals of individual and team accountability. Regarding the basic design of the wiki, there is indeed enhanced communication and cooperation, as long as all or most of the team members are invested in the wiki. If there is one particularly strong team member, he or she may take over, inhibiting the desired cooperation. The wiki assignment may be designed to avoid this potential issue. For example, each team member might need to claim a particular piece of the wiki as one for which they are responsible.

Fluidity. This element, related to flexibility, acknowledges the fact that the interface is not structured so that users have to work their way around it, and "also reinforces the blurring of traditional boundaries among educational resources." The interface allows users to focus on interaction and production of materials. As the tool used in the author's course, PBWorks scores well in this last regard. Changes in the assignment or course design would allow students to take advantage of other elements of fluidity, such as porous boundaries between resources.

Visualization. Transparent systems encourage users to incorporate visual elements through the ease of use of various media. While PBWorks is not designed as a repository for a particular type of media in the same way as is YouTube or Flickr, it does make it easy to embed links to social networking tools and a variety of media formats, and to add graphics directly. Although this component of the tool was evident to the instructor, it was not to most teams of students. The author hypothesizes that students in her classes have not fully made the leap from the traditional presentation of information to a much richer environment. She attempted to remedy the lack of students' understanding by not only discussing this in class, but also emphasizing in the grading rubric the need to incorporate effective visuals. She also added an assignment requiring the development of a social media tool, and this has enhanced the visual elements of the wikis. However, students have been slow to transition to this aspect of the medium.

Collaboration. Mackey indicates that "transparent systems blur the lines between individual and community, encouraging teamwork and collaboration, extending learning beyond the classroom...." Beyond this element which addresses the work of students in the author's course, he also mentions that open learning negates the model of "one-way delivery modes." This element of open learning has developed fully in the information literacy course's use of the wiki. Students are collaborating on what to add to the wiki, and working on it both during class and on their own time. The author has observed that most, if not all, teams attempt to make sure that each student has work represented on the wiki. While team-based learning completely discards the one-way delivery of information, the wiki extends the shared delivery model in a way entirely compatible with TBL.

Production. This element refers to the ability of users to produce content in a wide variety of formats. Mackey also addresses the incorporation of meta information to identify elements of the content. While meta information has not played a role in the information literacy course's use of the wiki, students are slowly becoming accustomed to producing project components in differing formats. However, this has not yet happened as a result of the wiki, but of explicit assignments requiring students to do so. As noted in the section on visualization, this is one area in which the author continues to struggle. The brief nature of the course—seven two-hour meetings—most likely has an impact on this element.

Publishing and Distribution. Because of the open nature of the products created or embedded in transparent systems, the review and editing of these products may be open as well, although it might be limited to particular individuals or groups. The author has found this aspect of the wiki to be particularly interesting. The first time she used one, she expected that students would want access to the wiki space to be limited to the students in the course. However, the third time she used the wiki, she asked students for permission to show their work at a conference presentation. The students were surprised that the wiki was not already fully available.

Student Perceptions of Wiki

In the last session of the first class in which she used the wiki, the instructor asked students to provide feedback on the use of teams and asked whether the wiki was a valuable part of the learning experience. She also asked students if they thought working on it contributed to their information literacy skill set. Responses about the wiki were mixed, but a majority, 11, felt that it was an important component of the course. Six students included both negative and positive comments, and three saw no value to its use.

The mixed comments focused on the fact that because students had been doing the work individually, the only purpose to the wiki was to organize a team's work. Another student mentioned that because the teams were large, it was difficult to gather around one computer when working on the team's wiki section. Another observed that structuring the appearance of the wiki stole time from the actual content, not understanding that structuring information is actually part of the content. Those who did not feel it was valuable mentioned that it seemed to be redundant, because they had already done individual assignments.

The positive comments focused on putting new skills into practice, motivating students to do their best work to help the team's wiki postings, and providing peer review. A suggestion was made to make the wiki content more interesting by expanding the scope of what teams include in the research guide.

The responses point to aspects of the wiki component that need to be adjusted, but validate the inclusion of the wiki in the course in the eyes of most students. Students recognized the interactive, collaborative, and publication elements connected with open learning. Many students also recognized the value of the additional digital literacy skills they were acquiring, skills that differ from how they typically interact with social media. Redesign of course elements, as well as explicit discussion about the reason for using a wiki and how it facilitates collaboration and evaluation, should allow students to grasp more fully the benefits of the medium.

ADDITIONAL METALITERACY ELEMENTS

The instructor was generally pleased with the impact that the changes in the final project had on a number of elements of the course. The convergence of the wiki-based research guide, founded on the core research-related components and the focus on the impact of information technology made for a more coherent course, with elements that were clearly appreciated by most students in the spring 2011 section. The students gained experience using one social media tool that allowed them to easily share their collaborative work. In addition, they achieved a better understanding of the features of a wiki, including the fact that others can make changes to it. The instructor will continue to use these innovations, with adjustments addressing student concerns, in forthcoming sections of the course. Indeed, she initiated several key changes to the course for the fall 2011 sections that have become important components of the course.

One of these changes involved asking the director of the campus art museum to come speak about visual literacy, as an expanded course component related to the data visualization unit. The second time that she presented this material, we built in an activity that utilized the team structure and really engaged students in deciphering an image. This collaboration has expanded the conception of information on the part of everyone involved.

A second change involved assigning students to explore and create using a second web-based presentation application of their choice. Suggestions included XtraNormal (www.xtranormal.com), Dipity (www.dipity.com), Prezi (http://prezi.com/index), and Splashup (http://splashup.com), but students were free to explore further. They were to use the application to provide information about their team's topic. In the two classes in which this has been assigned, none of the students had created a product using any of these tools, and most had never heard of them, with the exception of XtraNormal. The majority of students so far have selected Prezi for the assignment, though several have used XtraNormal (became unavailable in 2013), and students also discovered Nota (no longer extant) and Animoto (http://animoto.com). I expect that in the future more will already be familiar with Prezi. Many of those who have used it for class have indicated that they really like the tool, and quickly went on to using it for other purposes.

In another recent change, teams needed to add a section to their wiki space that provided the search terms they had used to find information on their topic. They were encouraged to use an online concept mapping tool to do this, such as bubbl.us (https://bubbl.us) or Mindomo (www.mindomo.com), thus enlarging their mastery of web-based applications. This seemingly minor addition actually was designed to address the metacognitive aspect of metaliteracy. The author believed that producing a public list would encourage team members to reflect upon their terms, and alter them as necessary. However, this assignment did not completely fulfill expectations. A colleague suggested asking students to prepare two lists: one of initial search terms and one of revised terms. This was implemented the next time the author taught the course, and proved to encourage student reflection and learning.

Table 6.1 provides a chart of the course objectives in relation to the core metaliteracy learning objectives, as described in the authors' 2011 article (Mackey & Jacobson, 2011), and the corresponding course elements. Although the course goals have not been updated recently, and cover all sections of the course, taught by a number of instructors who had to come to consensus on these common objectives, the chart shows the significant metaliteracy components. There should be a considerable overlap with a contemporary information literacy course, but this exercise is a useful one for highlighting particular areas needing attention. In table 6.1, format type and delivery mode receive extra emphasis, while the course objective "Students will be able to analyze the importance of information-related topics in today's world" is not sufficiently explicit about the key components of personal privacy, information ethics, and intellectual property issues, even though they are a strong theme in the course.

Despite these incremental changes, there are still limitations on what can be accomplished in a one-credit course that also has to teach basic research skills. In searching for solutions, the author thought of two possible approaches. One was very basic: to expand the course to two credits. The second was to develop a new course that would focus on social media and include a collaborative component.

TABLE 6.1

Mapping core metaliteracy learning objectives for UNL205x

UNL205x Learning Objectives	Core Metaliteracy Learning Objectives	Supporting Coursework in UNL205x
Students will be able to:		
Provide a rationale for the idea that not all information is created equal	Evaluate User Feedback as Active Researcher, Create a Context for User-generated Information, Evaluate Dynamic Content Critically	Course readings, team application exercises, blog posts, individual assignments, online research guide creation
Distinguish the differing strengths of various types of information sources	Understand Format Type and Delivery Mode	Course readings, team application exercises, individual assignments, online research guide creation
Locate efficiently a range of appropriate information sources	Understand Format Type and Delivery Mode	Team application exercises, individual assignments, online research guide creation
Critique information sources considering appropriate evaluative elements	Evaluate User Feedback as Active Researcher, Create a Context for User-generated Information, Evaluate	Course readings, team application exercises, blog posts, individual assignments, online research guide creation
Create and share information appropriate to a purpose using web-based applications	Produce Original Content in Multiple Media Formats Share Information in Participatory Environments	Individual web-based discovery and creation projects, team application exercises, online research guide creation
Analyze the importance of information-related topics in today's world	Understand Personal Privacy, Information Ethics, and Intellectual Property Issues	Assigned videos, blog postings, class discussions, online research guide creation

EVOLUTION TOWARD INFORMATION LITERACY AS A METALITERACY

Expanded Information Literacy General Education Course

Having more time with students would allow a stronger metaliteracy component in an information literacy course. Students would still be expected to become familiar with searching and evaluating traditional research tools, but would also have a chance to explore newer information sources, and to make comparisons between the two. The directed exploration of these contrasting but complementary tools would be illuminating to students. They tend to view online social technologies such as Twitter, blogs, and Facebook as leisure time pursuits (Head & Eisenberg, 2009, pp. 15–17). Might they have value when doing research? When would they be particularly useful? How might feedback from others affect one's own evaluation of the sources? In addition, would non-textual information prove valuable to their research? Scholars in particular fields look for visual images or graphic resources as a matter of course. But with enhanced access to such materials, should others be searching for them?

Transforming a one-credit course that meets for 14 contact hours into a two-credit course does not necessarily mean doubling the contact time. A blended course, making use of a variety of Web 2.0 communication media, might best emphasize facets of these tools. Students would continue to work in teams, sharing their work with other members of the class. As in the course described in the next section, Blackboard might be used to supplement other online resources. However, if the goal of the course is to introduce students to actual social media formats, utilizing a proprietary system that will not be a part of their life after college is not beneficial. Instead, "as producers of digital documents, information-literate individuals must make critical choices about the precise media format to articulate ideas and the online site or tool for doing so" (Mackey & Jacobson, 2011). Perhaps, rather than requiring that teams must present their work on a wiki, they themselves might select the best mechanism for communicating their work.

A New, Social Media-Focused Course

This is exactly what happened the following quarter, in an advanced information literacy course. The author and a colleague, Gregory Bobish, collaborated on a new course, UNL489, to delve more deeply into Web 2.0 information sources. This course, also just one credit but liberated from the need to teach students the basics of academic research, provided an excellent canvas for both the instructors and the students to investigate a number of online and social media tools in a structured environment. Team-based learning was used again, though with smaller teams, due to the low enrollment in the course (12 students). Teams were the perfect unit for the assignment the instructors had in mind: a remix project that could take any form. The teams were given leeway in both topic and format, as long as they were both connected with social media. All students in the course, with just two exceptions, had already taken a lower-level information literacy course. The two who had not were assigned a number of online tutorials to bring them up to speed with basic information literacy concepts and skills.

The course's description:

> Explore the burgeoning information environment, examining its cre-
> ation, availability, value, and your participation in creating information
> for others to use. This course will focus on today's technologies and
> their conveyance of information, both in the US and globally. Go beyond
> the knowledge learned in your information literacy general educa-
> tion course, and grapple with challenging issues that affect our lives
> daily. Assignments will culminate in team-based projects, creatively
> presented.

The two instructors were most interested in using this new course as a test bed
for the full panoply of elements found in the broader metaliteracy framework
of information literacy. Active engagement with new media was an essential
component of the course. Students were not only acting as consumers of
information in a wide variety of formats, but also manipulating that information in order to share it with others.

Critical evaluation of the information they found was an integral part of
the work in which students were engaged. Students were consciously aware of
this, and the instructors did not need to emphasize the importance of evaluation as much as in the lower-level, more traditional UNL205x course. The
students were frequently brought up short by the unfamiliarity of using nontraditional forms of information in the academic setting. They tried to identify experts on Twitter, and identify blogs of value to their topics. At times, it
seemed that Bobish and Jacobson were more comfortable with this situation
than were the students, which was surprising.

For their own part, the instructors found it very odd to break from the
mold of the more traditional information literacy class. While they both tend
to incorporate social media and new technologies into their lower-level course
to varying degrees, that course also teaches students basic information literacy concepts, from primary and secondary sources to how to cite information
correctly and issues connected to plagiarism. The sources the students find
to build their research guides are conventional. UNL489 gave the author and
her colleague the license to strike out in completely new directions, exploring
resources in formats that have only come into existence in the last few years.
More details are provided in the following section, written by the author's
co-instructor, Gregory Bobish. The librarian instructors had intertwined
goals, viewing this new course as a testing ground for metaliteracy, but also as
a way to determine which components might be adapted to enhance the basic
information literacy course so that it benefited more from the metaliteracy
aspects of information literacy.

Application Exercises to Enhance Metaliteracy Skills

BY GREGORY BOBISH

When planning for UNL489 began, the author of this section had recently pub-lished an article investigating the pedagogical benefits of using new technolo-gies in teaching information literacy concepts (Bobish, 2011). This article included sample exercises for each of the 87 learning outcomes of the ACRL (2000) *Infor-mation Literacy Competency Standards for Higher Education*, and the instructors were eager to incorporate some of these exercises into their new course, both because they involved aspects of metaliteracy vital to the course and to find out how they would work in practice.

There were a variety of challenges involved in adapting the more general exercises suggested in the original article to the specifics of UNL489. Some of these concerns would most likely be present in any class, such as changes that have taken place in the technologies themselves since the exercises were con-ceived. For instance, the social bookmarking site Delicious.com is mentioned in several exercises, and for a period of time it seemed that this site was going to disappear. Other web-based tools had different interfaces or altered function-ality that would affect the implementation of the sample exercises to varying degrees. Some of the exercises suggested in the article were simply not practical for a course of this short duration. Exercises that required students to follow a Twitter feed or Facebook group over time, examining its evolution and ideally beginning to participate in the discussion, could not be accommodated in the time frame available.

Other challenges arose because the instructors had decided to teach the course using the team-based learning method described earlier in the chapter. Since most of the exercises developed for the ACRL learning outcomes were designed for individual students, they needed to be adapted to fit this teaching methodology, which relies heavily on students working together to reach con-clusions about the material. As the following examples will show, this "challenge" actually expanded the scope of the exercises we used for UNL489 and allowed us to dig deeper into the content at the same time. Please see figures 6.1 and 6.2 for copies of the exercises.

EXERCISE 1

YouTube Video Removal Exercise

This exercise (for ACRL Standard 5, indicator 1, outcome d) as originally con-ceived reads:

> **d.** Demonstrates an understanding of intellectual property, copy-right, and fair use of copyrighted material

Media-sharing: Students find videos that have been removed from YouTube for intellectual property reasons. Students also attempt to find instances where embedding has been disabled, and discuss why this might happen. It interferes with advertising revenue, for one thing, as the band OK Go discovered when their record label disallowed embedding of their videos. Show examples of available copyrighted material that have not been removed, or that is even promoted by the creators, and discuss why the sharing might be beneficial. Have students present arguments either online or in class on both sides of the issue. Why is copyright important? Why is fair use important? How can a middle ground be reached? (Creative Commons is one possibility, but allow students to brainstorm before giving them this answer.) (Bobish, 2011)

FIGURE 6.1

YouTube video removal exercise

Name: _____

Team name: _____

This exercise deals with videos removed from YouTube due to copyright or other violations.

1. Individually, read the "Why was my video removed?" section of the Electronic Frontier Foundation website at www.eff.org/issues/intellectual-property/guide-to-youtube-removals. Then read the short section near the bottom of the page titled "Do I Have a Good Defense? Is my video a fair use?"

2. Individually, find a video on YouTube that has been, or should be, removed due to copyright violation(s). Determine who the original copyright holder is, if possible. (If it is a song, music video, or TV show, a web search of the title will often show who originally released it.) Write the URL for the video and the name of the original copyright holder here:

3. In your team, choose one video to focus on, and come up with at least 3 possible fair use defenses for keeping the video on YouTube. List them here:

    1.

    2.

    3.

---

4. In your team, if the video has not been taken down, consider why the copyright holder might not have pursued the issue. List your team's best reason here:

5. In your team, present and defend your reasons for keeping the video up.

The first major change we made to this exercise was to include a brief reading from the Electronic Frontier Foundation's website dealing with the issues surrounding removal of videos from YouTube, and how fair use principles might or might not apply (www.eff.org/issues/intellectual-property/guide-to-youtube -removals). This was done because although students in UNL489 were required to have taken a lower-level information literacy course or to have completed a series of online tutorials on important information literacy concepts, it was essential that they had a basic understanding of how copyright and fair use concepts related to the specific situation being examined in the exercise.

The next change involved what we were asking students to locate. The original exercise asked students to find videos that had been removed from YouTube for copyright reasons. We retained this element, but added the task of attempting to identify the original copyright owner. This was done to introduce the point, relevant to the course's final project (described below), that when remixing or otherwise using existing content, one of the many challenges is that the copyright owner might be difficult or impossible to find, even if the person posting the new video has the best intentions of getting permission.

These first two parts of the exercise were completed individually, and the changes were made mainly to more directly address the content of the course. The changes described below were necessary for the exercise to function in the team-based learning environment.

Once each individual had found a YouTube video that had been removed or that they felt should have been removed, they shared their videos with the other members of their team. Teams then chose one video to work on together, usually the video with the most obvious copyright problems. Teams' first task was to identify three possible fair use defenses for keeping the video available. If the selected video had not been taken down, the team was asked to discuss why it was still available given the copyright problems involved, and to decide as a team on the one best reason for this. Teams then presented the video to the class and defended their reasons for keeping the videos available. These changes essentially made the exercise more specific, requiring teams to state their strongest arguments rather than simply discussing the issues in a more informal way as suggested by the original article. The fact that teams had to defend their arguments before the rest of the class made intra-team discussion more focused and at the same time provided students with first-hand experience of how difficult it can be to sort out even the simplest of copyright questions.

EXERCISE 2

Primary Information: Finding Experts via Blogs and Twitter

The original exercise (for ACRL Standard 2, indicator 3, outcome d) reads:

> **d.** Uses surveys, letters, interviews, and other forms of inquiry to retrieve primary information
>
> **Micro-blogging:** Have students find people relevant to their topic who use Twitter, and begin to follow them. What are they currently doing/saying? Are the tweets useful on their own, or do they lead to more detailed primary information? (Bobish, 2011)

FIGURE 6.2
Finding experts via blogs and Twitter

Name: _____

Team name: _____

The point of this exercise is to find experts on your team's research topic who have blogs or Twitter accounts, and to follow them throughout the course to see what they are currently interested in. You may also be alerted to resources that you can use for your final remix project as these experts post about them.

1. Brainstorm with your team for 1–2 minutes. What kind of people might be talking/writing about our topic in blog/Twitter format?

2. Individually, start searching for blogs and Twitter accounts of people who are researching in your field. Use Google Blog search, or regular Google, or anything else you can think of. Note the names/blogs/Twitter handles of the people you find and consider which ones you'd like to bring to your team.

3. In your team, share the blogs/Twitter accounts you've found and decide on three of them that you'd like to post to your wiki as a team.

    1.

    2.

    3.

4. Using the handout, and asking questions if necessary, embed the Twitter accounts or blog RSS feeds into your team's wiki page so that whenever you log into the wiki, you'll see the latest postings from your experts.

5. Teams report out using whiteboards:
    a. Best expert with blog or Twitter feed
    b. How you found them
    c. One interesting fact about either the expert or your team's process of finding them or getting the source embedded into your blog

Due to the length of the course, and to the way teams were working in anticipation of the final project, we expanded this exercise so that students were not only beginning to follow experts, but were also examining previous tweets/blog entries to see if there was already a base of information to draw from.

Initially, teams had one to two minutes to brainstorm about who might be using the Twitter and blog formats to talk about their topics. Then, in a way similar to the copyright exercise above, they had some time to individually search for Twitter accounts and blogs to bring back to their teams for discussion. Teams were then required to decide on three Twitter accounts or blogs that they would use as ongoing information sources for the course, and ultimately for their final project.

Probably the most important change we made to this exercise was to require each team to embed the Twitter or blog feed into the team's wiki page, so that every time they visited the wiki page, they would see new information from the experts they had identified. In addition to providing teams with up-to-the-minute information on their topics, this gave each team a chance to learn the technical skills necessary to accomplish the task and to gain a deeper understanding of some of the technologies whose impact was the focus of the course.

Since the original exercise examples were somewhat generalized, much of our work in adapting them to UNL489 involved finding ways to inject more specific course content into their framework, while still respecting their pedagogical intent. Interestingly, we were able to expand the content covered by each exercise by making them more focused, as when the second exercise not only exposed students to the use of Twitter and blogs as sources of information but also provided them with knowledge of tools that they would end up using themselves later in the course. By altering or adding to the original exercise examples, we were able to get students more involved in using these technologies, rather than simply looking at what others were doing with them. This practical experience was not only one of the core goals of the course, but also prepared them for the hands-on work that would be necessary to succeed on their final project.

Remix Final Project

Although students viewed two remixes early in the quarter, and had been given a grading rubric for the remix, as the end of the course drew near, it appeared that the teams still were not completely clear about what they might produce. Bobish therefore wrote this description for students and posted it to Blackboard:

What is a remix?

(at least for the purposes of this course)

General points:

Be creative and enjoy the process—this is intended to be experimental, so try things you haven't done before. We'd like them to be well-done, but we're more concerned with the ideas than with the production quality.

We're not listing specific examples, because the goal of the project is for your group to decide how you will interpret the idea of a remix in terms of your topic. If you want to look at examples, you can google remix and find as many as you want, but be careful not to let the examples you find limit you to using their specific techniques. Leverage whatever expertise your group members have, and let that guide what you decide to do.

Remix specifics:

1. It is not just a collection of sources. A collection of sources is a bibliography, not a remix.
2. It is *composed of* multiple sources, in a variety of formats. You are actually re-using material you have found, rather than (or perhaps in addition to) creating your own content. You are transforming this content and using it in a way other than how it was intended to be used.
3. Your team's original sources should be cut up, and relevant pieces of them should be combined in some way (the particular way is up to you). Except in unusually long remixes, you won't be using any one source in its entirety.
4. The choice of the pieces and of how they are arranged and represented should make a point. That point should be your team's thesis statement.
5. Keep track of your team's process. Why did you end up creating what you did? What were some alternative options you thought about and why did you reject them? What obstacles did you face and how did you overcome them? Questions like these will not only help you focus your remix, but will also be useful as you present your remix to the class.

This clarification aided the teams, who then went into high gear. The three teams took very different approaches to their remix project. One team used a Facebook page as a launching point for a variety of resources connected to mobile devices and the social networking subculture. While this was not quite what the instructors had in mind as a remix, the students created a number of resources, using tools learned in class, to give a multi-faceted look at their topic. These resources included a Wordle, two uses of Dipity timelines, and a short remix of related YouTube videos.

Another team, one that contained a computer science major, created a video as their remix about the impact of Twitter. This was a more classic example of a remix, and was made possible because of his expertise.

The third team created the most unusual project, a physical book, yet one that called upon knowledge of various literacies (Minaut, 2011). The team selected R. L. Minaut as the pseudonym for the author, as in "really mean it." The topic was anonymity 2.0, and the web of materials in the volume includes a QR code that leads to an online dating service that does not safeguard clients' online personae, a take-off on *Strangers on a Train*, titled "Strangers on the Internet," and a section highlighting the increasingly organized nature of online gossip. One of the students on the team actually published the book, complete with ISBN, through Amazon's CreateSpace program (https://www.createspace.com), fitting well with the metaliteracy concept of producing and sharing information in the traditional publication mode, yet its contents are very different from what is found in a traditional printed volume.

EXPANDING DISCOMFORT, EXPANDING KNOWLEDGE

Information literacy skills focusing on the printed format of information would not be adequate for interpreting and evaluating the remix products produced by the students in this course. This applies, of course, not only to students who are learning, but to the teachers, who had different levels of experience with social media and Web 2.0. Yet both were learning constantly throughout the course, trying to stay one step ahead of the students when possible, but also acknowledging that it is appropriate to learn from them as well. Resources and applications on the web evolve constantly, and it is hard to stay up to date. And familiarity with what is available is simply the first step—then one must learn to use the tools. It is a daunting task to those of us who felt secure in their information literacy until just recently.

Looking back to just over a decade ago, to the turn of the 21st century, it is rather astonishing to realize what was, at the time, a cutting-edge course, would be hopelessly outdated today, in its original guise. Librarians have become blasé at the radically restructured information environment as consumers of that information and its attendant technology. The changes have been incremental, even though the increments are exceedingly short. The standards and accepted knowledge about the information environment, which instruction librarians valued at that time, have had to expand to adequately address today's dynamic online resources. Just as information literacy has indubitably altered to encompass new literacies and new modes of information production and sharing, those who help others to become more fully information literate have had to adapt to the changed information environment. We are teachers, but we have also become learners, which is not always the most comfortable situation. But learn we must, or we will have less and less to teach others.

REFERENCES

Association of College and Research Libraries. (2000). *Information literacy competency standards for higher education*. American Library Association. www.ala.org/ala/mgrps/divs/acrl/standards/standards.pdf

Bobish, Greg. (2011). Participation and pedagogy: Connecting the social web to ACRL learning outcomes. *The Journal of Academic Librarianship, 37*(1), p. 54–63.

Head, Alison J., & Eisenberg, Michael B. (2009). Lessons learned: How college students seek information in the digital age. http://projectinfolit.org/publications

Jacobson, Trudi E. (2004). Meeting information literacy needs in a research setting. In I. F. Rockman (Ed.), *Integrating information literacy into the higher education curriculum* (pp. 133–164). San Francisco, CA: Jossey-Bass.

Jacobson, Trudi E. (2011). Team-based learning in an information literacy course. *Communications in Information Literacy, 5*(2), 82–101.

Mackey, Thomas P. (2011). Transparency as a catalyst for interaction and participation in open learning environments. *First Monday, 16*(10).

Mackey, Thomas P., & Jacobson, Trudi E. (2011). Reframing information literacy as a metaliteracy. *College & Research Libraries, 72*(1), 62–78.

Michaelsen, Larry K., Knight, Arletta B., & Fink, L. Dee. (Eds.). (2004). *Team-based learning: A transformative use of small groups in college teaching*. Sterling, VA: Stylus.

Minaut, R. L. (2011). *Anonymity 2.0: Flooding the marketplace, the needle in the haystack, and the encyclopedia of crumbs*. Class project.

O'Malley, Kevin F. (2000). *Federal jury practice and instructions*. St. Paul, MN: West Group.

University at Albany, State University of New York. (2000). Undergraduate bulletin, 2000–2001. http://replay.web.archive.org/20010219002540/www.albany.edu/undergraduate_bulletin/general_education.html

University at Albany, State University of New York. (2002). Undergraduate bulletin, 2002–2003. http://replay.web.archive.org/20021216021103/www.albany.edu/undergraduate_bulletin/general_education.html#communication

Zazzau, Vivien. E. (2009). Exploring wikis in a library credit course. *Communications in information literacy, 3*(1), 58–64.

7

Exploring Digital Storytelling from a Metaliteracy Perspective

I N THIS CLOSING CHAPTER WE ANALYZE AN ONLINE COURSE IN digital storytelling from the lens of our metaliteracy model. This chapter compares the core metaliteracy learning objectives with the expected outcomes of this online course in the humanities. While digital storytelling was not initially designed with information literacy in mind, it embodies the learner-centered and metacognitive principles of metaliteracy, especially related to the idea of the reflective learner as producer of original information. This case study provides a practical model for instructors to apply metaliteracy across the curriculum and not only in courses that explicitly require specific information competencies. This chapter is informed by the experience and observations of one of the book's authors, Tom Mackey, who taught several sections of the course from 2009 to 2012 at the Center for Distance Learning (CDL) at Empire State College, SUNY.

This chapter starts by describing the Institutional Context for this course, as part of the successful online program at Empire State College, the largest single provider of online learning in the SUNY system. The next section, Digital Storytelling, describes this interdisciplinary and emerging area of study.

We discuss the overall Learning Design of the course, with an emphasis on the curriculum development process at CDL, and how this course evolved over several years. We also describe a freely available digital storytelling rubric that was repurposed as an OER used by the instructor and students. This leads to an examination of the learning objectives for this course and the Web 2.0 tools applied to support the objectives and encourage active participation and distribution of original digital content. We close this chapter with Mapping the Metaliteracy Model to Digital Storytelling to show how effectively the core metaliteracy principles align with the learning objectives for this course.

INSTITUTIONAL CONTEXT

SUNY Empire State College

In 1971 Empire State College was established as a nonresidential university college to provide open education to a wide range of learners with diverse backgrounds and interests. Ernest L. Boyer, renowned education scholar and former chancellor of SUNY, envisioned a nontraditional institution that meets students where they are through flexible approaches to learning. This radical idea reflected the era of the early 1970s and was focused on overcoming traditional barriers to higher education. As outlined in *A Prospectus for A New University College: Objectives, Process, Structure and Establishment*, the original vision for this college "transcends constraints of space, place, and time" and "represents an expression of faith in a more hopeful future, not yet shaped or perceived, in which higher education can open new paths of learning and fulfillment" (SUNY, 1971, p. 2). This idea for a flexible nonresidential institution was accomplished through a primary emphasis on the individual in pursuit of self-paced "individual student learning" that takes place "with the guidance and counseling of master teachers" (p. 2). This approach evolved over time into a mentor-learner model that guides students through a series of individual choices and multiple forms of study options that are independent and collaborative, as well as face-to-face, blended, and online.

The college encourages self-directed learning as part of the degree planning process to create a unique educational journey for every learner. This includes transcript review, to integrate previous study at other institutions, and prior learning assessment (PLA), to credential college-level learning gained through life experience. This distributed college format includes a network of regional center locations and smaller units throughout New York State, international partnerships in Lebanon, Greece, and the Czech Republic, and a successful online program that extends the reach of the institution beyond any geographic boundary. Empire State College is a part of SUNY, the largest public university system in the United States. SUNY includes 64 campuses throughout New York State, including community colleges, four-year comprehensives, and four research centers.

Benke, Davis, and Travers (2012) argue that "as a game changer and leader in open learning for the past forty years, SUNY Empire State College is undergoing a new era of innovation as it harnesses the affordances of emerging technologies to enhance its unique mentor-learning model and its expertise in assessing learning acquired outside the walls of the ivory tower" (p. 149). This new era means that in addition to several hallmarks of progressive education, such as guided independent study, group study, residencies, and online learning, the college has also expanded blended learning and open learning opportunities, including the development of MOOCs. In all of the diverse modes of study offered at the college, the learner is always at the center of individualized degree planning, working closely with a mentor.

At Empire State College, the curriculum itself is open because learners make decisions about the development of their degree concentrations. According to Sir John Daniel (2011), "Empire State College allows students to invent their own courses and programmes according to their interests and needs." In addition to the design of individualized degree plans, students are encouraged to make choices about the mode of study and to develop learning opportunities based on their own academic goals. Sir John Daniel argues:

> These dimensions of openness that were introduced by the UK Open University and Empire State College remained the principal expressions of openness in higher education for the next thirty years. Two dimensions—open admissions and distance learning—were widely copied and there are now millions of students in open universities around the world.

This combination of open and online learning allows the college to reach students throughout New York State, in every state in the country, and internationally. This approach has been appealing to adult learners who return to school after years of building a career or while raising a family. According to Benke, Davis, and Travers (2012) the mentor-learner model is central to this process and promotes active engagement in learning design that is ultimately rewarding and empowering beyond any particular study. The authors argue, "Learners note that although the degree planning and prior learning assessment processes are difficult, they develop self-awareness as learners and the capacity to continue their learning in work and other educational settings." This self-awareness embodies a metacognitive approach to higher education that makes learners cognizant of the pedagogical strategy and modality for each study, how all of the studies fit within a coherent degree plan, as well as how prior learning and transcript credit are assessed and formulated into the overall degree. Such flexibility and student involvement in the process is not typical at most learning organizations but is central to the philosophy of this progressive institution.

CDL

Empire State College has been a leader in distance education since the mid- to late 1970s. CDL was established in 1979 when two programs at the college combined: Extended Programs and the Center for Independent Study. According to Richard Bonnabeau, Extended Programs offered "degrees based on independent study materials and individualized learning contracts" and the SUNY Independent Study Program provided "modified British Open University materials to students scattered around the college and to students at other SUNY campuses" (1996, p. 83). CDL was initially a print-based program that experimented with a range of technologies in the 1980s and 1990s, such as closed circuit television, video conferencing, and Internet discussions via CAUCUS (Lefor, Benke, & Ting, 2001). By 2005, CDL had moved entirely to the web with a primary emphasis on asynchronous online learning. This led to considerable growth, to the point where it now accounts for half of the enrollments for the entire college.

Currently CDL offers nearly 500 online studies, including more than 450 structured content courses and multiple varieties of Independent Study and Educational Planning in which students learn the process of designing their unique degree plans. As an online program that emerged from the flexible and innovative Empire State College, it is philosophically grounded in the learner-centered, mentor-learner principles of the institution. All of the online students work closely with a mentor to design their degrees in the 12 areas of study offered throughout the college. As part of the degree planning process, students write a rationale essay that describes their degree plan and how the courses, transcript credit, and PLA fit together cohesively to constitute their concentration. This experience is metacognitive because students carefully reflect on their own education and the choices they make, rather than simply select courses in a traditional degree program. As part of their rationale essay, students write about the connections they plan to make in their degree and in future goals beyond college.

CDL's online courses are based on constructivist principles and promote active learning, collaboration, and problem-based learning. The courses include content from a variety of sources, including instructor commentary, required readings (including books ordered through an online bookstore), and external links to open resources. But the courses are not focused on memorizing content and instead emphasize online discussions, writing, and teamwork.

Courses are capped at 20 to 22 students, providing an individualized approach to online learning while promoting interaction and collaboration with peers. Students are encouraged to exchange ideas about course modules in online discussions as a primary activity and to engage in social learning through group work. The courses are enhanced with media resources as appropriate, such as digital images, virtual timelines, blogs, wikis, web-based multimedia, and explorations in mobile media. For instance, the interdisciplinary course The Future of Being Human integrates Second Life as an immersive activity to explore virtual identity (http://commons.esc.edu/smatresources).

In addition to online courses, CDL has taken a lead in open learning initiatives, offering the first ever MOOC in the SUNY system, Creativity and Multicultural Communication (www.cdlprojects.com/cmc11blog). CDL mentors Betty Hurley-Dasgupta and Carol Yeager developed this connectivist MOOC, or cMOOC, inspired by the work of George Siemens and Stephen Downes. According to Yeager and Hurley-Dasgupta, their approach to the MOOC format is "based on the theory of connectivism and the practice of Personal Learning Environments and Networked Knowledge that utilize metaliteracy within the connective Personal Learning Environments (PLEs)" (2012, p. 63). This first MOOC offered by CDL reached an international audience and was available to learners from Empire State College who completed this study for course credit. Hurley-Dasgupta and Yeager followed the first cMOOC with VizMath, an interdisciplinary exploration of mathematics (http://math.cdlprojects .com). The authors of this book, Tom Mackey and Trudi Jacobson, developed a Metaliteracy MOOC (http://metaliteracy.cdlprojects.com) in fall 2013 using the same connectivist model developed by the Hurley-Dasgupta and Yeager team. The cMOOCs have been developed outside the learning management system (LMS) and demonstrate that the open and online learning environment takes many forms while providing students with unique ways to pursue learning in collaboration with others. This sense of innovation exemplifies Empire State College as a learner-centered institution open to exploring novel ways to connect with students using a variety of emerging technologies.

College-Level Learning Goals

In 2011 Empire State College embarked on a college-wide planning process that developed the *Academic Plan 2011–2015* for the entire institution (Empire State College, 2011a). As part of this activity, the college defined seven learning goals for all students: active learning, breadth and depth of knowledge, social responsibility, communication, critical thinking and problem solving, quantitative literacy, and a combined approach to information and digital media literacy (Empire State College, 2011b, p. 8). This redefinition of information and digital media literacy integrates elements of both frameworks to: "Critically access, evaluate, understand, create and share information using a range of collaborative technologies to advance learning, as well as personal and professional development" (Empire State College, 2011b, p. 8). As this description of the united learning goal demonstrates, Empire State College supports the critical thinking dimension of information literacy (critically access, evaluate, and understand) with the learner-as-producer, or metaliterate aspects of digital media literacy (create and share information with collaborative technology). As part of the larger academic plan for the entire institution, the learning goals provide a comprehensive set of objectives for all learners across the college. It is within this context that an interdisciplinary course in digital storytelling plays an important role in showing how these goals and objectives are met through the creative production and distribution of learner-centered narratives.

DIGITAL STORYTELLING

Digital storytelling is an emerging area of study and pedagogical approach to teaching and learning with digital media. Two of the early founders of this movement are Joe Lambert and Dana Atchley, who started collaborating in the 1980s (Tucker, 2006, p. 54). According to Lambert, "Digital Storytelling uses computers to create media-rich stories and the internet to share those stories creating communites [sic] of common concern on a global scale" (www .nextexit.com/dap/whatis.html). After meeting in 1986, Lambert expressed interest in an idea Atchley had for an interactive stage show that incorporated multimedia to advance the narrative called *Next Exit* (www.nextexit.com/dap/conv1.html). This project led to a worldwide tour in the 1990s and is currently available as an interactive website with featured stories that were developed for those performances (www.nextexit.com/drivein/drivein_01.html). This approach to mixing media for narrative development can be traced back to the performance art experiments of Laurie Anderson in the 1970s (www.pbs.org/art21/artists/laurie-anderson) and to the eclectic pop art and media explorations of Andy Warhol in the 1960s. Of course the origins of storytelling can be traced back to oral traditions that predate both writing and print.

Digital storytelling has evolved with technologies and engages learners in diverse media, writing, and inventive narrative structures. According to ELI:

> Digital storytelling is the practice of combining narrative with digital content, including images, sound, and video, to create a short movie, typically with a strong emotional component. Sophisticated digital stories can be interactive movies that include highly produced audio and visual effects, but a set of slides with corresponding narration or music

> constitutes a basic digital story. Digital stories can be instructional, per-
> suasive, historical, or reflective. The resources available to incorporate
> into a digital story are virtually limitless, giving the storyteller enormous
> creative latitude. (http://net.educause.edu/ir/library/pdf/ELI7021.pdf)

As this definition indicates, digital storytelling combines personal narrative
and multimedia elements to tell a persuasive narrative. This expansion of traditional storytelling in virtual settings integrates a range of media formats
and is not limited to online audio and video. Today's social media environment features resources for photo galleries, virtual pin boards, immersive
virtual environments such as Second Life, interactive presentation tools such
as Prezi, wikis, and blogs that all offer potential for creating individual and
collaborative stories.

Alexander and Levine (2008) defined "Web 2.0 Storytelling" as "the telling
of stories using Web 2.0 tools, technologies, and strategies" (p. 42). According
to the authors, "Web 2.0 storytelling is a rapidly evolving genre, developing as
new platforms emerge and moving in pace with the creativity of the human
mind" (p. 56). This suggests unlimited capacity for new approaches to this
innovative format in personal and pedagogical contexts. In his book *The New
Digital Storytelling*, Bryan Alexander described the genre as "telling stories
with digital technologies" (2011, p. 3). He expands this definition further:

> Digital stories are currently created using nearly every digital device in
> an ever-growing toolbox. They are experienced by a large population.
> Their creators are sometimes professionals, and also amateurs. They
> can be deeply personal, or posthumanly otherwise, fiction and nonfic-
> tion, brief or epic, wrought from a single medium or sprawling across
> dozens. We are living in a time of immense creativity, with new oppor-
> tunities for creators appearing nearly every day. Several decades of
> energetic digital experimentation have borne fruit, and yet, in the larger
> historical frame, still these are early days of innovation. (2011, p. 3)

As Alexander points out, this is a time of incredible creativity and innovation,
brought about in many ways by open social technologies that have democratized the production and sharing of original and repurposed digital information. We have seen the proliferation of individual and collaborative narratives
on YouTube, Facebook, blogs, wikis, photo sharing sites, and through interactive gaming applications. Mobile technologies are further advancing the
creative production of personal narratives for capturing images, video, and
sound on the fly, and then producing and publishing to personal and shared
spaces.

As a genre grounded in the oral tradition of sharing ideas, digital storytelling offers much potential for inspiring the creative use of social technologies for formal and informal learning. This chapter describes an online course

about digital storytelling, but these approaches could be applied to studies in other disciplines as well. These techniques are practiced by independent media makers inspired to create and communicate a good story using freely available resources.

LEARNING DESIGN

The design of the Digital Storytelling course at SUNY Empire State College has progressed over several years and has recently undergone major revisions to integrate the use of Web 2.0 resources. In many ways the course has evolved with the web itself, from a static Web 1.0 perspective, with an emphasis on HTML coding, digital imaging, and file transfer protocol (FTP), to a dynamic Web 2.0 approach that features blogs, microblogs, and the design of multimedia projects with open resources. This allows students to learn both the theory and practice of digital storytelling. The course was first developed by Hilary McLellan who defined digital storytelling as "the art and craft of exploring different media and software applications to communicate stories in new and powerful ways using digital media" (2006, p. 66). The initial course design was informed by McLellan's approach and it has evolved over time to reflect changes in social media. In recent versions of the course, both Phylise Banner and Nicola Marae Allain contributed significant revisions based on Web 2.0 design principles.

Course development at CDL is a collaborative process that integrates the content expertise of faculty teams and colleagues at the center. CDL is organized into four interdisciplinary faculty teams: Business Management and Economics (BME), Science Math and Technology (SMAT), Social Science (Team Social), and Humanities. All new courses are proposed by faculty and reviewed by the academic team, and then submitted to a center wide Curriculum Committee. Once approved, courses are then placed into production, with faculty as content experts and Curriculum and Instructional Designers (CIDs) as co-developers, with a particular emphasis on technology and design. CDL faculty members are mentors and also play an additional role as Academic Area Coordinators (ACs) for concentration areas within college wide Areas of Study (AOS). The ACs oversee these curricular clusters, work closely with adjunct faculty, and make decisions regarding major and minor revisions, as well as new course development. Digital Storytelling, for instance, was a legacy course developed under the direction of an AC that then underwent two major revisions to reflect updates in changing technologies. This allowed the course to stay current and evolve as the media landscape altered, bringing forth opportunities to incorporate open resources for producing and sharing individual and collaborative narratives.

As the course advanced over time, it has promoted self-directed and collaborative activities using freely available Web 2.0 tools. The current AC for this course, Nicola Marae Allain (formerly Nicola Marae Martinez), who has expertise in digital media and digital learning environments, described the overall design of this study in the following way:

> Students in Digital Storytelling master at least one new tool every two to three weeks. In a distance learning environment, they do not receive one-to-one tutorial assistance as is common in the laboratory setting. Rather, they are directed to seek tutorial assistance in social media spaces such as YouTube, how-to.com and other World Wide Web resources that provide superb step-by-step instructions in video and with screencasts using a wide range of the very tools students are learning to master. In addition, digital media online courses have a student café in which students help each other learn some of the more difficult aspects of using Twitter and other social media tools. (Martinez, 2011, pp. 15–16)

Learners gain knowledge about the theory of digital storytelling while acquiring practical experience with several technology applications to produce their own projects. They examine resources as independent learners and also work together to solve problems if technical concerns arise. This interactive setting is reinforced through specific learning objectives and the adaptation of a digital storytelling rubric.

Learning Objectives

The Digital Storytelling course features six learning objectives that range from learning the theory and practice of the topic, to learning about new Web applications, to understanding effective design, to critically assessing digital projects. These objectives developed over time with input from the primary course developers Hilary McLellan, Phylise Banner, and Nicola Marae Allain. The complete list of objectives follows:

1. Students will learn about the theory and practice of digital storytelling across a range of media.
2. Students will learn about different applications of digital storytelling that have emerged and how these applications can be adapted to their professional work as well as their personal lives and those of their clients.
3. Students will learn about personal storytelling and how it can be implemented with digital media.

4. Students will learn about effective digital design.
5. Students will learn about new tools and frameworks for storytelling with digital media.
6. Students will be able to critically assess digital storytelling projects that they encounter.

The learning objectives for this course are advanced through several assignments: online course discussions (20%), virtual field trip discussions (20%), and story projects (60%). For instance, the first objective to "learn about the theory and practice of digital storytelling across a range of media" is addressed with course readings about the theory of the topic, virtual field trips to media sites that exemplify effective digital storytelling, and the development of several learner-centered digital media projects. Students are exposed to theoretical issues related to digital storytelling through readings from experts in the field, such as Bryan Alexander, and by watching online materials, such as the TED TALK with Jonathan Harris titled "The Web as Art" (www.ted.com/talks/jonathan_harris_collects_stories.html), and then conversing with peers about the readings and video in the online discussion. The asynchronous discussions provide opportunities for students to share reflections about the course content and to react to the observations of peers.

The second objective related to "different applications of digital storytelling" and how they are applied in personal and professional situations is reinforced through the web-based applications that are used by students to create their digital projects, and in how they discuss the context of this work in the LMS and with their blog postings. Students learn about several applications through their own creation of digital narratives and reflect on how the tools and concepts could be applied in a number of settings, both personal and professional. Students in the course share insights from their own individual and work life experience in the online discussions and blogs as related to major themes. Many of the adult learners in the course have a breadth of experience to call upon when exchanging ideas about ways that digital storytelling is applied in different settings. They share thoughts about how they would implement these tools in their current work environment or describe similar resources already in use.

The focus of the third objective on "personal storytelling and how it can be implemented with digital media" is met through many aspects of the course, including virtual field trips that provide convincing examples of personal narrative. For instance, one of the online journeys includes StoryCorps, which is described as "an independent nonprofit whose mission is to provide people of all backgrounds and beliefs with the opportunity to record, share, and preserve the stories of our lives" (http://storycorps.org/about). As noted at the Story-Corps website, this resource "has collected and archived more than 45,000 interviews with nearly 90,000 participants" (http://storycorps.org/about) and provides access to stories via the StoryCorps Listen page (http://story corps.org/listen) and NPR's *Morning Edition* (www.npr.org/series/4516989/storycorps). Students learn about personal narratives by studying the genre and listening to storytellers who express ideas with online media. They apply the theory of digital storytelling through dialogue with peers and with their own practice developing media projects. As part of the course requirements they also create and maintain an ongoing blog that offers their unique reflections as well.

The virtual field trips also support learning objective four related to "effective digital design" because each online journey includes high-quality web resources related to digital storytelling, as shown in the Interactive Narratives site (www.interactivenarratives.org). Samples of effective design are also available to students by accessing the We Tell Stories site (www.wetell stories.co.uk) featuring interactive stories such as "The 21 Steps" by Charles Cumming (www.wetellstories.co.uk/stories/week1). The inventive exemplars of the genre provide a creative context for students to gain insights about the process and to envision how their own ideas could take shape in digital forms. This objective is further supported by the virtual field trips because students describe their response to each journey in the online discussions, sharing specific observations and insights with other students. By doing so, the engagement with the digital environment becomes a collaborative process that supports a shared understanding of the issues involved. This approach is counter to the memorization of facts found in traditional settings and instead reinforces the social contexts for learning.

The fifth learning objective promotes "new tools and frameworks for storytelling with digital media" and is encouraged through the virtual field trips, as well as the development of several digital story projects using openly available resources on the web. Students learn new tools and approaches to storytelling by experiencing digital stories online, as well as through their own creation and sharing of original digital narratives designed for the course. This is an empowering process that shows students how to adapt to emerging technologies by learning a set of story tools for their own original productions. Students also gain insights about different frameworks for making digital stories, such as how to design an effective storyboard for translating creative ideas into tangible projects.

The sixth learning objective "to critically assess digital storytelling projects that they encounter" promotes a metacognitive component by requiring students to answer the same set of reflective questions throughout the term. This objective is also met through the other course elements, including the virtual field trips, the production of original digital projects, the review of stories created by peers, and ongoing interaction in the online discussions.

One central aspect of this critical thinking ability and metacognitive reflection is learning how to apply a digital storytelling rubric to the assessment of these projects. Throughout the course, students are asked to apply a rubric that was adapted from an open and freely available resource at the University of Houston (http://digitalstorytelling.coe.uh.edu/archive/pdfs/samplerubric.pdf). Learners use this tool to evaluate the virtual field trips and also to comment on the work of peers as the course develops. This process of ongoing reflection informs the design of their own original projects as well, providing opportunities for the students to create digital stories based on what they learn by using this structured analytical tool. As noted by Martinez (2011) this open resource supports critical thinking because "one way to foster critical analysis, evaluation and thinking is through the implementation of carefully designed rubrics that allow students to participate in peer critique and evaluate digital media artifacts" (p. 16). Martinez (2011) illustrated the ways this tool supports independent and collaborative learning:

> For example, in the Digital Storytelling course, students apply a digital storytelling rubric to the review and evaluation of professional digital stories, as well as those of their peers. The rubric used in CDL studies was adapted from a tool created to evaluate digital stories at the University of Houston. A wonderful side effect of applying this rubric to the analysis of different story projects is that students gain a strong grasp of commonly accepted criteria for the creation of digital stories as they evaluate them. It helps them understand where their own stories fit within the spectrum of other digital narratives. (Martinez, 2011, p. 16)

In this context, the rubric is not just a tool used by instructors to evaluate student work but rather an active resource for learners to expand their critical thinking related to how they analyze digital storytelling projects. This process recognizes the shifting role of learner as teacher in this environment by supporting peer review using the rubric, and by asking students to assess websites and media resources with the same analytical tool usually used by the instructor. It also provides an essential metacognitive component of self-reflection by encouraging students to think about their own learning using the rubric criteria.

Creating Digital Stories

The overall course design supports the learning objectives and reflects a scaffolding of technology use through individual and collaborative story projects. In the first assignment, students create an original word cloud using Wordle (www.wordle.net). Students go to the Wordle site, click the "create" button, and write a unique story into the text box (or copy and paste from a text document they created in advance). Wordle converts the text to a visual word cloud that provides the user with a number of different features to change color, font style, and layout. As part of this assignment, students are asked to explore all of these features to see how the styles change the visual aspect of their stories. While this is an individual story, the assignment has a collaborative component because the students save their Wordles in a directory for this course, allowing them to see all of the other projects created by peers (www .wordle.net/gallery?username=ESC_Storytelling). As such they know that the audience for this project extends beyond the instructor to include peers in the course as well as visitors to the Wordle site. The Wordle assignment supports the visual dimension of storytelling that illustrates the relationship between text and image. In this context, words become graphics based on several stylistic features and the visual organization of ideas.

At the start of the course, students are also required to establish a blog that is updated for every module, leading to at least seven blog postings throughout the term. The blog and the Wordle assignment coincide to encourage students to create a digital story and write a reflective blog posting early in the course. The blog is another space for storytelling, as students have the freedom to develop it in styles that range from personal to fiction to documentary.

After establishing the blog and creating the first Wordle assignment, the next project uses Animoto (www.animoto.com) to create a one-minute multimedia story. The Animoto site allows users to create and share presentations with pictures, text, and videos. Dynamic presentations are developed via mobile devices or computers and are styled with a wide selection of predesigned visual templates, font styles, and music. Once created, users share the media production at such sites as Facebook, Twitter, YouTube, or WordPress. The topic of the Animoto assignment is open-ended and requires only that the videos tell a story in some way. Students in the course, for instance, have used this tool to create personal narratives related to their family, work life, travel, or community. Students submit this project in the LMS through an Assignment Tool and share a link to their work in a special online discussion that enables them to discuss their work with peers.

After the first two digital stories using Wordle and Animoto, students are encouraged to develop a narrative using an application of their choice. This next project challenges students to evaluate, assess, and select a tool to create a new project. For this assignment students are asked to create a story about a special artifact from their lives. This is the thematic thread that is used to build a personal narrative. Students are encouraged to explore a wide selection of digital storytelling tools at "Cogdogroo" in wikispaces (http://cog dogroo.wikispaces.com/StoryTools) and then apply one of these resources to the development of the artifacts project. This leads to familiarity with a wide variety of tools since the students are making unique choices and then sharing those resources with peers. At this point in the course, many of the projects increase in complexity and quality because students have gained experience as digital storytellers and are able to make informed decisions when selecting resources and designing their narratives.

In the last project, students use VoiceThread (http://voicethread.com) to create an annotated story. VoiceThread allows storytellers to create a multimedia slideshow by uploading images, text, video, and audio. For this project, students develop a story with pictures, video, and/or text and then enhance their story with voice-over narration. This interactive site allows other users to add their own audio contributions, while providing a space for students to annotate other student projects as well. This assignment allows for student communication within each story space, and a peer evaluation component encourages reflective critique among student authors. In some ways this is one of the most complex assignments that culminates in the end result of students' knowledge acquisition throughout the course. Students integrate text, image, and narration in the VoiceThread project while providing an opportunity for peers to contribute a unique perspective on the narrative with their own voice commentary.

For every digital story created in this course, students are also required to think about each production by answering a set of questions that promote metacognitive reflection. When submitting each digital story in the LMS, using the Assignment Tool, students are required to reflect on all of the following questions (with responses viewed exclusively by the instructor as part of the assignment submission process):

- What inspired you to tell this story? Why is it important?
- Who was your intended audience? What emotions did you intend to evoke (if any)?
- What was your creative process during the activity?
- What technical considerations helped or hindered the project?
- What did you find most challenging? What was the highlight of the experience for you?
- What did you learn that will assist you in developing future digital stories?

These questions challenge students to think about their own creative process, including: the inspiration for the work, the targeted audience, emotional impact, potential technology challenges, individual highlights, and a self-assessment about what they learned through this experience and how this might impact future projects. Students use the same set of questions to self-assess their blog in the final module in the course. Collectively, this is an important metacognitive dimension of the course that supports learning objective five related to new tools and frameworks for creating digital media, as well as the sixth objective related to the critical assessment of digital stories. This set of questions provides students with an opportunity for continuous reflection on their own thinking about technology, digital storytelling, as well as their creative and technical processes as the course unfolds. This reflective component is a central part of the learning process that empowers the learners to self-assess their storytelling abilities in this interactive online setting.

As shown in this analysis of learning objectives and related story assignments, the focus of this course is on several interrelated activities, including interaction in the online discussions, the exploration of virtual field trips, and discussions about those online journeys, as well as the production of original stories using various applications. For every online discussion, students are required to post one response to the original set of instructor questions and at least two responses to peers, to promote interaction and dialogue. Every module includes multiple questions from the instructor related to the core themes. Students are asked to synthesize their ideas in response to the questions as part of a dialogue, rather than in short-answer format. Students are also asked to post responses to the blogs developed by peers. Collectively, this work supports the scope of learning objectives from theory to practice and the production of original media in digital storytelling.

MAPPING THE METALITERACY MODEL TO DIGITAL STORYTELLING

Although Digital Storytelling is not an information literacy course, there is a strong relationship between the technology and the overall learning design that reflects an expanded and comprehensive metaliteracy in practice. Martinez (2011) describes this intersection of learner-centered digital design and learning as "digital media literacy" (p. 16). Her description of learner engagement in this course through the original production of digital media projects is also consistent with the foundation elements of metaliteracy, especially related to producing, sharing, and communicating information. She wrote:

> This type of course, which has a focus on both storytelling and digital media mastery, provides all levels of students with the opportunity and skills to gradually acquire competency and literacy as the study evolves. In my experience, even the student with the least technical skill among her peers has been able to create a blog; learn Twitter; review, research and evaluate digital media resources; and create digital stories

> that combine elements of written narrative, audio commentating, visual
> resources, moving images and music. All of these skills form the build-
> ing blocks of digital media literacy. (Martinez, 2011, p. 16)

This course introduces learners to the development of original digital media projects using open resources. It also challenges them to gain critical thinking abilities in the evaluation of professional websites as well as their own work, and the digital stories created by peers. This online course does not require expensive software or specialized hardware to create personal narratives. Every student with computer and web access is able to link to the applications for creating and sharing the results of their work. The course itself is housed in the LMS, but it refers to several independent sites external to this environment and openly available on the web. This approach democratizes access to technology while promoting critical thinking and reflection by empowering learners to create and share their diverse stories online.

Digital Storytelling exemplifies many of the primary components of metaliteracy and supports the college-level learning goals at Empire State College related to information and digital media literacy. The focus on producing and sharing digital stories, and continuously reflecting on that work through collaborative dialogue, embodies the core principles of metaliteracy. This is an important consideration because it shows how key elements of metaliteracy may already be at play in our teaching and learning practices, while also demonstrating that we need to foreground the characteristics that support a comprehensive and unified approach identified in metaliteracy.

As we see in table 7.1, Mapping the metaliteracy model to digital storytelling, the original assertions we outlined in our article "Reframing Information Literacy as a Metaliteracy" can be mapped to the learning objectives for Digital Storytelling. Initially, we outlined seven learning objectives that constitute metaliteracy in practice. While these continue to develop and expand, the original objectives include the following:

1. Understand Format Type and Delivery Mode
2. Evaluate User Feedback as Active Researcher
3. Create a Context for User-generated Information
4. Evaluate Dynamic Content Critically
5. Produce Original Content in Multiple Media Formats
6. Understand Personal Privacy, Information Ethics and Intellectual Property Issues
7. Share Information in Participatory Environments

(Mackey & Jacobson, 2011, pp. 70–76)

This section will demonstrate that all of the metaliteracy learning objectives align well with the digital storytelling outcomes and are supported through

TABLE 7.1

Mapping the metaliteracy model to digital storytelling

Digital Storytelling Learning Objectives	Metaliteracy Learning Objectives	Coursework in Digital Storytelling
Students will learn about the theory and practice of digital storytelling across a range of media.	Understand Format Type and Delivery Mode	Course readings and online discussions, and virtual field trips
Students will learn about different applications of digital storytelling that have emerged and how these applications can be adapted to their professional work as well as their personal lives and those of their clients.	Produce Original Content in Multiple Media Formats	Course readings and online discussions, virtual field trips, and the creation of original story projects
Students will learn about personal storytelling and how it can be implemented with digital media.	Understand Personal Privacy, Information Ethics, and Intellectual Property Issues	Virtual field trips and the creation of original story projects
Students will learn about effective digital design.	Produce Original Content in Multiple Media Formats	Course readings and online discussions, virtual field trips, and the creation of original story projects
Students will learn about new tools and frameworks for storytelling with digital media.	Produce Original Content in Multiple Media Formats, Share Information in Participatory Environments	Virtual field trips and the creation of original story projects
Students will be able to critically assess digital storytelling projects that they encounter.	Evaluate User Feedback as Active Researcher, Create a Context for User-generated Information, Evaluate Dynamic Content Critically	Course readings and online discussions, virtual field trips, digital storytelling rubric, and the creation of original story projects

interactive assignments that promote dialogue, collaboration, producing and sharing digital information, and reflecting on the educational experience.

The first learning objective in Digital Storytelling to "learn about the theory and practice of digital storytelling across a range of media" relates to understanding the format type and delivery mode within emerging technology settings. As learners gain knowledge about the theoretical underpinnings of producing digital media projects, they need to have an understanding of how information formats vary within evolving modes of delivery. For instance, the way that visual, textual, and aural information is produced in Animoto is different from Wordle and VoiceThread. Wordle automatically converts text information to word clouds based on how often a particular word appears in the document. Wordle has limited stylistic choices while Animoto expands the type of visual information incorporated in a story to include pictures and videos. VoiceThread provides a higher level of interactivity than either Animoto or Wordle by providing viewers with the option to participate in the story by contributing their own audio narration. These differences in format type and delivery mode influence the theory and practice of telling digital stories and are essential considerations for both author and reader of the narratives.

The second objective in the course, to "learn different applications of digital storytelling that have emerged and how these applications can be adapted to their professional work as well as their personal lives and those of their clients" is primarily aligned with the metaliteracy objective to "produce original content in multiple media formats." As we have seen, the production and sharing of information in this course is central to becoming a digital storyteller. Similarly, the ability to produce original content in a range of media formats supports learners to become metaliterate in an evolving and participatory social media environment. Students in this course learn to adapt to different applications that are presented in each module. As shown in the Artifacts assignment, they also evaluate a wide range of tools in different multimedia formats and make an informed choice that suits their vision for the story they have in mind. This requires critical thinking that leads to the creative production of original content. These are interrelated competencies that are supported through metacognitive reflection and dialogue with peers.

Another connection between the digital storytelling and metaliteracy learning objectives is found in the third objective in the course to "learn about personal storytelling and how it can be implemented with digital media." This relates to the metaliteracy assertion to "understand personal privacy, information ethics and intellectual property issues." When designing original digital stories, learners need to have a deep understanding of the ethical and intellectual property dimensions of producing and sharing original and repurposed content. This is especially relevant in open learning and social media environments where information is transient and the delivery of information is circuitous through a vast network. Oftentimes digital information is collaboratively produced and shared, requiring an understanding of community standards for original and repurposed content and peer review. Today's learners need to understand copyright considerations as well as the options offered by the Creative Commons for both searching and sharing information and for licensing creative works. Since digital storytelling may involve personal narratives, the creator of these projects must be aware of audience considerations and the distinctions between personal and professional information. Further, the digital storyteller needs to reflect on how their personal narratives may be read in public settings. In the digital storytelling course, for example, many of the stories exist outside of the LMS in publicly available websites. The producer of these works must understand how to define privacy settings and to be aware of the full range of options for sharing digital stories online.

The fourth objective in Digital Storytelling, "students will learn about effective digital design," also connects to one of the core principles of metaliteracy, to learn how we "produce original content in multiple media formats." As shown in this case study, students learn about effective design through the production of their own work. But they also approach this from a theoretical perspective, completing course readings and taking virtual field trips to gain insights about effective design. They share observations about digital storytelling examples with peers and incorporate this knowledge into the production of their own narratives. As the course progresses, students reflect on their storytelling projects and think about how these experiences inform future work in this area.

Throughout this process, students work toward the fifth course objective, to "learn about new tools and frameworks for storytelling with digital media." This relates to the metaliteracy objective for producing information and also to "share information in participatory environments." Producing and sharing information are intertwined in this context as students learn about using digital technologies as active and creative contributors. At the same time, they learn about different approaches to narrative development, both individual and collaborative, and in various forms that are structured and linear, or decentered and fluid. The tools impact the storytelling and vice versa, as Wordle shows the potential for producing text as image, based on an original text document, and VoiceThread demonstrates the collaborative potential of annotating linear pictorial narratives within a learning community.

The sixth learning objective for this course indicates that "students will be able to critically assess digital storytelling projects that they encounter." This relates to at least three of the metaliteracy learning objectives: evaluate user feedback as active researcher, create a context for user-generated information, and evaluate dynamic content critically. As students gain analytic abilities in this course, it is important for them to understand how other participants actively engage and contribute through their own narratives. User feedback is relevant to online discussions, responses to blog postings, and through audio annotations contributed to the VoiceThread assignment. Reflective learners are continuously creating a context for these contributions by engaging in a conversation with other participants and analyzing the sources of the information provided through this exchange. The context created influences the way we think about a particular issue and may take shape in an online discussion, a collaborative wiki, a blog, or a collaborative presentation. In an open social media environment, participants must take a lead in how they organize and understand the many sources available and transform this information into meaningful knowledge. This involves the ongoing critical evaluation of dynamic content that is transient and transparent. In the Digital Storytelling course, students apply an open rubric to assist them in navigating virtual field trips and to better understand their own productions and those of their peers. The rubric is a useful tool in gaining this critical thinking perspective to evaluate active content and to become an effective information designer in digital domains.

As we have seen in this section, the core metaliteracy learning objectives can be mapped to the expected outcomes in Digital Storytelling. Although not originally designed from a metaliteracy perspective, the goals of this course to encourage the production and sharing of original digital stories online fit nicely into this unifying framework. While digital storytelling clearly lends itself to the original creation and distribution of digital narratives within a collaborative community, this same approach could be applied in other disciplinary settings as well to actively engage learners in metacognitive reflective practice.

CONCLUSION

This case study demonstrates the importance of institutional support for developing innovative learning opportunities for students. Many of these same techniques could be applied in other courses at a range of institutional settings and broad disciplinary contexts. The Digital Storytelling course examined in this chapter emerged within an online program at Empire State College that encourages experimentation and flexibility in learning design. As a progressive institution within the largest public university system in the country, Empire State College promotes self-directed learning that takes many forms, including guided independent study, group study, blended and online courses, mobile learning, MOOCs, and PLA to credential college-level learning. This sense of invention is grounded in the principles of individualized learning and metacognitive reflection as part of the degree planning process. This student-centered philosophy is supported by a dialogue with mentors and includes a tradition of self-direction and reflective practice. These same institutional values could be applied in other contexts as well to support flexibility and innovation in emerging modalities.

The Digital Storytelling course illustrates how the creative production and delivery of original artistic expressions can be supported with learning objectives. This work relates to writing, design, planning, critical thinking, collaboration, technology, and reflection. While this course examines the genre of digital storytelling itself, and places students in the role of producer and collaborator, similar techniques could be applied in courses outside this discipline as well to encourage creativity and self-reflection. Imagine the interactive and visual representations that learners could construct to expand knowledge in mathematics, lab sciences, social sciences, business, and professional studies. This course model is ideal because it demonstrates that in an open social media environment face-to-face computer labs or expensive technologies are not required to teach students how to produce meaningful projects. The instructor is a facilitator in this context who encourages independence and community as a means to self-discovery and the creation of new knowledge. In many ways the metacognitive questions that students respond to online are as important to this process as the tools themselves. Similarly, the shared rubric is another key component that encourages critical thinking and peer review. As we have seen, the design of this course, with a focus on clearly defined objectives and effective technology use, promotes an empowering approach to learning consistent with metaliteracy.

REFERENCES

Alexander, Bryan. (2011). *The new digital storytelling: Creating narratives with new media*. Santa Barbara, CA: Praeger.

Alexander, Bryan, & Levine, Alan. (2008, November/December). Web 2.0 storytelling: Emergence of a new genre. *Educause Review*. http://net.educause.edu/ir/library/pdf/ERM0865.pdf

Benke, Meg, Davis, Alan, & Travers, Nan. (2012). SUNY Empire State College: A game changer in open learning. In Diana G. Oblinger (Ed.), *Game Changers: Education and Information Technologies*. Educause. http://net.educause.edu/ir/library/pdf/pub720311.pdf

Bonnabeau, Richard F. (1996). *The promise continues: Empire State College the first twenty-five years*. The Donning Company.

Cumming, Charles. (2013). The 21 steps. *We Tell Stories* [Web site]. www.wetellstories.co.uk/stories/week1

Daniel, Sir John. (2011). UNESCO Bangkok Special Seminar 2012 (No. IV): The Future of (Open) Education. www.col.org/resources/speeches/2012presentations/Pages/2012-04-24.aspx

Educause Learning Initiative. (2007). 7 things you should know about ... Digital storytelling. http://net.educause.edu/ir/library/pdf/ELI7021.pdf

Empire State College. (2011a). Academic Plan 2011–2015. www.esc.edu/media/academic-affairs/oaa/Academic-Plan-1-11-2012.pdf

Empire State College. (2011b). Learning Goals. www.esc.edu/media/academic-affairs/College-Level-Learning-Goals-1-20-2012.pdf

Empire State College. (2013a). Distance learning catalog. www.esc.edu/distance-learning/catalog

Empire State College. (2013b). Math and science in your life: Science Math and Technology Resources at Empire State College. http://commons.esc.edu/smatresources

Empire State College. (2013c). Undergraduate degrees. www.esc.edu/degrees-programs/undergraduate-aos

Lambert, Joe. (n.d.). What is digital storytelling? A conversation with Dana Atchley on the subject of digital storytelling. www.nextexit.com/dap/whatis.html

Lefor, P., Benke, M., & Ting, E. (2001). Empire State College: The development of online learning. *The International Review of Research in Open and Distance Learning, 1*(2). www.irrodl.org/index.php/irrodl/article/view/22/363

Mackey, Thomas P., & Jacobson, Trudi E. (2011). Reframing information literacy as a metaliteracy. *College & Research Libraries, 72*(1), 62–78.

Martinez, Nicola Marae. (2011). Educating the digital citizen in the 21st century. SUNY Empire State College. *All About Mentoring*, (39), 13–19. www.esc.edu/media/ocgr/publications-presentations/All-About-Mentoring-Issue-39-2011.pdf

McLellan, Hilary. (2006). Digital storytelling in higher education. *Journal of Computing in Higher Education, 19*(1), 65–79.

Public Broadcasting System. (2001). About Laurie Anderson. *Art in the twenty-first century*. Art 21. www.pbs.org/art21/artists/laurie-anderson

State University of New York (SUNY). (1971). *A prospectus for a new university college: Objectives, process, structure and establishment*. http://suny-empire.esc.edu/media/ocgr/anniversary/esc40th/a-prospectus-for-a-new-university-college.pdf.SUNY. (2013). Short history of SUNY. https://www.suny.edu/student/university_suny_history.cfm

Tucker, Genevieve. (2006). First person singular: The power of digital storytelling. *Screen Education*, (42), 54–58. Communication & Mass Media Complete.

Yeager, Carol, & Hurley-Dasgupta, Betty. (2012). Reflections on MOOCdom—A dialogue on possibilities. *All About Mentoring*, (42), 63–68. www.esc.edu/media/ocgr/publications-presentations/All-About-Mentoring-Issue-42-Winter-2012.pdf

About the Authors

THOMAS P. MACKEY, PhD, is the dean at the Center for Distance Learning at SUNY Empire State College in Saratoga Springs, New York. His teaching and research interests include metaliteracy, information literacy, blended, open, and online learning, and social media. At Empire State College, he teaches online courses in digital storytelling and information design and co-developed Metaliteracy MOOC with Trudi E. Jacobson and colleagues from Empire State College and the University Libraries at the University at Albany. Tom is a member of the editorial team for *Open Praxis*, the peer-reviewed, international, open access, scholarly journal about research and innovation in open, distance, and flexible education published by the International Council for Open and Distance Education. He is a member of the SUNY Faculty Advisory Council on Teaching and Technology and the SUNY Learning Network Advisory Council. He participated in the Chancellor's Online Education Advisory Team that recommended adoption of the Open SUNY proposal. Tom has published four co-edited books with Trudi E. Jacobson for Neal-Schuman Publishers about faculty-librarian collaboration, including the most recent *Teaching Information Literacy Online* (2011). His research articles have been published in *First Monday, College & Research Libraries, Computers & Education, The Journal of General Education, College Teaching, Rhizomes, The Journal of Information Science,* and *The Journal of Education for Library and Information Science.* He may be contacted by e-mail at tom.mackey@esc.edu.

TRUDI E. JACOBSON, MLS, MA, is distinguished librarian and head of the Information Literacy Department at the University at Albany, SUNY. She teaches undergraduate information literacy courses. Her interests include the use of critical thinking and active learning activities in the classroom, particularly using Michaelsen's method of team-based learning. She was the principal investigator for a SUNY Innovative Instruction Technology Grant from 2012–2013 that created the Metaliteracy Learning Collaborative. The collaborative has developed a robust set of metaliteracy learning objectives and is working on a badging system. She is the co-author, with Lijuan Xu, of *Motivating Students in Information Literacy Classes* (2004) and co-editor, with Thomas P. Mackey, of four volumes that explore information literacy-related collaborations between faculty and librarians. She recently contributed to and co-edited *The Information Literacy User's Guide: An Open, Online Textbook,* a project undertaken by librarians in her department. She has published articles in a number of journals, including *The Journal of General Education, College & Research Libraries, portal, Communications in Information Literacy, Journal of Academic Librarianship, Research Strategies, College Teaching,* and *The Teaching Professor.* In 2009 Trudi won the Association of College and Research Libraries Instruction Section's Miriam Dudley Instruction Librarian Award. She may be contacted by e-mail at tjacobson@albany.edu.

Index

Locators in *italic* refer to figures/tables/diagrams

CPSIA information can be obtained at www.ICGtesting.com
Printed in the USA
LVOW01s2353070414

380749LV00015B/307/P